LITERARY TERMS

A Dictionary

THIRD EDITION, REVISED AND ENLARGED

Karl Beckson
and Arthur Ganz

ANDRE DEUTSCH

First published in Great Britain 1990
by André Deutsch Limited
105-106 Great Russell Street, London WC1B 3LJ

Copyright © 1960, 1975, 1989,1990 by Karl Beckson and
    Arthur Ganz
A revised and enlarged edition of *A Reader's Guide to
Literary Terms*, copyright © 1960 by Karl Beckson
and Arthur Ganz

British Library Cataloguing in Publication Data

Beckson, Karl, *1926-*
    Literary terms: a dictionary.
    1. Literature. Encyclopaedias
    I. Title II. Ganz, Arthur
    803'.21

ISBN: 0 233 98558 1 hardback
       0 233 98561 1 paperback

Printed in Great Britain by
Billing and Sons Limited, Worcester

To Estelle Beckson
and
Jack Ganz

Preface

In his dictionary of the English language, Dr. Samuel Johnson defined *lexicographer* as a "harmless drudge." The authors of *Literary Terms: A Dictionary* express the hope that their drudgery has in fact produced relatively little harm, considering the vexed nature of their subjects: literature and its terminology. At any rate, the generous reception of the first two editions of this book led us to assume that we had succeeded in our intention, as stated in the Preface to the second edition: "to provide a guide to literary terminology detailed enough for the writer or teacher yet clear enough for the student or general reader."

Since the appearance of the second edition in 1975, new developments in literary criticism (with its inevitable efflorescence of fashionable terminology) have grown so alarmingly that we were convinced that a third edition was called for. We have, accordingly, added such new terms as *deconstruction, Russian Formalism, feminist criticism, reader-response criticism, hermeneutics,* and *anxiety of influence.* Moreover, we have revised a number of terms to clarify or expand existing discussions. We have also updated bibliographical citations to encourage readers to pursue their interests further.

As in the previous edition, we employ boldface for terms used in the course of defining other terms so that the reader may consult those in boldface for further discussion. In some cases, such as in the entries on rhyme and tragedy, we group several terms together instead of directing the reader to various other parts of the book. Systematic use of this volume is possible by consulting at the back the Selected List of Entries, which arranges terms by subject.

Finally, once again we wish to thank students, teachers, and friends who have generously offered us comments and advice.

K.B.
A.G.

Abbreviations

abbr.	abbreviated
ca.	about
cf.	compare with
e.g.	for example
i.e.	that is

Prosodic symbols

ᴜ	either a short vowel or an unaccented syllable
′	an accented syllable
-	a long vowel
ˋ	a light or secondary stress
‖	a caesura, or pause
/	a virgule, which separates metrical feet

Letters of the alphabet are used to designate rhyming words in verse (as *abab*) and superior numbers, where appropriate, to designate the number of feet in a line (as $a^4b^3a^4b^3$).

LITERARY TERMS: A DICTIONARY

A

abecedarius: See **acrostic.**

ab ovo: Latin: "from the egg." Beginning a narrative from its logical beginning rather than, as in the traditional **epic,** in the middle of things, *in medias res.* Both terms are used in Horace's *Ars Poetica* (ca. 9 B.C.).

abstract: 1. A summary of a book or document. 2. As opposed to *concrete.* A sentence can be described as abstract if it makes a general statement about a class of persons or objects ("Men are weak") or if its subject is an abstraction—that is, a quality considered apart from its object—such as *wealth, beauty,* or *deepness.* "Honesty is the best policy" is an abstract statement, but "Hotchkiss is a thief" is concrete. The latter statement refers to a particular object rather than to a general class of objects.

Absurd, Theater of the: See **Theater of the Absurd.**

academic drama: See **school plays.**

acatalectic: A term applied to verse which is metrically complete. If a verse lacks one or more unaccented syllables in its final foot, it is called "catalectic" (noun form, "catalexis"), or "truncated." (A line from which the initial syllable or syllables are missing is called "headless.") If a verse contains an extra syllable, it is called "hypercatalectic," "hypermetrical," "redundant," or "extrametrical." In the following quatrain by Blake, the first line is headless, the third acatalectic, and the second and fourth hypercatalectic:

> When / Sir Josh / ua Rey / nolds died
> All Na / ture was / degrad / ed;
> The King / dropp'd a tear / into / the Queen's Ear,
> And all / his Pic / tures Fad / ed.

accent: The stress placed upon certain syllables in a line of verse. Stresses are determined by word, rhetorical, and metrical accent. *Word accent* refers to the natural stress pattern of the word itself, as in *cóndŭct*, the noun, or *cŏndúct*, the verb. *Rhetorical accent* is the stress put on a word because of its function or importance in the sentence, and *metrical accent* is the stress pattern established by the meter. When the metrical accent forces a change in the word accent, the phenomenon is called "wrenched accent." This may be the result of simple ineptitude in the poet, but it is also a characteristic of both folk and literary ballads.

> This Hermit good lives in that wood
> Which slopes down to the sea.
> How loudly his sweet voice he rears!
> He loves to talk with marinéres
> That come from a far countrée.
>
>   Coleridge, *The Rime of the Ancient Mariner*

See **ictus; primary and secondary accent; thesis.**

accentual verse: See **meter.**

acrostic: A poem in which letters of successive lines form a word or pattern. In a true acrostic, the initial letters form the word; in a mesostich, the middle letters do so, and in a telestich, it is the terminal letters. A cross acrostic forms the pattern with the first letter of the first line, the second letter of the second line, etc. If the pattern consists of the letters of the alphabet in order, the acrostic is called an "abecedarius," as in the following, which is given in part:

> An Austrian army awfully array'd,
> Boldly by battery besieged Belgrade.
> Cossack commanders cannonading come
> Dealing destruction's devastating doom.
>
>   Alaric Watts

act: One of the major divisions of a play. In Classical theory, a play is divided into five acts, but the number was reduced in the nineteenth century. Most modern plays employ three acts, although many have only two or eliminate act structure entirely and use only scene divisions.

action: Though critics employ the term *action* to refer to the succession of events in a play or novel, a distinction may be made between the physical action and the psychological action, consisting of a character's internal conflicts or the clash of wills between characters. In *Hamlet*, for example, the physical action is considerable—indeed, it is one of the busiest plays in dramatic literature—but this external action derives from an equally significant inner action involving the self-doubts of both the Prince and Claudius. Between them, there rages a psychological as well as a political struggle, from which the tragic circumstances emerge. The question of whether plot or character—outer action or inner action—is more important has been much disputed; it has not been, nor is it likely to be, settled. See **plot**.

aesthetic distance: The distance that must exist between a work of art and the reader or beholder so that it may achieve its intended effect. Thus "distanced," the reader experiences the power of the literary work, but his experience is controlled by that work's formal qualities. He does not, therefore, confuse art with "life." A knowledgeable spectator in the theater may deplore the actions of the villain, but he does not rush onstage to succor the heroine. A problem for the reader, the critic, and the artist may be underdistancing, which can distort the experience by excessive subjectivism, or overdistancing, which may debilitate the artistic experience.

The term *aesthetic distance* is used synonymously with *psychical distance*, coined by Edward Bullough in 1912, when he wrote: "Distance is obtained by separating the object and its appeal from one's own self, by putting it out of gear with practical needs and ends."

See Edward Bullough, *Aesthetics: Lectures and Essays*, ed. Elizabeth M. Wilkinson (1957).

Aestheticism: A literary and artistic movement of the nineteenth century, emerging in France and developing in England and other European countries. Unlike the mere devotion to beauty that characterizes aestheticism in other historical periods, nineteenth-century Aestheticism generally held that life should be lived as art and that art should be independent of social, political, or moral teaching. Hence, the doctrine of *l'art pour l'art* ("art for art's sake"), a concept derived from Kant's view of art as "purposiveness without purpose," is central to Aestheticism. (The term *l'art pour l'art* was first used by Benjamin Constant in his *Journal intime*, February 11, 1804.)

In France, the divorce of art from utility was enunciated as a manifesto by Théophile Gautier in his preface to his novel *Mademoiselle de Maupin* (1835) and developed by such writers as Baudelaire and Mallarmé. In England, the concept of artistic autonomy had its roots in such early-nineteenth-century writers as Coleridge, Leigh Hunt, and Arthur Hallam; in the United States, Poe, writing in "The Poetic Principle" (1850), spoke of the "poem written solely for the poem's sake."

As a widespread phenomenon in literature, painting, and book design, Aestheticism in England may be traced from the 1870's to the end of the century. The Aesthetes were inspired by such figures as Keats, who had suggested, in an ambiguous phrase in his "Ode on a Grecian Urn," an equivalence between Beauty and Truth; the Pre-Raphaelites, particularly Rossetti, whose devotion to art was legendary; Swinburne, who argued for artistic autonomy and who symbolized the artist in conflict with his society; and Whistler, who brought a new artistic consciousness to painting. In particular, however, the Aesthetes looked to Walter Pater as their "Master," whose *Studies in the History of the Renaissance* (1873) Oscar Wilde called his "golden book" and to which Arthur Symons referred as "the most beautiful book of prose in our literature." In the conclusion to his work, Pater urged his readers to live with aesthetic intensity, "to burn always with [a] hard, gemlike flame," and spoke of the "love of art for art's sake." But Pater did not advocate an unbridled hedonism (as Wilde thought he had) but an intellectually passionate aestheticism, which, though opposed to didacticism, did not rule out the moral effect of art; indeed, in "Style" (1888), Pater insisted that great art was possible only if it enlarged "our sympathies with each other."

By the 1890's, Aestheticism became more flamboyant and daring: Wilde's *Salomé* and Aubrey Beardsley's androgynous, perverse figures in his illustrations for the play typify what was called **Decadence.** Yet the Aesthetic Movement, in its opposition to nineteenth-century didacticism, focused attention on the autonomy of art and thus prepared the way for such later developments as **Imagism** and the **New Criticism.**

See Holbrook Jackson, *The Eighteen Nineties* (1913); William Gaunt, *The Aesthetic Adventure* (1945); R. V. Johnson, *Aestheticism* (1969); Ruth Temple, "Truth in Labelling: Pre-Raphaelitism, Aestheticism, Decadence, Fin de Siècle," *English Literature in Transition*, 17 (1974), 201–17.

aesthetics: From Greek: *aisthetikos*, "sense perception." A term introduced into philosophical discussion in the mid-eighteenth century to refer to explorations of the nature of art and its place in human experience. As a branch of philosophy, aesthetics is largely concerned with general principles rather than with evaluations of specific works of art.

In the past, aestheticians attempted to define Beauty. The objective view, held by Plato and Aristotle, was that Beauty resided in the object; the subjective view, held by Hume, was that it was that which pleases the beholder. Attempting to resolve the conflict, Kant suggested that subjective views may have universal validity.

Modern aestheticians, however, have devoted their attention to other matters: for example, they have explored the relationship of art to truth, whether subjective or objective, and the nature of the aesthetic experience in the beholder. The idea of Beauty is now usually regarded as a problem for the semanticist rather than for the literary critic and aesthetician, for whom Beauty is not the principal value in judging art.

See Albert Hofstadter, *Truth and Art* (1965); Harold Osborne, ed., *Aesthetics in the Modern World* (1968).

affective fallacy: In *The Verbal Icon* (1954), W. K. Wimsatt, Jr., and M. C. Beardsley have defined the affective fallacy as "a confusion between the poem and its *results* (what it *is* and what it *does*). . . . It begins by trying to derive the standard of criticism from the psychological effects of the poem and ends in impressionism and relativism. . . . the poem itself, as an object of specifically critical judgment, tends to disappear." Wimsatt and Beardsley's work has been influential in reinforcing the New Critics' concentration on actual texts rather than peripheral matter.

In "The 'New Criticism': Some Qualifications," *Literary Essays* (1956), David Daiches questions the validity of the affective fallacy: "The value of literature surely lies in its actual or potential effect on [experienced and sensitive] readers. . . . To deny this is to fall into the 'ontological fallacy' of believing that a work of art fulfills its purpose and achieves its value simply by *being*, so that the critic becomes concerned only to demonstrate the mode of its being by descriptive analysis." See **New Criticism**.

affective stylistics: See **reader-response criticism**.

afflatus: See **inspiration**.

Age of Reason: See **Enlightenment, the**.

agon: Greek: "a contest." That part of a Greek drama in which two characters, each one aided by half the chorus, indulge in verbal conflict.

Agrarians: See **Fugitives and Agrarians**.

alazon: See *miles gloriosus*.

alba: See *aube*.

alexandrine: 1. In French, a verse of twelve syllables containing four (sometimes three) accents. It is used for elevated verse such as that of the classical tragedies. 2. In English, an iambic hexameter verse is often called an alexandrine.

Alienation Effect: See **Epic Theater**.

allegory: An extended narrative that carries a second meaning along with the surface story. The continuity of the second meaning involves an analogous structure of ideas or events (frequently historical or political); this extended metaphor distinguishes allegory from mere allusion or symbolic ambiguity. Hence, though such a work as *Moby Dick* has a rich symbolic structure accompanying the surface narrative, one that offers multiple interpretations, it lacks the continuity of analogous meanings essential to allegory. In general, then, allegory limits the possibility of interpretation once the surface narrative yields the allegorical analogy.

Landscapes and characters in allegory are usually incarnations of abstract ideas, and characters may even bear such names as Death, Fellowship, Good Deeds, and Beauty (as in the medieval morality play *Everyman*) and Christian, Faithful, and Mr. Worldly Wiseman (as in Bunyan's *Pilgrim's Progress*). In these moral allegories, the narrative "level" provides entertainment while the allegorical "level" instructs.

It is often said that allegory "both conceals and reveals." In political allegory, the author may disguise his criticism or satire for fear of reprisal, but perception of the analogy between the narrative and contemporary events reveals the intended meaning. In Orwell's *Animal Farm*, on the other hand, the political allegory of the Bolshevik Revolution and subsequent Stalinist excesses is little concealed by the surface; discovery of the allegorical design is one of the delights of the fable.

Allegory is not only a literary mode but, by extension, a method of critical analysis as well. Thus, critics sometimes interpret works allegorically where they perceive coherent analogies between characters and abstract ideas. In recent years, critics have used Freudian psychology to interpret allegorically such a work as Hawthorne's *The Scarlet Letter* (Hester as Ego; Rev. Dimmesdale as Superego; and Chillingworth as Id) and myth to find universal analogies inherent in a concrete narrative, as in *The Rime of the Ancient Mariner*, which depicts the cursed wanderer who has offended God.

See Angus Fletcher, *Allegory: Theory of a Symbolic Mode* (1964); John MacQueen, *Allegory* (1970); John Whitman, *Allegory: The Dynamics of an Ancient and Medieval Technique* (1987).

alliteration: The close repetition of consonant sounds, usually at the beginning of words; also called "head rhyme."

> To sit in solemn silence in a dull, dark dock,
> In a pestilential prison, with a life-long lock,
> Awaiting the sensation of a short, sharp shock,
> From a cheap and chippy chopper on a big, black block!
> W. S. Gilbert, *The Mikado*

Anglo-Saxon prosody was based on alliteration rather than rhyme.

allusion: A reference, usually brief, to a presumably familiar person or thing. For example, the poem below contains, and depends upon, a reference to the phrase "in Abraham's bosom."

> Mary Ann has gone to rest
> Safe at last on Abraham's breast,
> Which may be nuts for Mary Ann,
> But is certainly rough on Abraham.
> Anonymous

altar poem: See *carmen figuratum.*

ambiguity: In *Seven Types of Ambiguity* (1938; rev. ed., 1947), William Empson uses this word to refer not to carelessness that produces two or more meanings where a single one is intended but to the richness of poetic speech which can be brought about by "any verbal nuance, however slight, which gives room for alternative reactions to the same piece of language." Although Empson does not demand that his distinctions be regularly observed, for purposes of classification he groups his ambiguities into seven categories:

1. A word or syntax can be effective in several ways at once.
2. Two or more meanings may make up the single meaning of the writer.
3. In a pun two ideas can be given simultaneously.
4. Different meanings can combine to make clear a complicated state of mind in the writer.
5. An image or figure may lie halfway between two ideas.
6. The reader may be forced to invent interpretations because the things said are contradictory.
7. Two meanings may be contradictory and show a fundamental division in the author's mind.

Because of the pejorative connotations of the term *ambiguity,* other critics have suggested *multiple meaning* and *plurisignation* as alternate terms.

amphiboly (-e; -ogy; -ogism): An ambiguity induced either by grammatical looseness (in the sentence "I stood by my friend crying," we do not know who cried) or by the double meanings of words (the sentence "A dark horse has won the triple crown" may refer either to a rare achievement in horse racing or to an obscure cardinal's election to the papacy). Prophecies with double meanings, such as those made by the witches to Macbeth, may also be called amphibolies.

amphibrach: A metrical foot of three syllables, consisting of one long syllable flanked by two short ones or, in accentual poetry, of one accented syllable flanked by two unaccented ones.

> I sprang to / the stirrup, / and Joris, / and he;
> I galloped, Dirck galloped, we galloped all three . . .
>> Browning,
>> "How They Brought the Good News from Ghent to Aix"

amphimac: A metrical foot of three syllables, consisting of one short syllable flanked by two long or, in accentual poetry, of one unstressed syllable flanked by two stressed.

> Live thy life,
>> Young and old,
> Like yon oak,
> Bright in spring,
>> Living gold.
>> Tennyson, "The Oak"

anabasis: Greek: "a going up." The rising of an action to its climax.

anachronism: Something placed in an inappropriate period of time. An anachronism may be unintentional, such as the clock in *Julius Caesar*, or deliberate, such as Shaw's reference to the Emperor in *Androcles and the Lion* as "The Defender of the Faith."

anacoluthon: A sentence which does not maintain a consistent grammatical sequence. In the following sentence, which contains an example of the fabled dangling participle, the subject is *water* when it should be *Hotchkiss:* "Going down for the third time, the water closed over Hotchkiss's head."

anacreontic verse: Verse in praise of wine, women, and Epicurean pleasures generally, after the manner of Anacreon, sixth-century-B.C. Greek poet, as in the following stanza of Alexander Brome's "To His Friend That Had Vowed Small Beer":

> Leave off, fond hermit, leave thy vow,
>> And fall again to drinking:
> That beauty that won't sack allow,
>> Is hardly worth thy thinking.
> Dry love or small can never hold,
> And without Bacchus Venus soon grows cold.

anacrusis: An extra unaccented syllable or group of syllables at the beginning of a verse which regularly starts with an accented syllable, *e.g.*, *To* in line four below:

> Seamen three! What men be ye?
> Gotham's three wise men we be.
> Whither in your bowl so free?
> *To* rake the moon from out the sea.
> > Thomas Love Peacock, "Three Men of Gotham"

anagnorisis: See **tragedy.**

anagogical: See **four levels of meaning.**

anagram: A word or name resulting from the transposition of letters. For example, the title of Samuel Butler's satirical narrative *Erewhon* is an anagram for the word *nowhere.*

analects: A group of short passages, usually collected from the works of one author.

analogy: A resemblance between two different things, sometimes expressed as a simile.

> 'Tis with our judgments as our watches, none
> Go just alike, yet each believes his own.
> > Pope, *An Essay on Criticism*

analytic bibliography: See **bibliography.**

anapest: A metrical foot consisting of two unstressed syllables followed by one stressed syllable. Except for the first foot of lines two and three, all the feet in the following stanza are anapests:

> Oh, he flies / through the air / with the great / est of ease.
> This daring young man on the flying trapeze.
> His figure is handsome, all girls he can please,
> And my love he purloined her away.

anaphora: The repetition of an identical word or group of words in successive verses or clauses.

> I gave her Cakes, and I gave her Ale
> > I gave her Sack and Sherry;
> I kissed her once and I kissed her twice,
> > And we were wondrous merry.
> > > Anonymous

anastrophe: The deliberate inversion of the common order of words. The first and fourth lines of the following stanza have normal word order while the second and third are examples of anastrophe:

> He took his vorpal sword in hand:
>> Long time the manxome foe he sought—
> So rested he by the Tumtum tree,
>> And stood awhile in thought.
>>> Lewis Carroll, "Jabberwocky"

ancients and moderns, quarrel between: A widespread debate in the seventeenth and eighteenth centuries, particularly in France and England, among those who argued for or against the idea that there had been progress in science and the arts. The increase in nationalistic pride and the challenge to established authority provide the background of the quarrel. Among the moderns, Aristotle and Homer were frequently attacked because both had been regarded for centuries as infallible. In *The Passions of the Mind* (1649), Descartes asserted: "What the ancients have taught is so scanty and for the most part so lacking in credibility that I may not hope for any kind of approach toward truth except by rejecting all the paths which they have followed." However, Boileau and Racine, among others, defended the ancients, for French poetry had drawn inspiration from Classical models.

The debate reached England in Sir William Temple's *An Essay upon Ancient and Modern Learning* (1690), which supported the ancients and rejected the idea of progress in learning, a position opposed by William Wotton in *Reflections upon Ancient and Modern Learning* (1694). Swift, upholding Temple and the ancients, satirized the controversy in *The Battle of the Books* (1704). Unlike many French moderns, the English generally granted superiority to the ancients in the arts. Addison, in *The Spectator*, No. 160 (1711), regarded Homer as a natural genius, and Alexander Pope in *An Essay on Criticism* (1711), like many Neoclassicists, urged the moderns to imitate the ancients in order to re-create Nature:

> Learn for ancient rules a just esteem:
> To copy nature is to copy them.

See J. B. Bury, *The Idea of Progress* (1920); Richard Foster Jones, *Ancients and Moderns: A Study of the Rise of the Scientific Movement in Seventeenth-Century England* (2nd ed., 1961).

Angry Young Men: A term characterizing a group of British writers of the 1950's whose work expressed bitterness and social disillusionment. The term, taken from Leslie Paul's autobiography, *Angry Young Man* (1951), has been widely used to describe the protagonists, as well as the authors, of such works as Kingsley Amis's *Lucky Jim* (1954) and John Osborne's *Look Back in Anger* (1956), though both authors have angrily denounced the term. Other writers, such as Colin Wilson (*The Outsider*, 1956), John Braine (*Room at the Top*, 1957), and John Wain (*Hurry On Down*, 1953), have also had the term applied to them.

Though the Angry Young Men cannot be regarded as constituting a "movement" (indeed, they have turned their anger, real or feigned, on one another), there are common elements in their work: questioning the value of idealistic commitment in a world that seems to lack worthwhile causes, these authors, most of them from the lower classes, have created a kind of hero (more accurately, **anti-hero**) who rebels against the Establishment, rails against its constraints, and sometimes strives for individual integrity. None of these authors has proposed or devised a new aesthetic; rather, they have used traditional forms and styles in the drama and novel to express their hostilities.

See Kenneth Allsop, *The Angry Decade* (1958).

annal: A yearly record of historical events. An annal is less extensive in scope than a **chronicle.**

annotation: A textual comment in a book. Annotations may range from a reader's penciled comments in the margins of a page to an editor's printed notes which clarify the meaning of the text.

antagonist: The major character in opposition to the hero or protagonist of a narrative or drama. In Melville's *Billy Budd* the antagonist is Claggart.

antepenult: The third syllable from the end of a word. The *nal* of *analogy* is the antepenult.

anthology: A collection of poetry or prose, sometimes divided into categories such as lyric verse, satiric verse, etc. *The Greek Anthology* is perhaps the most famous.

anticlimax: Literally, an effect which works against the climax, frequently a descent from a noble or lofty tone to one noticeably less exalted. If the descent is sudden, the effect is often comic, as in this stanza from Canto I of Byron's *Don Juan*, in which the youthful hero begins to feel the first impulse of love:

> He pored upon the leaves, and on the flowers,
>   And heard a voice in all the winds; and then
> He thought of wood-nymphs and immortal bowers,
>   And how the goddesses came down to men:
> He missed the pathway, he forgot the hours,
>   And when he looked upon his watch again,
> He found how much old Time had been a winner—
> He also found that he had lost his dinner.

anti-hero: A type of hero lacking the traditional heroic qualities (such as courage, idealism, and fortitude), frequently a pathetic, comic, or even antisocial figure. Though elements of the anti-hero may be traced to such a character as Don Quixote (in whose madness the quality of idealism takes on ironic dimensions), the type developed in the nineteenth and twentieth centuries: the anti-hero finds commitment to ideals difficult or impossible because of his sense of helplessness in a world over which he has no control (*e.g.*, Dostoevsky's narrator in *Notes from the Underground* and Arthur Miller's Willy Loman in *Death of a Salesman*) or whose values he suspects. In his rejection of conventional values and his final acceptance of his status as outcast, Meursault, of Camus's *The Stranger*, emerges as a representative anti-hero. Lieutenant Henry, the central figure of Hemingway's *A Farewell to Arms*, voices a particularly explicit rejection of the traditional warrior-hero's values: "I was always embarrassed by the words *sacred, glorious, sacrifice.* . . ."

anti-masque: See **masque**.

anti-novel: See **New Novel**.

antistrophe: The second of the stanzas which make up the triad of the Pindaric ode. See **ode**.

antithesis: A rhetorical figure in which sharply opposing ideas are expressed within a balanced grammatical structure, as in the first line of this couplet by Pope:

> Worth makes the man, and want of it, the fellow;
> The rest is all but leather or prunella.
> *An Essay on Man*

antonym: A word that means the opposite of another. *Heavy*, for example, is the opposite of *light*, *strong* of *weak*, etc.

anxiety of influence: A term used by Harold Bloom in *The Anxiety of Influence: A Theory of Poetry* (1973) to describe the determination of major poets "to wrestle with their strong precursors, even to the death." "Immense anxieties of indebtedness" result as these poets deliberately "misread" the works of prior poets in order to "clear imaginative space for themselves." Employing the psychoanalytic concept of the Oedipus complex, Bloom suggests that anxiety indicates an unconscious struggle against the poetic father, the precursor, in the quest for artistic self-identity. Bloom says in illustration, *"The Ballad of Reading Gaol* becomes an embarrassment to read directly one recognizes that every lustre it exhibits is reflected from [Coleridge's] *The Rime of the Ancient Mariner.*" Bloom concludes that Wilde "lacked the strength to overcome his anxiety of influence."

See Harold Bloom, *A Map of Misreading* (1975); David Fite, *Harold Bloom: The Rhetoric of Romantic Vision* (1985).

aphaeresis: The dropping of an initial letter, syllable, or sound, as in the development of the word *special* from *especial*.

aphorism: A short, pithy statement of a truth or doctrine; similar to an apothegm or maxim. An example is Pope's "The proper study of mankind is man" (*An Essay on Man*).

apocope: The dropping of a final letter, syllable, or sound, as in the development of *curio* from *curiosity*.

apocrypha: Writings of uncertain or unknown authorship. The term, applied to the Biblical *Apocrypha* (books in the Greek version of the Old Testament but not in the Hebrew Bible), is also used to designate literary works of doubtful authorship. Some scholars, for example, believe that the play *Pericles, Prince of Tyre*, is apocryphal, that is, not Shakespeare's. See **canon.**

Apollonian and Dionysian: Terms used by Nietzsche in *The Birth of Tragedy* (1872) to account for the dual impulses that result in the tragic experience. The Apollonian impulse (named after Apollo, the god of dream and illusion) is the desire to create a world of serenity and harmony; the Dionysian impulse (named after Dionysus, god of intoxication, who symbolically represents the unrestrained forces of nature) is, conversely, the desire to express irrationality, barbaric frenzy, "*excess* in pleasure, grief, and knowledge."

Nietzsche rejected the widely held idea that Greek tragedy exhibited the traditional classical values of "noble simplicity and calm grandeur," as Winckelmann had stated. The Dionysian impulse, associated with non-rational, unconscious forces found in primitive ritual, was the true source of the tragic experience, "a manifestation and illustration of Dionysian states, as the visible symbolization of music, as the dream-world of Dionysian ecstasy." The Apollonian values of repose and harmony, Nietzsche believed, had been incorrectly understood: "Tragedy must really be symbolized by a fraternal union of the two deities: Dionysus speaks the language of Apollo; Apollo, however, finally speaks the language of Dionysus. . . . Tragedy is the Apollonian materialization of Dionysian insights and effects." In short, Apollo provides the mask; Dionysus, the inspiration. The result of Dionysian tragedy, Nietzsche maintains, is that "the state and society and, quite generally, the gulfs between man and man, give way to an overwhelming feeling of unity leading back to the very heart of nature."

The influence of Nietzsche has been considerable on subsequent critics and artists, who, like Thomas Mann, Eugene O'Neill, and D. H. Lawrence, give expression to his ideas without employing his terminology.

See Patrick Bridgwater, *Nietzsche in Anglosaxony: A Study of Nietzsche's Impact on English and American Literature* (1972).

apologue: See **fable.**

apology, the: Greek: "defense." A work written to defend the writer's ideas or to clarify a problem. Plato's *Apology*, in which Socrates defends himself before the governing body of Athens, is perhaps the most notable example. In English, Sir Philip Sidney's *Apologie for Poetrie* (1580) discusses poetical practice, while in *Apologia Pro Vita Sua* (1864), Newman defends some of his convictions.

aporia: See **deconstruction.**

aposiopesis: An abrupt breaking off in the middle of a sentence without the completion of the idea, often under the stress of emotion. In the closet scene from *Hamlet*, the Prince, while raging against Claudius, is startled by the sudden entrance of the ghost:

> Hamlet: A murderer, and a villain;
>   A slave that is not twentieth part the tithe
>   Of your precedent lord; a vice of kings;
>   A cut-purse of the empire and the rule,
>   That from a shelf the precious diadem stole,
>   And put it in his pocket!
> Queen: No more!
> Hamlet: A king of shreds and patches,—
>   *Enter Ghost*
>   Save me, and hover o'er me with your wings,
>   You heavenly guards! What would your gracious
>   figure?

apostrophe: A figure of speech in which a person not present or a personified abstraction is addressed. The heroine of Fielding's *Tom Thumb* is apostrophized thus:

> Oh! Huncamunca, Huncamunca, oh!
> Thy pouting breasts, like kettle drums of brass,
> Beat everlastingly loud alarms of joy;
> As bright as brass they are, and oh, as hard;
> Oh! Huncamunca, Huncamunca, oh!

More strictly, an apostrophe (Greek: "a turning away") is a digression in a speech, a turning away to address a judge or someone absent, and by extension a similar break in a poem.

apprenticeship novel: See *Bildungsroman.*

apron stage: The apron is that part of the stage which projects beyond the proscenium arch. Any stage which consists primarily or entirely of an apron and on which the action is not seen as framed within the proscenium may be called an apron stage.

The Elizabethan theater, for which Shakespeare designed his plays, was built around such a stage.

Arcadia: Though originally a mountainous district in the Peloponnesus, Arcadia symbolized in the pastoral verse of the Classical poets, *e.g.*, Vergil's *Eclogues,* the harmony and simplicity of an imagined Golden Age. Arcadia is populated by shepherds and shepherdesses who, removed from the complexities of actual life, both urban and rural, devote themselves to their flocks and their songs. The Renaissance saw the development of the Arcadian prose romance, of which the *Arcadia* of Sannazaro and that of Sir Philip Sidney are the most notable examples. See **pastoral.**

See Robert E. Stillman, *Sidney's Poetic Justice: The Old Arcadia, Its Eclogues, and Renaissance Pastoral Traditions* (1986).

archaism: A word or phrase which is no longer used in actual speech. The use of archaisms has been a common device in poetry up to the twentieth century. The words *quoth, eftsoons,* and the spelling *dropt* were all archaic at the time these lines were written:

> He holds him with his skinny hand,
> "There was a ship," quoth he.
> "Hold off! unhand me, grey-beard loon!"
> Eftsoons his hand dropt he.
> Coleridge, *The Rime of the Ancient Mariner*

archetype: From the Greek: *archē*, meaning "original" or "primitive," plus *typos*, "form." The term, employed by the psychoanalyst C. G. Jung, has been used in the **New Criticism** since the 1930's to characterize a pattern of plot or character which evokes what Jung calls a "racial memory." Thus, the voyage in *The Rime of the Ancient Mariner* is an archetype of the spiritual journey which all men experience, the Ancient Mariner himself an archetype of the man who offends God. Such "primordial images," as Jung calls them, lie in the "collective unconscious," which is the repository of the experience of the race.

See Maud Bodkin, *Archetypal Patterns in Poetry* (1934); see also **criticism; myth.**

argument: 1. A brief abstract or summary of the plot prefixed to a literary work or to a section of it. Dryden's translation of Vergil's *Aeneid*, for example, contains an "Argument" preceding each book of the poem.

2. A division of a **speech.**

arsis: See **thesis.**

art for art's sake: See **Aestheticism.**

aside: In the theater, a short passage spoken in an undertone, usually directed to the audience. By convention, the aside is presumed to be inaudible to other characters on the stage and, most important, presumed to be true, for villains and dissemblers habitually reveal their true motives and thoughts only to the audience. This device has rarely been used since the end of the nineteenth century, when it was prominent in melodrama. For a related device used by a character when he is alone onstage, see **soliloquy.**

assonance: The close repetition of similar vowel sounds, usually in stressed syllables. Assonance is found in each line of the following quatrain:

> Twinkle, twinkle, little star,
> How I wonder what you are!
> Up above the world so high,
> Like a diamond in the sky.
>   Anonymous

atmosphere: The mood which is established by the totality of the literary work. Foreshadowing, though related to atmosphere, is primarily a plot device. In the first act of *Macbeth*, the presence of the three witches establishes the atmosphere of the play, which is dark and somber, but what they say is a foreshadowing of the evil which is later dramatized.

attitude: See **tone.**

aube (or *aubade*): French: "dawn" (or "dawn song"). In French medieval poetry, a song of regret, usually in dialogue form, sung by lovers who must part at dawn. (In Provençal verse, such a poem is called an "*alba*.") The most famous English example occurs in Shakespeare's *Romeo and Juliet*, when the lovers must part after their wedding night:

Juliet: Wilt thou be gone? it is not yet near day:
It was the nightingale and not the lark,
That pierc'd the fearful hollow of thine ear;
Nightly she sings on yon pomegranate tree:
Believe me, love, it was the nightingale.

Romeo: It was the lark, the herald of the morn,
No nightingale: look, love, what envious streaks
Do lace the severing clouds in yonder east:
Night's candles are burnt out, and jocund day
Stands tiptoe on the misty mountain tops.

autobiography: From Greek: "self-life-writing." An account of one's own life, generally a continuous narrative of major events. An autobiography differs from a **memoir**, which has a different focus, or a diary and journal, both of which lack continuity and are generally kept for the author's private purposes (though often prepared for publication). Since there is no prescribed form or subject matter for an autobiography other than the author's experience of life, the *Confessions* of St. Augustine and Rousseau as well as T. S. Eliot's *Four Quartets* and Yeats's *Collected Poems* have often been called "spiritual autobiographies." James Olney has consequently written that "what is autobiography to one observer is history or philosophy, psychology or lyric poetry, sociology or metaphysics to another." Psychoanalytic critics regard the writing of an autobiography as the author's attempt to "reconstruct the self"—in short, as a therapeutic method of alleviating inner tensions.

See James Olney, ed., *Autobiography: Essays Theoretical and Critical* (1980); Estelle C. Jelinek, ed., *Women's Autobiography: Essays in Criticism* (1980).

autotelic: The idea that a work of art is autonomous—that is, self-contained as an aesthetic entity and not propagandistic or morally instructive. Thus, the autotelic work is valued not for its "usefulness" or for its "information" but for its capacity to evoke an imaginative world that enables the reader to be simultaneously engaged in its tensions but detached from its moral consequences. The term *autotelic*, related to *art for art's sake* (see **Aestheticism**), was first widely used in **New Criticism.**

avant-garde: French: "vanguard." In literature, a term designating new writing that contains innovations in form or technique.

See Richard Kostelanetz, ed., *The Avant-Garde Tradition in Literature* (1982).

B

ballad: A narrative poem, usually simple and fairly short, originally designed to be sung. Ballads often begin abruptly, imply the previous action, utilize simple language, tell the story tersely through dialogue and described action, and make use of refrains. The folk ballad, which reached its height in Britain in the sixteenth and seventeenth centuries, was composed anonymously and handed down orally, often in several different versions. The literary ballad, consciously created by a poet in imitation of the folk ballad, makes use (sometimes with considerable freedom) of many of its devices and conventions. Coleridge's *Rime of the Ancient Mariner*, Keats's *La Belle Dame sans Merci*, and Wilde's *Ballad of Reading Gaol* are all literary ballads.

See Alan Bold, *The Ballad* (1979).

ballade: A fixed verse form derived from Old French poetry. In its most common form, the ballade consists of three stanzas and an envoy, a short concluding stanza often addressed to a person of importance. The meter is usually iambic or anapestic tetrameter, and the rhyme scheme is regularly *ababbcbC* in each of the octaves and *bcbC* in the envoy. (Capital letters represent lines repeated as refrains. Some eight-line ballades have double refrains, with the fourth line repeated in each octave and in the envoy, thus: *bBcB*.) There is also a ten-line ballade, in which the rhyme scheme is *ababbccdcD* in the stanzas and *ccdcD* in the envoy. The double ballade contains six eight- or ten-line stanzas, still limited to three or four rhymes respectively, but often omits the envoy. In the *chant royal*, there are five eleven-line stanzas rhyming *ababccddedE* and an envoy rhyming *ddedE*. The *chant royal* is rare in English; the ballade in general tends to be used for light verse.

ballad stanza: A quatrain of alternating tetrameter and trimeter lines rhyming *abcb*:

> Ben Battle was a soldier bold,
>   And used to war's alarms;
> But a cannon-ball took off his legs,
>   So he laid down his arms.
>   Thomas Hood, "Faithless Nellie Gray"

bard: A word originally used to refer to an ancient Celtic order of minstrel-poets who composed and sang verses celebrating the achievements of chiefs and warriors; now a synonym for *poet*.

baroque: A style (or, as some critics insist, a cluster of related styles) dominant in the period between the Renaissance and the Neoclassical age (or from the late sixteenth to the eighteenth century). First used by art historians in the mid-eighteenth century to criticize bizarre or extravagant seventeenth-century architecture, the term *baroque* (derived from the Portuguese *barroco*, referring to an irregularly shaped pearl) has lost its pejorative connotations and has been extended to the other visual arts, to music, and to literature. The essential differences, however, between literature and the other arts have made the term *baroque* imprecise; it is still undergoing critical refinement.

In general, however, the term *baroque* is used to characterize a literary style that employs ingenious and startling conceits to express and resolve the tensions between spiritual aspiration and fleshly impulse and to dramatize and transcend the paradoxes inherent in man's relationship to time and eternity. Such a style attempts to express and reconcile the disharmonies and radically divergent polarities of existence by means of expanded vision and heightened sensibility. Some **Metaphysical poetry,** particularly that of Crashaw, has, for example, been called "baroque."

See Lowry Nelson, *Baroque Lyric Poetry* (1961); Robert T. Petersson, *The Art of Ecstasy* (1970); Frank J. Warnke, *Versions of Baroque: European Literature in the Seventeenth Century* (1972).

bathos: 1. A sudden and ridiculous descent from the exalted to the ordinary, especially when a writer, striving for the noble or pathetic, achieves the ludicrous. The term *bathos* was first used in this sense by Alexander Pope in his essay *On Bathos, or, Of the Art of Sinking in Poetry* (1728), a comic treatise inspired by Longinus's *On the Sublime* (ca. A.D. 1). *Bathos* and *anticlimax* are sometimes synonymous, but where anticlimax may be a deliberate device, bathos is always unintentional.

2. By extension, *bathos* has also come to signify sentimentality or excessive pathos.

beast epic: In the Middle Ages, a sequence of stories, the characters of which were animals who had human characteristics. Designed as **allegory,** the beast epic satirized aspects of contemporary life, especially the court and the Church.

The precise origin of the genre has been a subject of much speculation, but it is probably most indebted to Aesop's *Fables*, in particular to the story of the sly fox and the sick lion, the fable which became the central episode in the first beast epic, *Ecbasis captivi* (ca. 930), *The Prisoner's Escape*. Thereafter, the figure of the clever rogue called, in English, Reynard the Fox became a central character in the beast epic along with Chanticleer the Cock, Noble the Lion, Ysengrim the Wolf, and others. Interpreted allegorically, Reynard was seen as the Church, Noble as the King, and Ysengrim as the barons.

The most famous beast epic of the time was *Le Roman de Renard* (twelfth century); in England, the genre became widely known when a Flemish version was translated and printed by Caxton in 1481. Earlier, however, Chaucer, in the "Nun's Priest's Tale" of *The Canterbury Tales*, had told the tale of Chauntecleer the cock and the fox as a separate story. In the Renaissance, Spenser's *Mother Hubberds Tale* continued the tradition of the beast epic, and in 1793 Goethe utilized the genre in his *Reineke Fuchs*, which contained political and social satire.

Beat Generation: A group of American writers (chiefly poets) of the 1950's and 1960's whose work gave expression to their alienation from society. The term *Beat* implies that these writers felt themselves to be "beaten" by modern life; however, the novelist Jack Kerouac used the term (also regarded as an abbreviation of "beatific") to suggest that his generation of writers was on a new spiritual quest (he once said, "The Beat Generation is basically a religious generation"), though their interest in drugs, sex, speed, and four-letter words shocked some of their first readers.

Kerouac's popular novel *On the Road* (1957), with its romantic nihilism, its rejection of political and social values, and its centering on self, gave the Beat Generation not only a local habitation and a name but also considerable notoriety; however, the first Beat novel was probably John Clellon Holmes's *Go* (1952), which depicts the Beat scene in New York in the 1940's. Beat writers, such as Allen Ginsberg, Gregory Corso, and Lawrence Ferlinghetti, never attempted a uniform aesthetic, but their poetry, usually in **free verse,** is characterized by colloquial diction and rhythms. The sudden death of Kerouac in 1969 (brought on by excessive drinking) seemed to have officially ended the era of the Beat Generation.

See S. P. Rosenbaum, ed., *The Beat Generation: A Collection of Memoirs, Commentary, and Criticism* (1975); John Tytell, *Naked Angels: The Lives and Literature of the Beat Generation* (1976); Fred W. McDarrah, *Kerouac and Friends: A Beat Generation Album* (1985).

beginning rhyme: Rhyme at the beginnings of lines, a device rarely used. (See Sidney Lanier's *The Symphony*.)

belles-lettres: Literally, "fine letters," the term has been used interchangeably with *literature,* though current usage restricts its meaning to lighter writings or to appreciative essays on the beauties of literature.

bestiary: A collection of descriptions of animals, some of them fabulous, such as the unicorn. The origins of such lore are traceable to a time before ancient Greece. In the fifth century B.C., Herodotus collected oral accounts, as did Aristotle a century later in his *Historia animalium.* The first to discuss the relationship of theological symbolism to animals was Plutarch, who stated that the Egyptians believed that animals revealed mystical truths about the gods.

At the beginning of the twelfth century, Latin bestiaries were popular in England and on the Continent. These elaborate and ornate picture books, used to inculcate moral and religious doctrine, were produced in monasteries for some two hundred years.

bibliography: A list of books or shorter works on a particular subject or a list of the works of a particular author or authors. Among the various kinds of bibliographies, the *enumerative* bibliography is perhaps the simplest, for it generally gives such basic information as the author's name, the title of the work, the place and year of publication, and the publisher. A *descriptive* bibliography, which includes all of the details generally found in an enumerative bibliography, contains such additional information as a description and analysis of a book's format, including its pagination, binding, and title page in order to distinguish the first **edition** from subsequent editions and additional printings. An *analytic* bibliography, which includes all that is generally found in a descriptive bibliography, also contains a thorough description of the physical makeup of the book, such as its **signatures,** press numbers (small numbers at the foot of a page in books published between the seventeenth and nineteenth centuries to indicate which press the sheet was printed on when more than one press was involved), ornaments, paper, watermarks, ink, and size of type.

Two other terms are widely used: A *primary* bibliography, such as Stuart Mason's *Bibliography of Oscar Wilde* (1914), is a listing of books, articles, and reviews written by an author (in this case, Wilde); a *secondary* bibliography, such as E. H. Mikhail's *Oscar Wilde: An Annotated Bibliography of Criticism* (1978), is a listing of books, articles, and reviews written by scholars and literary critics.

Bildungsroman: A term frequently used by German critics; a *Bildungsroman* (*Bildung*, "formation"; *roman*, "novel") is a portrait of the youthful development of a central character. Examples are Dickens's *David Copperfield*, Mann's *The Magic Mountain*, and Samuel Butler's *The Way of All Flesh*. *Bildungsroman* is used interchangeably with *Erziehungsroman* (*Erziehung*, "upbringing" or "education"), a novel of initiation and education in life. See *Künstlerroman*.

See Jerome H. Buckley, *Season of Youth: The Bildungsroman from Dickens to Golding* (1974); Randolph P. Shaffner, *The Apprenticeship Novel* (1984).

biography: An account of the life of a person. The modern biography, which is based on careful research and which is relatively dispassionate in attitude, is a comparatively recent form. Classical and medieval biographies were generally written to illustrate a thesis. In the typical saint's life, for example, the subject was reduced to an illustration of the qualities of a Christian saint. The Renaissance and the Reformation, however, produced a new emphasis on the individual, and by the time that Boswell wrote the life of Dr. Johnson, the development of the modern biography was substantially complete. The subjectivity of the Romantics, later reinforced by Freudian theory, has produced the biography which attempts to re-create the inner life of its subject. Recently, the techniques of the novel have begun to influence the writing of biography, as in the work of André Maurois.

See Alan Shelston, *Biography* (1977); David Novarr, *The Lines of Life: Theories of Biography, 1880–1970* (1986).

black humor: Writing in which grotesque or horrifying elements are sharply juxtaposed with humorous or farcical ones. In medieval medicine the black humour was the black bile, one of the bodily fluids, an excess of which produced melancholy. (See **humours.**) In modern literary usage, however, the sense of this term is distinct from its older meaning. Although in 1939 the French Surrealist writer André Breton called a collection of writings an *Anthologie de l'humour noir*, the terms *black humor* and *black comedy* only came into general use in the early 1960's, especially in describing the works of such American writers as Nathanael West, Vladimir Nabokov, and Joseph Heller. The aim of the black humorist is not to blend the serious and the comic, as in Chekhov, or to satirize through exaggeration, as in Swift, but to shock and disorient the reader, forcing him to laugh while recognizing a horrifying and disoriented world. The term has also been applied to such plays of the **Theater of the Absurd** as Ionesco's *The Lesson* and *The Chairs*. A related, but more limited, term is *gallows humor*, which refers to joking with the idea of death, especially under macabre circumstances.

See Bruce Jay Friedman, ed., *Black Humor* (1965); Douglas M. Davis, ed., *The World of Black Humor: An Introductory Anthology of Selections and Criticism* (1967); Matthew Winston, "*Humour noir* and Black Humor," in *Veins of Humor*, ed. Harry Levin (1972).

blank verse: Although verse described as *blank* is, strictly, no more than unrhymed, the term is limited to unrhymed iambic pentameter. Blank verse was first used in English by Surrey in his translation of Vergil and first appeared in the drama in Sackville and Norton's *Gorboduc* (acted 1561), later becoming the standard verse form of the Elizabethan theater. It was chosen by Milton for *Paradise Lost* and has since been used more than any other form for serious verse in English.

Bloomsbury Group: A circle of English writers, artists, and intellectuals who frequently held informal artistic and philosophical discussions in Bloomsbury, a section of London near the British Museum, from around 1907 to the 1930's. The group included, at various times, the novelists E. M. Forster and Virginia Woolf, the art critics Roger Fry and Clive Bell, the painter Duncan Grant, the economist John Maynard Keynes, and Leonard Woolf, who, with his wife, Virginia, founded the Hogarth Press, which published many works by Bloomsbury's adherents.

In their discussions, the members of the group examined such concepts as art, beauty, conduct, and friendship. Some members were influenced by G. E. Moore's *Principia Ethica* (1903), which proposed that "the most valuable things, which we know or can imagine, are certain states of consciousness, which may be roughly described as the pleasures of human intercourse and the enjoyment of beautiful objects"; these states are, according to Moore, not only the *"raison d'être* of virtue" but the "rational ultimate end of human action and the sole criterion of social progress."

Though many members of the Bloomsbury Group would probably have agreed with the values here affirmed by Moore—an aversion to moral prudery and an admiration for sensitivity, friendship, civilized tolerance, as well as an appreciation of beauty—the wide range of interests and temperaments in the group precluded any uniform aesthetic or philosophic attitudes. Moreover, despite the importance of their achievements in twentieth-century art and literature, they did not effect a sharp break with the past. As Michael Holroyd has written in *Lytton Strachey and the Bloomsbury Group* (1971): ". . . most of the Bloomsbury writers and artists were unable finally to sever the umbilical cord joining them to the inherited traditions of the past. . . . They modified, romanticized, avoided those traditions with varying degrees of success. . . . they were, in the words of Roger Fry himself, 'the last of the Victorians.' "

See Quentin Bell, *Bloomsbury* (1968); Leon Edel, *Blooms-bury: A House of Lions* (1979); S. P. Rosenbaum, *Victorian Bloomsbury: The Early Literary History of the Bloomsbury Group* (1987).

bombast: Originally referring to a stuffing made of cotton or horse-hair to produce bulges that fashion demanded during the Eliz-abethan period in England, the term came to mean inflated language such as that sometimes employed by dramatists of the day, as in this passage from Marlowe's *Tamburlaine the Great:*

> And here in Afric, where it seldom rains,
> Since I arriv'd with my triumphant host,
> Have swelling clouds, drawn from wide-gasping wounds,
> Been oft resolv'd in bloody purple showers,
> A meteor that might terrify the earth,
> And make it quake at every drop it drinks.

boulevard drama: Originally the body of plays produced in the late nineteenth century for the major theaters of Paris by such writers as Labiche and Halévy. The term is now applied to plays, usually comedies of some sophistication, designed primarily as com-mercial products. In the modern English theater, many of Noël Coward's plays are examples of boulevard drama.

bourgeois drama: A term widely used to describe the modern re-alistic drama dealing with the problems of middle-class char-acters.

bouts-rimés: Sets of rhyme words unattached to verses. At various times since the seventeenth century, the making of impromptu verses to fit *bouts-rimés*, or preconceived rhyme words, has been a fashionable pastime.

bowdlerize: Derived from Dr. Thomas Bowdler's expurgation of "offensive" passages from *The Family Shakespeare* (1818), which removed "whatever is unfit to be read by a gentleman in a company of ladies," the term now refers to the prudish expur-gation of any supposed indecency.

Breton lay: See **lay.**

broadside: A sheet of paper, generally of large size, with printed matter on only one side. It is designed for distribution or posting.

burlesque: A work designed to ridicule attitudes, style, or subject matter by handling either an elevated subject in a trivial manner or a low subject with mock dignity. *Burlesque* is the general term for various types of satirical imitation; it is useful to distinguish it from *parody*, which refers to a specific subgenre. A parody ridicules a serious literary work or the characteristic style of an author by treating the subject matter flippantly or by applying the style to an inappropriate, usually trivial, subject. Thus, the libretto of Gilbert and Sullivan's *Patience* is not a parody since it does not ridicule another work by comically imitating its style or subject matter; rather, it is a satire of the attitudes of **Aestheticism.** The following stanzas by Robert Southey are parodied by Lewis Carroll:

> "You are old, Father William," the young man cried;
>   "The few locks which are left you are gray;
> You are hale, Father William,—a hearty old man:
>   Now tell me the reason, I pray."
>
> "In the days of my youth," Father William replied,
>   "I remembered that youth would fly fast,
> And abused not my health and my vigor at first,
>   That I never might need them at last.
>   Southey, "The Old Man's Comforts
>   and how he gained them"
>
> "You are old, Father William," the young man said,
>   "And your hair has become very white,
> And yet you incessantly stand on your head—
>   Do you think, at your age, it is right?"
>
> "In my youth," Father William replied to his son,
>   "I feared it might injure the brain;
> But now that I'm perfectly sure I have none,
>   Why, I do it again and again."
>   Carroll, "Father William"

Among the various forms of comic imitation is the pastiche, a work made by pasting together scraps from different parts of an artist's work or from the works of various artists. Sometimes such a combination aims at creating a new work, as when a number of airs are strung together in a medley. Usually, however, the intention is satirical, and in its most common English usage, the term *pastiche* is a synonym for *parody*. In French, *pastiche* refers to an imitation of a literary work or style, often to ridicule it.

Like parody, travesty also ridicules a specific work or literary form by comic mimicry. Its technique is to employ an inelegant or coarse style for a more elevated subject, as in Samuel Butler's *Hudibras* (1663), which mocks then current Puritanism by describing the misadventures of Sir Hudibras in **doggerel,** thereby creating a travesty of the **chivalric romance:**

> When civil fury first grew high,
> And men fell out, they knew not why;
> When hard words, jealousies, and fears,
> Set folks together by the ears,
> And made them fight, like mad or drunk,
> For Dame Religion as for Punk. . . .

The mock epic, another form of burlesque, renders a trivial subject ridiculous by treating it with the elaborate and dignified devices of the **epic.** The masterpiece of the mock epic in English is Pope's *The Rape of the Lock,* in which the theft of an elegant lady's lock of hair by one of her beaus is presented as though it were an event of momentous importance. Beginning with a solemn statement of his theme ("What dire offense from amorous causes springs"), Pope introduces the usual epic features, such as supernatural machinery, **epic simile,** a voyage to the underworld, grandiose orations, and mighty battles—all used to describe the trivia of an elegant afternoon, as here, where the heroine's victory in a card game is portrayed as though it were a Homeric battle:

> An Ace of Hearts steps forth: the King unseen
> Lurked in her hand, and mourned his captive Queen:
> He springs to vengeance with an eager pace,
> And falls like thunder on the prostrate Ace.
> The nymph exulting fills with shouts the sky;
> The walls, the woods, and long canals reply.

The style of the mock epic is called the "mock heroic," which is often employed in works that do not mock the epic form. The stylistic intent, however, is similar to that in mock epics: to satirize their subjects by inflating them with false dignity. In Oscar Wilde's *The Importance of Being Earnest*, characters discuss absurd events, such as being "born, or at any rate, bred" in a handbag, with portentous solemnity.

See John D. Jump, *Burlesque* (1972); Joseph A. Dane, *Parody* (1988).

burletta: In the eighteenth- and nineteenth-century English theater, a short comic play with music. A considerable amount of music was essential to these productions in order to evade the law which limited legitimate drama to the patent theaters. A well-known nineteenth-century burletta was *Tom & Jerry! or Life in London,* produced at the Adelphi in 1821 and 1822.

Burns stanza: A six-line stanza, $aaa^4b^2a^4b^2$, named after the Scottish poet Robert Burns:

> Ha! whare ye gaun, ye crawlin' ferlie?
> Your impudence protects you sairly:
> I canna say but ye strunt rarely
>   Owre gauze an' lace;
> Though, faith! I fear ye dine but sparely
>   On sic a place.
>   "To a Louse"

The Burns stanza is a variant of the **tail-rhyme stanza.**

buskin: A half-boot covering for the foot and leg which reached to the calf; worn by actors in ancient Greek tragedy. Comic actors wore a low shoe or sock. "To put on buskins" consequently means to act or write tragedy.

Byronic hero: The type of hero modeled after Byron's central figures in such works as *Childe Harold's Pilgrimage* (1812–18), *Manfred* (1817), and *Cain* (1821). This figure is derived from such diverse sources as the **Sturm und Drang,** a German literary movement in the late eighteenth century; the conventional villain-hero of the **Gothic novel** (who is preoccupied with a secret sin later revealed in the novel and is generally portrayed as dark, handsome, with melancholy, brooding eyes); and various other figures by whom the Romantics were intrigued, such as the Wandering Jew, Prometheus, Goethe's Faust, and Milton's Satan.

The Byronic hero is a rebel, proudly defiant in his attitude toward conventional social codes and religious beliefs, an exile or outcast hungering for an ultimate truth to give meaning to his life in a seemingly meaningless universe. An individualist with an extraordinary capacity for passion, he suffers deeply from remorse over a moral or spiritual transgression; through his solitary wanderings among awesome landscapes, he yearns to purge himself of demonic self-destructiveness. Despite his "crime" or "sin," he remains a sympathetic figure, for he is not guilty of intentional cruelty. His nobility in grief inspires awe; his capacity for eloquence testifies to his extraordinary sensibility.

Later varieties of the type appear in Charlotte Brontë's Rochester, the hero of *Jane Eyre* (1847), and Emily Brontë's Heathcliff, the hero of *Wuthering Heights* (1847), as well as innumerable works of nineteenth-century Continental literature.

See Peter Thorslev, *The Byronic Hero* (1962).

C

cacophony: Discordant or harsh sounds which are frequently introduced for poetic effect. Cacophony may perhaps be the result of difficulty of articulation, though the image presented also influences the readers. In these lines by Browning, the image of sudden flame combines abrupt rhythms and explosive consonants to produce a cacophonous effect:

> A tap at the pane, the quick sharp scratch
> And blue spurt of a lighted match.
> "Meeting at Night"

cadence: The natural rhythm of language determined by its inherent alternation of stressed and unstressed syllables. When more precisely used in verse, the term *cadence* refers to the arrangement of the rhythms of speech into highly organized patterns. See **free verse.**

caesura (cesura): A pause in a line of verse dictated not by metrics but by the natural rhythm of the language. There is usually a caesura in verses of ten syllables or more, and the handling of this pause to achieve rhythmical variety is a test of the poet's ability. Note Pope's skill in shifting the caesura in this passage:

A little learning / / is a dangerous thing;
Drink deep, / / or taste not the Pierian spring:
There shallow draughts / / intoxicate the brain,
But drinking largely / / sobers us again.
An Essay on Criticism

canon: A body of writings established as authentic. Used particularly in reference to Biblical writings which have been received as authentic or authorized for the Christian Bible, the term is also used to designate an author's works which are accepted as genuine, such as Shakespeare's canon of thirty-seven plays. The term is likewise used by the Roman Catholic Church, which has a "Saints' Canon," a list of those who have been "canonized," *i.e.*, authorized by the Church.

canso (also **chanson**): In Provençal verse, a love lyric. See **troubadour.**

canticum: Parts of a Latin drama either sung or chanted. See **diverbium.**

canto: Italian: "song." A major section of a long poem. Dante's *Divine Comedy* and Byron's *Childe Harold*, for example, are divided into cantos.

canzone: A Provençal or Italian lyric, sometimes designed to be sung to music, often on the subject of love. The *canzone* had no fixed form but consisted of a series of stanzas of from seven to twenty lines, predominantly hendecasyllabic (*i.e.*, eleven syllables), and a concluding **envoy.** *Canzoni* were written by, among others, Dante, Petrarch, and Tasso. In English, Spenser's "Epithalamion" shows the influence of the *canzone*; W. H. Auden uses the term as the title of one of his poems.

capa y espada: Spanish: "cloak and sword." The comedies of such sixteenth- and seventeenth-century Spanish playwrights as Lope de Vega and Calderón de la Barca, dealing with love and intrigue among the aristocracy.

caricature: In literature, a character consisting of certain selected features exaggerated for comic effect. In Etherege's *The Man of Mode; or, Sir Fopling Flutter*, Sir Fopling, as the name suggests, is a caricature of the Restoration fop.

carmen figuratum: Latin: "a shaped poem," the verses of which are so arranged that they form a design on the page. When the design is an object, such as a cross or an altar, it is usually the theme of the poem. Dylan Thomas's "Vision and Prayer" is such a poem, but the type is most common in the Renaissance, as exemplified in George Herbert's "The Altar":

> A broken ALTAR, Lord, thy servant reares,
> Made of a heart, and cemented with teares,
>> Whose parts are as thy hand did frame;
>> No workman's tool hath touch'd the same.
>>> A   HEART   alone
>>> Is   such   a   stone
>>> Thy power doth cut,
>>> Wherefore each part
>>> Of my hard heart
>>> Meets in this frame,
>>> To praise thy name.
>> That if I chance to hold my peace
>> These stones to praise thee may not cease.
> O let thy blessed SACRIFICE be mine,
> And sanctifie this ALTAR to be thine.

In recent years, the vogue of shaped verse, called "concrete poetry," has become a worldwide phenomenon. Often the poems consist of single letters, words, or phrases in a variety of type styles and colors, all of which challenge the reader to perceive the shape and theme.

See Emmett Williams, ed., *An Anthology of Concrete Poetry* (1967); Mary Ellen Solt, ed., *Concrete Poetry: A World View* (1968).

carpe diem: Latin: "seize the day." A theme characteristic of a considerable body of poetry, most of it lyric. A *carpe diem* poem advises the reader, or the person it addresses, to enjoy the pleasures of the moment before youth passes away.

> What is love? 'Tis not hereafter;
> Present mirth hath present laughter;
>> What's to come is still unsure.
> In delay there lies no plenty;
> Then come kiss me, sweet and twenty,
> Youth's a stuff will not endure.
>> Shakespeare, *Twelfth Night*

catachresis: 1. The application of a word to something which it does not denote. Examples are the use of *individual* for *person* or *chronic* for *severe*. 2. Any strained or forced figure of speech. In Crashaw's "On Our Crucified Lord Naked and Bloody," Christ's blood is referred to as a garment, his body a wardrobe:

> Th'have left thee naked Lord! O that they had!
> This Garment too I would they had deny'd.
> Thee with thyselfe they have too richly clad,
> Opening the purple wardrobe of thy side.
> O never could bee found garment too good
> For thee to weare, but these, of thine owne Blood.

catalectic, catalexis: See **acatalectic.**

catastrophe: See **Freytag's Pyramid.**

catharsis: See **tragedy.**

Cavalier drama: In the 1630's, Queen Henrietta Maria, wife of Charles I of England, extended royal patronage to the performance at court of a type of play now called "Cavalier drama." These plays, always decorous and solemn, drew their materials from Greek romances, which were avidly read at court.

The background of the typical Cavalier play involves political and military conflict between two or three neighboring states. In the elaborate plot, crews of pirates either capture the central characters or rescue them from sinking ships. The ladies, always beautiful and virtuous, are in love with men who are always valiant and honorable. A lustful villain, a **stock character** in Cavalier drama, and numerous other impediments prevent the marriage which appears to be the natural course for the central figures. In time, however, all obstacles are removed; the play may therefore end in wedlock.

The florid dialogue, compounded of artifice and bombast, is in rhythmic prose, frequently arranged and printed to give the impression of blank verse. The most notable writers of this kind of drama were Thomas Killigrew and Sir John Suckling. With the Civil War and the ascendancy of Cromwell in the 1640's, Cavalier drama came to an end.

See Alfred Harbage, *Cavalier Drama* (1936).

Cavalier poetry: Verse written by courtiers of Charles I (reigned 1625–49), generally in praise of wine, women, song, and the King. Inspired by Jonson's graceful lyrics, the Cavalier poets regarded themselves as members of the "Tribe of Ben" in their concern for precise diction and concise form. Among the most distinguished of the Cavalier poets were Thomas Carew, Richard Lovelace, and Sir John Suckling. Though not a courtier, Robert Herrick is sometimes included in the group.

See Robin Skelton, *The Cavalier Poets* (1960).

Celtic Renaissance: See **Irish Literary Renaissance.**

Celtic Twilight: A term used to suggest an atmosphere much admired by some Irish writers of the late nineteenth century who, interested in supplying Ireland with a romantic past, attempted to create in their work a dreamy, shadowy vision of Celtic myth and legend. In *The Wanderings of Oisin* (1889), for example, W. B. Yeats suggests remote, heroic times by means of legendary figures, many references to "dream" and "shadow," and a style characterized by such phrases as "dove-gray" and "pearl-pale." The poet of the Celtic Twilight is concerned with an unreal world, more beautiful than the real. A leader in the **Irish Literary Renaissance,** Yeats called one of his books *The Celtic Twilight* (1893). James Joyce ridiculed the phenomenon in his phrase "cultic twalette."

See Austin Clarke, *The Celtic Twilight and the Nineties* (1969).

cesura: See **caesura.**

Chain of Being: The idea that the universe, as an organic unity, consists of a series of links and gradations of beings and objects arranged in a hierarchy of existence from the least significant to the source of creation, God Himself, toward which all things yearn.

Developed from Plato's theory of Ideas in the seventh book of *The Republic* (ca. 385 B.C.) and from the idea of the divine Demiurge in Plato's *Timaeus*, which depicts the creation of the phenomenal world from the Demiurge's own fecund nature, the Chain of Being embodies what philosophers have called "the principle of plenitude": all possible forms become actual within the hierarchy, extending from the eternal (or transcendent) Supreme Being to the sensible (or temporal) world, which is governed by time and change. The perfect Supreme Being, by its very nature a creative force, "overflows" with an infinite variety of forms without discontinuity. Thus, the divisions between forms in the animate and inanimate orders of existence are imperceptible.

Since, for the Neo-Platonists, the divine One does not "choose" to create but overflows into a multiplicity of forms, theologians in the Middle Ages brought this idea more into harmony with Christian doctrine by asserting that God, in His infinite goodness, "wills" the creation of all things. In retaining the idea of continuity, they envisioned the Chain of Being in the following form (here summarized):

> God
> Angels
> Man
> Animals
> Plants
> Stones

Man, as pivotal being uniting natural and supernatural orders of existence, shares with the angels eternal spirit and intelligence (in man, reason governed by logic; in angels, intuitive intelligence); with the animals and plants, man shares the capacity for reproduction and feeling. Some of these philosophical ideas are given expression in Hamlet's famous speech:

> What a piece of work is a man, how noble in reason, how infinite in faculties, in form and moving how express and admirable, in action how like an angel, in apprehension how like a god: the beauty of the world, the paragon of animals. . . .

By the early eighteenth century, the German philosopher Leibniz, starting from the assumption that God creates out of his goodness and perfection, developed the idea of a perfect world implicit in the principle of plenitude. Our perception of imperfection or evil, Leibniz argues, is the result of man's limited view of universal harmony. Leibniz's philosophical optimism—that this is the best of all possible worlds—was ridiculed by Voltaire in *Candide* (1759) and affirmed by Pope in *An Essay on Man* (1734):

Of systems possible, if 'tis confessed
That Wisdom Infinite must form the best,
Where all must full or not coherent be,
And all that rises rise in due degree;
Then in the scale of reasoning life, 'tis plain,
There must be, somewhere, such a rank as man. . . .
See, through this air, this ocean, and this earth,
All matter quick, and bursting into birth. . . .
Vast chain of being! which from God began,
Natures ethereal, human, angel, man,
Beast, bird, fish, insect, what no eye can see,
No glass can reach! from Infinite to thee,
From thee to nothing. . . .

See Arthur O. Lovejoy, *The Great Chain of Being* (1936); E. M. W. Tillyard, *The Elizabethan World Picture* (1948).

chain verse: Verse in which the stanzas (occasionally lines) are linked by rhyme or various patterns of repetition. The **villanelle** is an example of chain verse.

chanson de geste: French: "song of deeds." An Old French epic form which flourished between the eleventh and fourteenth centuries, describing the deeds of a historical or legendary hero. Many of the stories were concerned with Charlemagne and his knights. Some of the *chansons* dealt with battles against the Saracens, while others told of rebellion and disloyalty among Charlemagne's nobles. Later, such romantic elements as giants, fairies, and love affairs between Christian knights and Saracen maidens were introduced. There are about eighty surviving examples of the *chanson de geste,* of which the best known is *La Chanson de Roland.*

See William Calin, *The Epic Quest: Studies in Four Old French Chansons de Geste* (1966).

chansonnier: A collection in manuscript of Provençal troubadour poems.

chant royal: See **ballade.**

chantey (chanty, shantey): A sailor's song sung while at work.

chapbook: A pamphlet hawked about the streets of London by peddlers or "chapmen," particularly from the sixteenth through the eighteenth centuries. These pamphlets contained such miscellaneous matter as ballads, romances, and lives of notorious criminals.

character, the: A literary genre, especially popular in the seventeenth and eighteenth centuries, deriving from the *Characters* of Theophrastus (died 278 B.C.). The character is a brief essay describing the virtues or vices of a particular social type, such as the fop or the country squire.

Chaucerian stanza: See **rhyme royal.**

chiasmus: Greek: "placing crosswise" (the Greek chi is written as the letter X). A passage consisting of two balanced parts which have their elements reversed, as in the allusion to the hanged felon in Oscar Wilde's *The Ballad of Reading Gaol:*

> For his mourners will be outcast men,
>   And outcasts always mourn.

Chicago critics: A group associated with the University of Chicago between the 1930's and the 1950's, who emphasized a close reading and analysis of texts in order to redefine the various **genres** of literature. *Critics and Criticism: Ancient and Modern* (1952) contains essays by the most prominent Chicago critics: W. R. Keast, Richard McKeon, Norman MacLean, Elder Olson, Bernard Weinberg, and R. S. Crane, its editor. Influenced by the analytic and cultural implications of Aristotle's *Poetics*, these critics—sometimes called Neo-Aristotelians—were not only interested in developing a methodology for the analysis of "concrete artistic wholes" but also concerned with the relationship of criticism to the humanities. The Chicago critics differed from those associated with the **New Criticism** in their concern with the distinctions among genres rather than in the latter's examination of the uniqueness of poetry without differentiating among the various kinds.

chivalric romance: See **romance.**

choriamb(us): A foot of verse consisting of two stressed syllables flanking two unstressed, as in Swinburne's poem "Choriambics":

> Sweet the / kisses of death / set on thy lips,
>   colder are they / than mine;

> Colder surely than past kisses that love
> poured for thy lips as wine.

In a choriambic line, the first foot is a trochee, the last foot an iamb.

chorus: The chorus, from which the Greek drama developed, was originally a group of masked male dancers who sang or chanted as part of the ceremonies at religious festivals. As the Greek drama progressed, the role of the chorus altered and its importance diminished. In Aeschylus, the chorus often takes part in the action; in Sophocles, it is a commentator; and in Euripides, the chorus is primarily a lyric element. The Romans took the chorus from the Greeks; the Elizabethans imitated it from the Romans. The chorus, however, which was never made an integral part of English drama, was often reduced by the Elizabethans to a single figure who gave the prologue and epilogue and sometimes introduced major sections of the play, as in Shakespeare's *Henry V*. In modern plays, choruses are rare; when they appear, they may be either multiple, as in T. S. Eliot's *Murder in the Cathedral*, or single, as in Arthur Miller's *A View from the Bridge*.

chronicle: A record of events in historical order. The medieval chronicles, which occasionally contained legendary material, were composed in either verse or prose. They were based on the local records of the annalists and listed rather than evaluated events.

chronicle play: A dramatization of material taken from the chronicle histories of England, the most widely used of which were those of Holinshed and Hall. Such plays were very popular in Elizabethan England. At first they were scenes loosely strung together, but they soon developed greater unity and, in such plays as Marlowe's *Edward II* and Shakespeare's *Henry IV* (also called "history plays"), became subtle studies of character.

See Irving Ribner, *The English History Play in the Age of Shakespeare* (rev. ed., 1965).

Classical: A word that has carried so many different meanings at different times that no single meaning can any longer be said to appertain to it, this term should be used with discretion. Originally the *scriptor classicus* was one who wrote for the upper classes, as opposed to the *scriptor proletarius*, who wrote for the lower; soon, however, *classical* was applied to writing considered worthy of preservation and study; then the term *Classical* (in this usage always capitalized) referred simply to the literature of Greece and Rome; later it meant literature composed in imitation of the Graeco-Roman; and finally it was applied to literature which, though perhaps opposed to the ancient in concept and form, was worthy to be called "classical" because of the height of its achievement. In common use, the term *classical* is applied to literature which has at least some of these characteristics: balance, unity, proportion, restraint, and what Winckelmann called "noble simplicity and quiet grandeur."

classicism: The principles held to be the bases of classical art. See above.

clerihew: The invention of Edmund Clerihew Bentley (1875–1956), a clerihew contains two couplets which humorously characterize a person whose name is one of the rhymes. One of Bentley's original clerihews, inspired, according to G. K. Chesterton, by a chemistry lecture, is as follows:

> Sir Humphry Davy
> Abominated gravy.
> He lived in the odium
> Of having discovered sodium.

cliché: A timeworn expression which has lost its vitality and to some extent its original meaning. The use of clichés generally reveals a failure of the imagination. Several are included in the following sentence:

> Beckson and Ganz, *busy as bees*, are *working like dogs* to obtain *filthy lucre*.

Occasionally writers use clichés which are distorted for humorous effect, as in the case of *bated breath* in the poem below:

> Sally, having swallowed cheese,
> Directs down holes the scented breeze
> Enticing thus with baited breath
> Nice mice to an untimely death.
>   Geoffrey Taylor, "Cruel Clever Cat"

climax: The moment in a play or story at which a **crisis** reaches its highest intensity and is resolved. The major climax may be preceded by several climaxes of lesser intensity. See **Freytag's Pyramid; plot.**

cloak and sword play: See *capa y espada.*

closed heroic couplet: See **heroic couplet.**

closet drama: 1. A play written to be read rather than performed, *e.g.*, Byron's *Manfred.* 2. A play which, though intended to be performed, has survived as literature rather than as theater, *e.g.*, Shelley's *The Cenci.*

c.m.: The abbreviation for **common measure,** also called **hymnal stanza.**

comédie larmoyante: French: "tearful comedy." The sentimental comedy in eighteenth-century France. In response to the changing tastes of the age, a comedy developed which aimed to produce not critical laughter but pleasurable tears. These were usually evoked by the misfortunes of a virtuous heroine. The *comédie larmoyante* is not much admired today, but it is part of the drama of private emotion, which has characterized much of the modern theater. Among the practitioners of this genre were Philippe Destouches and, especially, Nivelle de La Chaussée.

comedy: Any literary work, but especially a play, less exalted and less serious than a tragedy, commonly having a happy ending. The term is flexible enough to include the satirical laughter of Aristophanes, the religious exaltation of Dante, and the near-tragedy of Chekhov. See **high comedy; low comedy; humor.**
    See Harry Levin, *Playboys and Killjoys: An Essay on the Theory and Practice of Comedy* (1987).

comedy of humours: See **humours.**

comedy of intrigue: See **intrigue.**

comedy of manners: A comedy concerned with the intrigues, regularly amorous, of witty and sophisticated members of an aristocratic society. The actions of those who oppose or ineptly imitate the manners of that society are the subjects of much raillery and laughter. Examples are the comedies of such Restoration play-wrights as Etherege and Congreve.

See Dale Underwood, *Etherege and the Seventeeth-Century Comedy of Manners* (1957); David L. Hirst, *Comedy of Manners* (1979).

comic relief: A comic element inserted into a tragic or somber work, especially a play, to relieve its tension, widen its scope, or heighten by contrast the tragic emotion. See, for example, the drunken porter's speech in Shakespeare's *Macbeth*.

commedia dell'arte: In medieval Italy, *arti* were groups of artisans or guilds. Thus, the *commedia dell'arte* was the comedy of the professional actors. These professional troupes, which came into prominence around the middle of the sixteenth century, worked primarily from skeletal scenarios which they filled out with dialogue and stage business, improvised in detail, though often rehearsed in essence. The companies consisted of about a dozen actors who played rigidly typed roles, such as Pantalone, the old man; Arlecchino, the lively clown; Il Capitano, the braggart soldier, etc. Masks and traditional costumes were worn by the clowns and old men. In the scenarios, most of which derived ultimately from Roman comedy, the young lovers, aided by their clever servants, outwitted their elders and attained money and happiness. The traditions of the *commedia dell'arte*, or masked comedy, were influential in the drama of the sixteenth and seventeenth centuries and, to some extent, survive today.

See Allardyce Nicoll, *The World of Harlequin* (1963).

common measure (c.m.): See **hymnal stanza.**

commonplace book: A notebook in which ideas and quotations are collected and grouped according to subject.

common rhythm: See **running rhythm.**

comoedia erudate: Latin: "learned comedy." In the Renaissance the learned imitations of Classical comedies by such writers as Aretino, Ariosto, and Machiavelli, whose *Mandragola* is the best-known example. Such plays were chiefly concerned with re-working the complicated intrigues inherited from the Roman **New Comedy.**

comparative linguistics: See **linguistics.**

compensation: The method of adjusting for omitted unstressed syllables in a line of metrical verse. Though an omitted syllable may be compensated for in the succeeding line, it is usually added to a foot in the same line or its place is taken by a pause. In the following stanza by Tennyson, where all four lines are trimeter, the stresses on and pauses after the words of the first line compensate for the missing syllables:

> Break, break, break,
> On thy cold gray stones, O sea!
> And I would that my tongue could utter
> The thoughts that arise in me.

complaint: A lyric poem, common in the Renaissance, which bewails the misery of the speaker, who is often someone whose beloved is unresponsive or absent. Occasionally, however, a complaint may be humorous, as in "The Complaint of Chaucer to His Empty Purse":

> To you, my purse, and to non other wight
> Compleyne I, for ye be my lady dere!
> I am sory, now that ye be light.

conceit: From Italian: *concetto*, "conception." A fanciful image, especially an elaborate or startling analogy. Petrarchan conceits are conventional comparisons imitated from the love sonnets of the Italian poet Petrarch. Such conceits were satirized by Shakespeare in the sonnet that begins "My mistress' eyes are nothing like the sun; / Coral is far more red than her lips' red." The Metaphysical conceit, characteristic of Donne and other Metaphysical poets of the seventeenth century, is a comparison, often elaborate, extended, or startling, between objects which are apparently dissimilar. Donne, having noted a flea which has sucked blood both from himself and from his mistress, who is about to exterminate it, exclaims:

> Oh stay, three lives in one flea spare,
> Where we almost, yea more than married are.
> This flea is you and I, and this
> Our marriage bed, and marriage temple is.
> > "The Flea"

See K. K. Ruthven, *The Conceit* (1969).

concordance: An alphabetically organized index of words in a text (such as the Bible) or in the work of a major author. Thus, a concordance of the works of Shakespeare lists the words used in the plays as well as the places where they may be found.

concrete poetry: See *carmen figuratum.*

concrete universal: A term invented by W. K. Wimsatt (*The Verbal Icon*) to refer to the idea, common in the history of criticism, that the work of art unifies the particular and the general. Although from one point of view the work of art is the sum of its disparate details (analogous to the denotation of a word in the logical sense—see **meaning**) and thus concrete, if the work is successful, says Wimsatt, these details coalesce into a totality, a "central abstraction" (analogous, as above, to connotation) which is the universal and which can be expressed only through the work.

confessional literature: A type of autobiography, confessional literature involves the revelation by an author of events or feelings that normally are discreetly concealed. The Romantic tendency to explore the depths, as well as the heights, of the soul has made the confession a characteristically, though not exclusively, Romantic form. For examples, see Jean-Jacques Rousseau's *Confessions*, Thomas De Quincey's *Confessions of an English Opium-Eater*.

confidant (confidante, fem.): A character in drama or fiction, a trusted friend to whom the protagonist reveals his most intimate feelings and intentions. Thus, Shakespeare uses Horatio, who has little effect on the plot, as a device to reveal Hamlet's plans to the audience. The device of the confidant eventually became so conventionalized that in the eighteenth century Sheridan made fun of it in *The Critic*, which contains the stage direction, "Enter Tilburina, stark mad in white satin, and her confidante, stark mad in white linen."

conflict: In drama and fiction, the opposition of two forces or characters. Conflict may occur: (1) within one character (Macbeth's reverence for Duncan and his desire to kill him); (2) between a character and society (Jude, in Hardy's *Jude the Obscure*, cannot surmount the social barriers which prevent him from obtaining a university education); (3) between two characters, each of whom tries to impose his will on the other (in its simplest form, the hero and villain of melodrama).

connotation: The implications or suggestions that are evoked by a word. Connotations may be (1) highly individual, based on associations because of pleasant or unpleasant experiences in a person's life; (2) general, or culturally conditioned, as in the word *anarchist*, which commonly evokes a picture of a large black-bearded man holding a bomb. See **denotation; meaning.**

consistency: The quality of internal coherence in the parts and in the tone of a literary work. Thus, a manipulation by the author to avoid the catastrophe in what appears to be a tragedy may be a violation of consistency in the work. The term may also be used to describe a character whose actions and speeches are in accord with his image as established by the author.

consonance: 1. The close repetition of identical consonant sounds before and after different vowels, such as "flip—flop," "feel—fill."

 2. Some writers accept as consonance the repetition of consonant sounds at the ends of words only, as in "east—west," or "hid—bed." Emily Dickinson uses consonance in place of rhyme in these quatrains:

> 'T was later when the summer went
> Than when the cricket *came*,
> And yet we knew that gentle clock
> Meant nought but going *home*.

> 'T was sooner when the cricket went
> Than when the winter *came*,
> Yet that pathetic pendulum
> Keeps esoteric *time*.

conte: See **tale.**

contextualism: A term used by Murray Krieger in *New Apologists for Poetry* (1956) to characterize an autonomous poetic context separated from non-poetic "contexts"—that is, references to external reality. In a poem, the only appropriate "context"

for analysis is the poem itself, a concept associated with New
Criticism.

convention: A generally accepted literary device or form. At a theatrical performance, for example, the audience accepts a set of
conventions: As the curtain (itself a convention) goes up, the
spectators see a three-walled room, but by another convention
the absence of the fourth wall is ignored. The action may be
surrounded by obviously false scenery painted on a flat canvas,
but this artificiality is also ignored. The arrangement of the fur-
niture, all of which faces the audience, and the gestures and
projected voices of the actors are dramatic conventions which,
though not "true to life," are necessary to the presentation of
the action. Consequently, if a character speaks in iambic pentameter verse, the audience is not startled by the unreality of
his speech, for convention is a necessary device in all literature.

copyright: Until the fifteenth century, when printing came into
prominence, there was no need to provide for the protection of
literary rights. However, when the pirating of works became a
problem, rulers granted exclusive rights to printers' guilds, which
then regulated the practices of their members.

The first English copyright law, in 1710, gave protection to
the author for fourteen years, renewable once for a like number
of years. The earliest American copyright laws, modeled after
the British, were enacted by individual states between 1783 and
1786; in 1790, the first federal copyright law was enacted. The
current copyright law, enacted in 1976, provides protection during the author's life and for fifty years after his or her death
(without need to renew) and extends to all copyrightable works,
whether published or unpublished, such as books, periodicals,
manuscripts, musical works (including accompanying words),
dramatic works (including any accompanying music), pantomimes and choreographic works, graphic and sculptural works
(including maps, models, globes), motion pictures, and sound
recordings. (Not protected by copyright are ideas, subject matter, and titles, since the law covers only the unique expression
in a work). If a copyright existed before January 1, 1978, when
the new law took effect, it now has a term of seventy-five years,
consisting of the original term of twenty-eight years and a re-

newal of forty-seven years (failure to renew results in loss of protection).

Today, most countries acknowledge the resolutions formulated at the Bern Convention (1886) and the numerous subsequent revisions. The signers agreed that literary material copyrighted in one country would receive protection in other signatory countries. Most countries, including those in the British Commonwealth, grant protection for the lifetime of the author and for fifty years thereafter. The United States was never a party to the Bern union, but American works are protected in signatory countries if published in one of those countries simultaneously with their publication in the United States.

See William S. Strong, *The Copyright Book: A Practical Guide* (1984); William F. Patry, *The Fair Use Privilege in Copyright Law* (1985).

counterplot: See **subplot.**

coup de théâtre: A striking, unexpected, and theatrically effective turn of events in a play. An extraordinary *coup de théâtre* occurs in Act V, Scene vi, of Webster's *The White Devil,* when Flamineo, who has been shot by his sister, Vittoria, and his mistress, Zanche, finding that they do not intend to follow him in death, springs to his feet and exclaims: "Oh cunning devils! now I have tried your love, / And doubled all your reaches.—I am not wounded."

couplet: Two successive lines of verse, usually rhymed and of the same meter. The following stanza consists of a pair of couplets:

> Lizzie Borden with an axe,
> Hit her father forty whacks,
> When she saw what she had done,
> She hit her mother forty-one.
> Anonymous

courtesy book: A type of conduct book popular in the Renaissance. It described the training and manner of life appropriate to a gentleman, a man who was to be a soldier, an adviser to his prince, and a gallant and accomplished courtier. The most famous example of this genre is Castiglione's *The Courtier.*

courtly love: A philosophy of love which exerted an important influence on medieval and Renaissance literature. The term *courtly
love* was derived from *amour courtois* ("courteous love"), coined
by Gaston Paris in 1883 to describe what Maurice Valency calls
in *In Praise of Love* (1958) "a new concept of manhood, the idea
of the gentleman, the *courtois.*"

The ideas associated with courtly love—a compound of such
elements as the attitudes of the Provençal troubadours, conventions drawn from Ovid, and the medieval veneration of the Virgin
Mary—were codified at the end of the twelfth century by An-
dreas Capellanus in *The Art of Honest Love* (sometimes called
The Art of Courtly Love).

Aristocratic and chivalric, courtly love was extramarital and,
as a result, secret. The lover, usually a knight, was expected to
languish, become pale, and be subject to fits of sighing, trem-
bling, and weeping. The lady whom he desired had to be of
noble birth; in the process of venerating her from afar, the knight's
spirit was ennobled so that he could perform deeds worthy of
his love. Once accepted by his lady, he vowed eternal faithfulness. Though adultery was a possibility, often the knight was
satisfied with innocent intimacies.

For Dante and other writers of the **dolce stil nuovo,** courtly
love takes on a Platonic and religious character: the beloved does
not inspire the lover to perform chivalric deeds but leads him
to a vision of God. The earlier code of courtly love, emphasizing
the sensual, dominates the characters of Chaucer's *Troilus and
Criseyde*.

See C. S. Lewis, *Allegory of Love* (1936); F. X. Newman, ed.,
The Meaning of Courtly Love (1968); Bernard O'Donoghue, *The
Courtly Love Tradition* (1982).

Cowleyan ode (irregular ode): See **ode.**

cradle books: See **incunabula.**

craft cycle: See **miracle play.**

crisis: A brief period of time in a story or play when a conflict is
intensified to the point where a resolution must occur. In the
course of an action, there may be several crises, each of which
precedes a **climax.** In *Hamlet*, for example, a major crisis occurs

during the play scene. The climax is reached when Claudius, having witnessed a representation of his own crime, rises from his chair, calls for lights, and rushes off.

criticism: The evaluation of literary works, including classification by genre, analysis of structure, and judgment of value. Though all critical activity ultimately reflects the individual's response to a literary work, there are several approaches that reveal the range of possible bases for the act of judgment. The following is a formal classification of some of the more important modes of literary criticism:

The *moralistic* approach, which has had the longest history, begins with Plato, who excluded most poets from his ideal Republic because of their harmful moral effect on the populace. In their depiction of flawed tragic figures, playwrights instilled corresponding weaknesses in their spectators, Plato argued, convinced that audiences identified too closely with such figures; he also condemned contemporary comedy, which, he believed, catered to man's lower appetites rather than his higher faculties. In Plato, as in all moralist critics, the underlying assumption is that art, as a significant formative agent in man's moral and spiritual development, should be didactic—that is, it should teach by presenting a moral vision of reality.

The *impressionistic*, or *aesthetic*, approach, which gained widespread acceptance in the late nineteenth century, involves the critic's personal and subjective response to a literary work. As Anatole France stated, such a critic reveals "the adventures of a sensitive soul among masterpieces," and Walter Pater, in his preface to *Studies in the History of the Renaissance* (1873), affirmed that "the first step toward seeing one's object as it really is, is to know one's own impression as it really is. . . . The aesthetic critic, then, regards all the objects with which he has to do, all works of art, and the fairer forms of nature and human life, as powers or forces producing pleasurable sensations, each of a more or less peculiar kind. This influence he feels, and wishes to explain, analyzing it, and reducing it to its elements." Such a critic reveals his understanding of a work of art in artistically shaped prose, which he regards as an art in itself. Echoing Anatole France and Pater, Oscar Wilde, in his essay "The Critic as Artist" (1890), wrote that impressionistic criticism was "the only civilized form of autobiography" and that the critic's "sole aim is to chronicle his own impressions."

The *biographical* approach proceeds on the assumption that by examining the facts and motives of an author's life, the critic can illuminate the meaning and intent of his work. Thus, such a critic attempts to discover analogues between the work and the writer's life by identifying such elements as characters modeled after real people and incidents derived from personal experience. In the case of such semi-autobiographical novels as Joyce's *A Portrait of the Artist as a Young Man* and Thomas Wolfe's *Look Homeward, Angel*, such an approach may be illuminating. Nevertheless, biographical critics recognize the essential differences between the structure of fiction and autobiography. While the latter inevitably involves selection and arrangement, fiction, no matter how closely related to the facts of an author's life, is free to invent new incidents and characters to meet the demands of art.

The *sociological*, or *historical*, approach, as its name implies, assumes that the relationship between art and society is organic and indivisible, that a work of art is not only a reflection but also a product of its social and historical milieu. Marxist critics, for example, interpret literature as a manifestation of the class struggle, as an instrument, in short, to advance their cause. But sociological or historical criticism need not be so narrow in its approach, for many critics, without preconceived ideological convictions, such as F. O. Matthiessen, in *American Renaissance* (1941) and L. C. Knights, in *Drama and Society in the Age of Jonson* (1937), have examined the relationship between art and social forces.

The *psychological* approach, chiefly inspired by the development of psychoanalysis in the twentieth century, has concentrated not only on the effect of the author's unconscious mental activity during the creative process but also on the interpretation of structure and character, frequently in psychoanalytic terms. The classic example is Ernest Jones's *Hamlet and Oedipus* (1949), in which both Hamlet and Shakespeare are subjected to such an examination. Despite its obvious limitations (a literary character is never the equivalent of a human being, nor can an author, long dead, be accurately subjected to psychoanalytic study), such an approach may be illuminating when used with discretion, especially in dealing with such a work as D. H. Lawrence's *Sons and Lovers*, in which the Oedipus complex is of central importance.

The *archetypal* approach involves a systematic analysis of universal motifs and patterns, such as the Rebel Against Authority or the Cursed Wanderer. Archetypes, as Jung suggested, emerge from the collective unconscious (the repository of inherited racial memories) and manifest themselves in myths, dreams, and literature. In addition to Jung's study of archetypes, the great work of Sir James Frazer, *The Golden Bough* (12 vols., 1890–1915), has been of prime importance to critics in its delineation of mythic patterns among ancient peoples. Literary artists as well have been profoundly affected by the study of myth: T. S. Eliot, for example, drew inspiration from Frazer's work and from Jessie Weston's *From Ritual to Romance*, a study of the Grail legend and related myths and rituals.

The *formalist* approach, stressing the essential structure of a literary work, is primarily concerned with the linguistic texture, not with the "message" which a work is presumed to communicate. In short, the formalist critic is less concerned with what a work "says" than how it achieves its effects. In his analysis of the structure of metaphor, paradox, irony, tone, and other interacting elements, the formalist critic (also variously called "ontological" or "New" critic) assumes that the literary work is a unique organism. Though an author's life and times may be of interest, ultimately the work as such must be examined for its form and effect. Critics of the **New Criticism** have cited, as one limitation of this critical discipline, an insufficient concern with values other than structural ones.

See Stanley Edgar Hyman, *The Armed Vision* (rev. ed., 1955); David Daiches, *Critical Approaches to Literature* (1956); Northrop Frye, *Anatomy of Criticism* (1957); Wilbur Scott, ed., *Five Approaches of Literary Criticism* (1962).

cross acrostic: See **acrostic.**

crown of sonnets: A poem comprising seven sonnets, which are interlinked. The final line of each stanza is also the first line of the next. The last line of the seventh sonnet is also the first line of the opening sonnet. For an example, see Donne's "La Corona."

curtain raiser: A one-act play or other entertainment which is performed at the beginning of a program. In the late nineteenth and early twentieth centuries, curtain raisers served to entertain the audience while latecomers arrived; in this way, the main play of the evening could be presented without distraction.

curtal-sonnet: A term used by Gerard Manley Hopkins in the preface to *Poems* (1918) to describe a shortened form of the sonnet, which he invented. Instead of the traditional fourteen lines, he reduced the number to ten and a half, divided into two stanzas, one of six lines, the other of four, with a "half-line tailpiece." In *Poems*, there are two curtal-sonnets, "Pied Beauty" and "Peace," which is given below:

> When will you ever, Peace, wild wooddove, shy wings shut,
> Your round me roaming end, and under be my boughs?
> When, when, Peace, will you, Peace? I'll not play hypocrite
> To own my heart: I yield you do come sometimes; but
> That piecemeal peace is poor peace. What pure peace allows
> Alarms of wars, the daunting wars, the death of it?
>
> O surely, reaving Peace, my Lord should leave in lieu
> Some good! And so he does leave Patience exquisite,
> That plumes to Peace thereafter. And when Peace here does house
> He comes with work to do, he does not come to coo,
>   He comes to brood and sit.

D

dactyl: A metrical foot consisting of three syllables, the first stressed, the other two unstressed.

> / u u / u u / u u /
> A was an / archer, who / shot at a / frog;
> B was a butcher, and had a great dog;
> C was a captain, all covered with lace;
> D was a drunkard, and had a red face.
>   Anonymous

Dadaism: Founded by Tristan Tzara in Zurich duing World War I, Dadaism was a nihilistic movement in art and literature which protested against logic, restraint, social convention, and literature itself. (Though some Dadaists claimed that the word *dada* was selected arbitrarily, the term is also believed to have expressed what the members of the group wanted in literature and art—masculinity instead of femininity, *dada* as opposed to *mama*.)

To demonstrate their contempt for civilization, they painted shocking pictures, wrote nonsensical poems, and arranged bizarre theatrical presentations in theaters and cabarets. One Dadaist, Marcel Duchamps, sent a toilet bowl to be exhibited at a sculpture show in Paris, but it was returned promptly. Hugo Ball, having composed a "sound poem," read it in a cabaret while dressed with blue cardboard on his legs, a removable scarlet collar, and a blue-and-white-striped top hat. It begins "gadji beri bimba / glandridi lauli lonni cadori."

Dadaism, flamboyant and self-conscious, spread to Germany, Holland, France, Italy, and Spain but waned shortly after the end of the war. By the early 1920's, André Breton was establishing **Surrealism**, its successor.

See Hans Richter, *Dada: Art and Anti-Art* (1965); William S. Rubin, *Dada, Surrealism, and Their Heritage* (1968).

dandyism: The elegance in dress and manners (especially as embodied in the Prince Regent's friend George "Beau" Brummell) that, in French and English literature, sometimes became a symbol for a rejection of nineteenth-century bourgeois society and a claim of superiority to its values. The view that the dandy is a heroic individualist in revolt against a decadent society is exemplified in Baudelaire's essay "Le Dandy." In the writings of Oscar Wilde the dandy is often a wit whose epigrams suggest that he lives by a code of aesthetics rather than morals. Other writers associated with the tradition of dandyism are Jules Barbey d'Aurevilly in France (*Du Dandysme et de Georges Brummell*) and Bulwer-Lytton in England (*Pelham*).

See Ellen Moers, *The Dandy: Brummell to Beerbohm* (1960).

débat: One of the most popular literary forms of the twelfth and thirteenth centuries (it survived through the fifteenth century), the *débat* was a contest frequently involving a question of theology, politics, morality, courtly matters, or love. After the *débat* had been argued by two personifications or abstractions, it ended in a decision arrived at by a judge.

Decadence: In its most general sense, the term *decadence* refers to any period in art or literature which is in decline as contrasted with a former age of excellence, as, for example, the "silver age" of Latin literature (Tacitus, Martial, Lucan, etc.) as opposed to the preceding "golden age" (Vergil, Horace, Ovid, etc.).

More specifically, *Decadence* designates a literary movement originating in nineteenth-century France which emphasized the autonomy of art, the hostility of the artist to bourgeois society, the superiority of artifice to nature, and the quest for new sensations. (Many of these elements are also associated with **Aestheticism,** which some literary historians insist is virtually indistinguishable from Decadence except for the latter's cultivated perversity.) The young Decadents of the time venerated Baudelaire's *Les Fleurs du mal (The Flowers of Evil)* and trumpeted Gautier's dictum that art should be independent of moral and social concerns. Self-consciously and flamboyantly, they published, briefly, *Le Décadent* (1886), the journal of the movement.

In Huysmans's novel *À Rebours* (1884), which Arthur Symons called "the breviary of the movement," Des Esseintes, its central character, typifies the Decadent who is affected by the *maladie fin de siècle* ("end-of-the-century illness"), which Symons characterized as "the unreason of the soul," the result of spiritual confusion. Abnormal in his tastes and behavior, Des Esseintes, with his bizarre curiosity, seeks to replace the natural with the unnatural in his search for new experiences.

In England, George Moore, announcing himself in *Confessions of a Young Man* (1888) as "feminine, morbid, perverse," wrote what was perhaps the first English "manifesto" proclaiming Decadence. Later, Arthur Symons, in "The Decadent Movement in Literature" (1893), referred to the literature of the movement as "a new and beautiful and interesting disease," an indication of moral and spiritual perversity. Much of the English Decadence, though perhaps diseased, was deliberately posed and designed to be startling. Among the representative figures are Oscar Wilde and Aubrey Beardsley.

See A. E. Carter, *The Idea of Decadence in French Literature 1830–1900* (1958); Barbara Charlesworth, *Dark Passages: The Decadent Consciousness in Victorian Literature* (1965); John M. Munro, *The Decadent Poetry of the Eighteen Nineties* (1970); Ian Fletcher, ed., *Decadence and the 1890s* (1979); R. K. R. Thornton, *The Decadent Dilemma* (1983).

decasyllabic verse: Lines consisting of ten syllables.

> Say what strange motive, Goddess! could compell
> A well-bred Lord t'assault a gentle Belle?
> O say what stranger cause, yet unexplored,
> Could make a gentle Belle reject a Lord?
> Pope, *The Rape of the Lock*

deconstruction: A term coined by the contemporary French philosopher Jacques Derrida and used primarily to designate the mode of literary criticism practiced, since the publication of Derrida's seminal works in the late 1960's, by his American followers, among the most influential of whom have been the Yale critics J. Hillis Miller and Paul de Man. Western philosophy, Derrida says, has traditionally involved a "metaphysics of presence," a claim that by avoiding the dangerous ambiguities of writing, one could through the directness of the spoken word be in contact with absolute Truth, with certain meaning, with a final ground, with essence or center. This "logocentric" view (the word as Truth, even the Word of God) had accorded speech primacy over writing because the conjunction of speaker and auditor supposedly guaranteed comprehension by the hearer of a truth fully known to the speaker. But following Nietzsche's argument that philosophy's claim of access to Truth rested on a repression of the elusively figurative nature of language, Derrida has insisted that all linguistic communication is characterized by radical uncertainty (that it is in this sense "writing").

To demonstrate the illusoriness of total understanding, Derrida has expanded upon and qualified the contention of the Swiss linguist Ferdinand de Saussure that there is no absolute equivalence between the "signifier" (the particular word or "speech event") and the concept "signified" and his view that language was not a system of positive designations but a system of negative differentiations (the identity of each signifier lying not in any essence of its own but in its being distinguishable from others). In addition, Derrida posits the idea that the imperfect signifying of language in effect *defers* the expression of full present meaning to some indefinite future. These qualities of distance and deferral inherent in the nature of language Derrida expresses in his punning neologism *différance*, a playful distortion of *différence* (the French verb *différer* carries the meaning of both "differ" and "defer"). Thus Derrida argues that the *appearance* of determinate meaning derives in each instance from what he calls a "trace," the unconscious sense of alternative past and future meanings as inevitably present in the very act of differentiating and deferring that constitutes the effort to achieve that meaning. Since writing must function within the limited realm of signification, Derrida denies that there is anything accessible outside the text and invites the reader to enter into a free play of interpretation that never claims to achieve a final totalizing of meaning.

Responding to this invitation, Derrida's literary followers have produced a criticism that "deconstructs" (the term suggests analysis rather than destruction) its texts, drawing out through close explication the contradictory elements within them until the "aporia," the point at which incompatible meanings become immutably irreconcilable, is reached. Doing so generally involves detailed verbal analysis to reveal the multiple meanings of key terms, even by examining their etymological roots. Deconstructive writing tends to blur the distinction between literature and criticism in the kind of work it does partly because of a desire to transcend familiar critical style, approaches, and attitudes but also because of the sense that a text seen as a chain of signifiers cannot produce another text that will contain its totalized Truth but only a further chain of signifiers.

Inevitably such a criticism has been controversial. Deconstructive criticism has been called "formalist" or "aesthetic" in approach because of its focus on the text as a self-contained linguistic entity. (Such strictures have also been raised in regard to both the New Criticism and Russian Formalism.) For similar reasons this critical enterprise has sometimes been judged as merely a playful academic exercise. The most telling charge leveled against deconstruction, however, has been that of nihilism. If discourse is divorced from intention and can never achieve decidable meaning, then—the complaint goes—it is no more than an endless echoing in a void. To this accusation there are various responses: that deconstructive interpretation does not so much deny the commonsense view of meaningful language as suspend it to make certain kinds of investigations possible, that such an approach does not destroy meaning but reveals its multiplicity, that its practice is a heroic confrontation of the abyss of undecidability as well as a joyous affirmation of the freedom offered by such undecidability. The range of attack and defense suggests why this movement has been so significant in recent literary criticism. It should be borne in mind that for a deconstructionist, committed to the indeterminacy of the text, any circumscribed description of deconstruction, such as this one, is bound to be invalid.

See Jacques Derrida, *Of Grammatology* (1967; English trans., 1976); Jacques Derrida, *Writing and Difference* (1967; English trans., 1978); Geoffrey Hartman, *Criticism in the Wilderness* (1980); Barbara Johnson, *The Critical Difference* (1980); Jonathan Culler, *On Deconstruction* (1982).

decorum: In Classical and later criticism, the idea that each of the elements of a work should fit appropriately into the whole and, especially, that the style of a passage should be suitable to the occasion and the character. Thus, a king should speak, not like an ordinary man, but in a grand and kingly manner. In Books I and II of *Paradise Lost*, for example, the fallen angels do not address each other colloquially but in a high, rhetorical style suitable to the great occasion with which they are concerned.

denotation: The thing or situation to which a word refers, exclusive of attitudes or feelings which the writer or speaker may have; a word's most literal and limited meaning. Thus, the denotation of *elephant* is a large, five-toed mammal with an extraordinary proboscis and long tusks of ivory. If the word, however, suggests to the listener or reader *clumsiness* or *remarkable memory*, it has acquired **connotations**. See **meaning**.

denouement: French: "unknotting." The events following the major climax of a plot. Sometimes, however, *denouement* designates only a final scene in which mysteries are unraveled and misunderstandings set straight. The denouement of Shakespeare's *A Midsummer Night's Dream* consists of the final rearrangement of the lovers and their subsequent marriages. In Shaw's *Major Barbara*, the "unknotting" occurs in Act III, in which Barbara finds a new faith to replace that which Undershaft had destroyed at the end of Act II, the climax of the play.

description: In a literary work, description, by presenting details of time, place, character, and social setting, creates the "world" in which the story moves. Whereas novelists in the past have exhaustively described environment as though distinct from character, many writers since the late nineteenth century have conceived of social setting as virtually inseparable from character. More recently, writers under the influence of psychological theory have utilized the **stream of consciousness,** a technique for depicting the fragmentary conscious and semiconscious thoughts of their characters, as a mode of description.

descriptive bibliography: See **bibliography.**

descriptive linguistics: See **linguistics.**

detective story: A narrative in which a mystery, frequently involving murder, is unraveled by a detective. First established as a distinct literary form by Poe in "Murders in the Rue Morgue" (1841), the detective story generally contains at least some of the following conventions: the seemingly perfect crime; the dull-wittedness of the police; the detective's confidant, who lacks his associate's brilliance but who always asks questions which clarify the situation; the suspect who appears guilty from the circumstantial evidence but who is later proved innocent; the sensational **denouement,** in which the detective explains in minute detail who killed whom and how. The method of discovery is, of course, deductive, for it is generally axiomatic that the sleuth should not be in possession of clues of which the reader is unaware. By ingenious plotting, the writer of the detective story invites his reader to match wits with the central character as both uncover clues leading to the culprit. By extension, many literary works, such as *Oedipus Rex* and *Hamlet*, may also be called "detective stories," since the hero in both plays seeks to unravel a mystery involving a murder. Some modern detective stories have ceased to be strict puzzles; instead, they emphasize the psychological implications of a crime or the violent adventures of the protagonist.

See Julian Symons, *Mortal Consequences: A History from the Detective Story to the Crime Novel* (1972); LeRoy Panek, *An Introduction to the Detective Story* (1987).

deus ex machina: Latin: "god out of the machine." In Greek drama, the use of a god lowered by a mechanism of some sort onto the stage to rescue the hero or untangle the plot. Euripides uses this device in half of his extant plays, while Aeschylus and Sophocles avoid it in most of theirs. In the *Poetics*, Aristotle, condemning the use of the *deus ex machina*, argues that the **denouement** of the plot must grow from the action itself. By extension, the term refers to any artificial device for the easy resolution of all difficulties. Serious modern writers avoid the *deus ex machina*, though it has sometimes been used in comedy. Brecht and Weill employ the device at the conclusion of the *Threepenny Opera* in the form of a proclamation by Queen Victoria which saves Mac the Knife from hanging.

deuteragonist: The second actor in Greek drama, added by Aeschylus, often synonymous with **antagonist**, although the deuteragonist could, when necessary, assume more than one role. In subsequent usage, the term has been applied to the character of second importance, such as Claudius in *Hamlet*. See **protagonist; tritagonist.**

dialogue: 1. The speeches of characters in a narrative or a play, especially the latter. In earlier literature, the dialogue of at least the principal characters made no pretense of being like the actual conversation of men. It was elaborate, deliberately heightened, usually in verse. Realistic dialogue was limited to comic characters or to those on a comparatively low social level. In modern plays, however, the dialogue is usually designed to imitate ordinary speech, although, when examined closely, it will regularly be found to be far more selective and highly organized. Modern novelists, relishing the directness and immediacy of dialogue, have made it prominent in their works till, in the **stream-of-consciousness** novel, they have produced a form made up almost entirely of the dialogue of the mind with itself.

2. A literary genre in which characters discourse at length on a given topic. See Dryden's "Essay on Dramatic Poesy" and Wilde's "The Critic as Artist," as well as the Socratic dialogues of Plato.

diary: See **autobiography.**

dibrach: See **pyrrhic.**

diction: The choice and arrangement of words in a literary work. Diction varies according to the ends a writer wishes to achieve. The kind of diction will, consequently, be decided by the nature of the literary form, the subject, and the style of the day. Thus, the ornate, balanced rhetoric of much eighteenth-century prose, considered elegant in its time, is deemed inappropriate in modern writing. Dr. Johnson's opening lines in his "Life of Dryden" may serve as an example of the diction which we now admire but rarely imitate:

> Of the great poet whose life I am about to delineate, the curiosity which his reputation must excite, will require a display more ample than can now be given. His contemporaries, however they reverenced his genius, left his life unwritten; and nothing, therefore, can be known beyond what casual mention and uncertain tradition have supplied.

Attempting to bring loftiness and distinction to his subject, Johnson here utilizes a diction suitable for his end. In a biography of the young Johnson, a modern scholar, James L. Clifford, uses homely diction in the opening lines of *Young Sam Johnson* to achieve a direct and forceful beginning:

> "Sept. 7, 1709, I was born at Lichfield." Samuel Johnson's pen scratched across the paper. In the drab quarters just above the ground floor of No. 1 Inner Temple Lane, he was beginning an account of his own early years. At intervals he made half whistling sounds and soft clucking noises with his tongue, or talked to himself in a low voice.

didactic: When the primary aim of a work of literature is to expound some moral, political, or other teaching, it is called "didactic." Ever since Plato banished the poets from his Republic, the relation between literature and doctrine has been a point of contention in a continuing dispute about the nature and function of art. If literature is a unique form of discourse and the function of the writer is different from that of the politician on the platform or the clergyman in the pulpit, then the didactic element may be considered irrelevant or intrusive and *didacticism* a derogatory word. On the other hand, many remarkable literary works—Dante's *Divine Comedy*, for example, or Milton's *Paradise Lost*—are didactic, at least in intent. The didactic element in these works, however, does not dominate them; it forms only a part of the aesthetic experience. Pending settlement of the dispute, this term may be most appropriately used to describe a work rather than to judge it. See **moral**.

digest: 1. A publication devoted exclusively or primarily to abridgments of books or articles that have previously appeared elsewhere. 2. The abridgment itself.

dime novel: See **penny dreadful**.

dimeter: A verse of two metrical feet. The third and fourth lines of a limerick are regularly dimeter, as below:

> There once was a sculptor named Phidias,
> Who did things that were perfectly hideous.
> He carved Aph / rodite,
> Without an / y nightie,
> Which shocked the overfastidious.

dipody: Two metrical feet considered as a unit. The use of the dipody as a unit of measure (an iambic hexameter, for instance, would consist of six iambs or three dipodies) is not usually characteristic of English prosody.

dirge: A lyrical poem or song of lament originally composed in commemoration of the dead and chanted at Roman funeral processions or banquets. Similar in intent, the Greek threnody and monody are also dirges, the latter sung by one person. In Shakespeare's *The Tempest*, the dirge appears as a poignant, mournful lyric when Ariel sings of Ferdinand's lost father:

> Full fathom five thy father lies;
> Of his bones are coral made:

> Those are pearls that were his eyes:
>   Nothing of him that doth fade
> But doth suffer a sea-change
>   Into something rich and strange.
>   Sea-nymphs hourly ring his knell:
> Hark! now I hear them,—ding-dong, bell.

dissociation of sensibility: In his essay "The Metaphysical Poets" (1921), T. S. Eliot complained that the fusion of thought and feeling characteristic of the **Metaphysical poets** had been progressively lost in the seventeenth century, particularly through the influence of Milton and Dryden—a loss, insisted Eliot, "from which we have never recovered." Whereas the Metaphysical poets, as well as the Elizabethan and Jacobean dramatists, "possessed a mechanism of sensibility which could devour any kind of experience" and felt "their thought as immediately as the odour of a rose," such poets as Tennyson and Browning produced only ruminations. As examples of modern poets who had successfully avoided the dissociation of sensibility, Eliot mentioned the late-nineteenth-century French poets Tristan Corbière and Jules Laforgue, who had an admitted influence on his own work. Since the 1950's, Eliot's analysis, once widely accepted by advocates of the New Criticism, has had much less influence among critics.

See T. S. Eliot, *Selected Essays* (2nd ed., 1960); Frank Kermode, *Romantic Image* (1957), Chapter VIII.

dissonance: 1. The juxtaposition of harsh or jarring sounds or rhythmical patterns; a synonym for **cacophony.**

2. The close repetition of consonant sounds; a synonym for **consonance.**

3. The juxtaposition of closely related but not identical vowel sounds in one or more lines, as in the various "o" and "a" sounds in this stanza:

> In a coign of the cliff between lowland and highland
>   At the sea-down's edge between windward and lee,
> Walled round with rocks as an inland island,
>   The ghost of a garden fronts the sea.
>   Swinburne, "A Forsaken Garden"

Since definitions 1 and 2 already have appropriate synonyms, the word *dissonance* may best be limited to the sense of definition 3.

distich: A verse unit consisting of two successive lines, generally rhymed and self-contained in meaning, especially that used in Greek and Latin elegiac verse. See **couplet; elegiac meter.**

distributed stress: See **hovering accent.**

dithyramb: 1. Originally a Greek choral song, probably sung at the sacrifice to Dionysus. The meters were varied, the tone vehement and passionate. Aristotle says that tragedy was, in origin, associated with the dithyramb. 2. Any poem of dithyrambic character.

diverbium: In Latin drama, dialogue verse which is spoken. See **canticum.**

divine afflatus: See **inspiration.**

doggerel: Rough, crudely written verse, usually humorous, though sometimes unintentionally so. The earliest use of the term may be Chaucer's reference to "rym dogerel" in "The Tale of Sir Thopas," a **burlesque** of a **medieval romance,** in *The Canterbury Tales.* In Swift's "The Author's Manner of Living," a mild self-derision animates this comic doggerel:

> On rainy days alone I dine,
> Upon a chick, and pint of wine.
> On rainy days, I dine alone,
> And pick my chicken to the bone:
> But this my servants much enrages,
> No scraps remain to save board-wages.

dolce stil nuovo: Italian: "sweet new style." Though Dante uses this phrase in the "Purgatorio" of the *Divine Comedy* (Canto XXIV, line 57), to characterize his style and that of certain of his predecessors, particularly Guido Guinicelli, it indicated an attitude toward women and earthly love rather than a literary "style." In the poetry of Guinicelli, the idea is advanced that the essential quality of the "gentle heart" is love kindled by God. The woman, embodying God's beauty and truth, arouses in the gentle heart

that love which has its source in God. As the "lover" revolves about the woman, she leads him to Divine Love and Truth by purifying his earthly desires so that he may achieve saintliness. In short, the beauty of the woman's body, the physical manifestation of the beauty of her soul, becomes the vehicle for her lover's union with God. By combining earthly and divine love, the *stilnovist* poets in the late thirteenth century established a new set of poetic attitudes under the animus of Christianity. The roots of this doctrine lay in troubadour verse and song which were designed for courtly or aristocratic audiences. Dante's *Divine Comedy* is an example, in epic form, of the *dolce stil nuovo*. A survival of the style appears later in Spenser's *Faerie Queene*.
See Maurice Valency, *In Praise of Love* (1958).

domestic tragedy: A serious play, generally realistic in style, with its protagonist drawn from the lower or middle classes and its action concerned with personal or domestic matters rather than high politics. The term has been applied to such plays as Lillo's *The London Merchant* or Hebbel's *Maria Magdalena* and even to the plays of Ibsen and other modern dramatists, but it is often limited to the Elizabethan domestic tragedy, which includes such plays as *Arden of Feversham*, *A Warning for Fair Women*, and *A Woman Killed with Kindness*.

donnée: French: literally, "the given fact." The fundamental elements of a work, such as its subject or characters, which the writer develops. The term was first widely used in English criticism by Henry James, who wrote in his essay "The Art of Fiction" (1884): "We must grant the artist his subject, his idea, his *donnée:* our criticism is applied only to what he makes of it." In restricting criticism to a writer's handling of the given material of a work of art and avoiding a preconceived idea of what it ought to be or do, James reveals his indebtedness to nineteenth-century **Aestheticism** and anticipates a basic tenet of the **New Criticism**.

Doppelgänger: See **Double, the.**

Double, the: A device whereby a character is self-duplicated (the *Doppelgänger,* "mirror image," or "alter ego"), as in the case of Leggatt and the Captain in Conrad's *The Secret Sharer,* or divided into two distinct, usually antithetical, personalities, as in Stevenson's *The Strange Case of Dr. Jekyll and Mr. Hyde*, which objectifies the internal struggle of good against evil.

Masao Miyoshi, in *The Divided Self: A Perspective on the Literature of the Victorians* (1969), outlines three categories of the Double: the formal (an author's conscious use of the device to express the theme of a work); the thematic or ideological (a philosophical view of self-alienation argued through divided characters); and the biographical (a revelation of the author's own unconscious divisions). Since these categories are themselves merely formal, not mutually exclusive, such a work as Wilde's *The Picture of Dorian Gray* can embrace all three.

The widespread use of the Double in nineteenth and twentieth-century literature (*e.g.*, Mary Shelley's *Frankenstein*, Dostoevsky's *The Double*, Joyce's *Ulysses*, Virginia Woolf's *Mrs. Dalloway*, and John Knowles's *A Separate Peace*) suggests to many critics the increasing awareness that the "self" is in reality a composite of many "selves." Moreover, since Freud and psychoanalytic theory (with its concepts of ego, id, and superego), there has been an increasing interest in the problem of the "divided self."

See Robert Rogers, *A Psychoanalytic Study of the Double in Literature* (1970); Karl Miller, *Doubles: Studies in Literary History* (1985).

double rhyme: See **rhyme**.

drama: In the most general sense, any work designed to be represented on a stage by actors. More strictly, however, a drama is a serious play (though it may end either happily or unhappily) dealing with a problem of importance but not aiming at tragic exaltation. This usage of the term originated in mid-eighteenth-century France, when Diderot and later Beaumarchais adopted the word *drame* to describe their plays of middle-class life. In modern usage, however, the term *drama* is frequently extended to all serious plays. For specific types of plays, see the listing under "Dramatic Types" at the end of this book.

See S. W. Dawson, *Drama and the Dramatic* (1970).

drama of sensibility: See **sentimental comedy**.

dramatic irony: See **irony.**

dramatic lyric: See **dramatic monologue.**

dramatic monologue: A poem consisting of the words of a single character who reveals in his speech his own nature and the dramatic situation. Unlike the stage soliloquy, in which place and time have been previously established and during which the character is alone, the dramatic monologue itself reveals place, time, and the identities of the characters. Called a "dramatic lyric" by Browning, who brought the form to its highest development, the dramatic monologue discloses the psychology of the speaker at a significant moment. Though Browning entitles one of his poems "Soliloquy of the Spanish Cloister," it is, in reality, a dramatic monologue, its opening a striking example of the speed with which he establishes character and situation:

> Gr-r-r—there go, my heart's abhorrence!
>   Water your damned flower-pots, do!
> If hate killed men, Brother Lawrence,
>   God's blood, would not mine kill you!

In modern literature, the dramatic monologue has been used by such poets as T. S. Eliot in "The Love Song of J. Alfred Prufrock" and by Yeats in the "Crazy Jane" poems.

See Robert Langbaum, *The Poetry of Experience: The Dramatic Monologue in the Modern Literary Tradition* (1957); Alan Sinfield, *Dramatic Monologue* (1977).

dramatic proverb: See *proverbe dramatique.*

dramatis personae: The characters in a play. Frequently a list of the characters, with an indication of their relationships, is printed at the beginning of a play. See **persona.**

dramaturgy: The composition of plays. The term is sometimes used to include the acting as well as the writing of drama.

dream allegory: A type of medieval poem in which the major portion involves a dream of allegorical significance. *The Romance of the Rose*, a widely read French dream allegory of the thirteenth century, established some of the conventions of the form: the idyllic garden in which the dreamer finds himself; the characters with such allegorical names as Fear, Chastity, Hypocrisy, etc.; physical struggles representing spiritual and moral conflicts. As Paul Piehler states in *The Visionary Landscape: A Study in Medieval Allegory* (1971): "Typically the dreamer is profoundly disturbed by some spiritual crisis; he has a vision of mysterious import which is interpreted by persons in spiritual authority, and the effect of the vision and its interpretation is to resolve the crisis, often raising him to a higher spiritual state."

The Romance of the Rose provided a model for other dream allegories of the time. Chaucer, for example, wrote four: *The Book of the Duchess, The House of Fame, The Parliament of Fowls*, and the "Prologue" of *The Legend of Good Women*. A contemporary of his, William Langland, used the form for *Piers Plowman*.

droll: A short, comic piece, often coupled with dancing, performed most often at fairs during the Commonwealth (1649–60) in England. Since the government had closed the theaters and forbidden full-length plays, the performances of drolls, often comic scenes extracted from earlier plays, were among the few ways of evading the Puritan edicts.

dumb show: In medieval and Renaissance drama, that part of a play performed in pantomime as a summary of the action or an indication of its theme. In *Hamlet*, the dumb show precedes the spoken lines of *The Murder of Gonzago* (the play presented before Claudius and Gertrude), which has marked similarities to the murder of Hamlet's father. According to Dieter Mehl, in *The Elizabethan Dumb Show* (1965), the term may also be used for "all cases where one or more characters advance and retire without having spoken," as in De Flores's brief appearance between Acts II and III of Middleton's *The Changeling*, when he hides a rapier behind a door.

duodecimo: Latin: "twelfth" (abbr. 12mo or 12°). The size of a book (about 5 × 7½ inches) derived from printing on sheets which are folded into twelve leaves or twenty-four pages. See **folio.**

duologue: A conversation between two characters in a play or story. See **dialogue.**

duple meter or **rhythm:** One with two syllables to the metrical foot.

dystopia: See **utopian literature.**

E

echo verse: 1. A line and an "echo" which repeats the final syllables with a change in meaning. 2. A poem made up of such lines.

> Shepherd: Echo, I ween, will in the woods reply,
> And quaintly answer questions: shall I try?
> Echo: Try.
> What must we do our passion to express?
> Press.
> How shall I please her, who ne'er loved before?
> Be Fore.
> What most moves women when we them address?
> A dress.
> Say, what can keep her chaste whom I adore?
> A door.
> Jonathan Swift, from "A Gentle Echo on Woman"

eclogue: From Greek: "selection." Originally a short poem or a section of a longer one. Later, the term was applied to the bucolic or pastoral poems of Vergil. In the Renaissance it came to designate any verse dialogue on pastoral themes, such as Spenser's *Shepheardes Calender.* By the eighteenth century, when town eclogues appeared, the term referred simply to the form. In such modern poems as Frost's "Build Soil" and MacNeice's "Eclogue from Iceland," as well as Auden's "Age of Anxiety," the eclogue has openly become a vehicle for the poet's political and social ideas.

edition: The total number of copies of a work printed from a single set of type. If, following a first edition, changes are made in the original setting-up of type, the book is printed as a second edition. The term *impression,* though related to *edition,* refers to the total number of copies printed at one time while the type or plates are in the press. Thus, an edition may go to several impressions, or printings, before a second edition is published.

The term *issue*, lacking a precise meaning, generally refers to a form of a book in which new material has been added to the original printing or a new arrangement adopted. Frequently, however, the term *reissue* may refer to the reprinting of a book with no changes. Sometimes different paper may be used for an impression; an inexpensive book may be printed on cheap paper while a de luxe "issue" may also appear. The term *issue* here merely refers to the different paper used.

In older books, the terms *impression* and *edition* are virtually inseparable, since type was broken up after a first printing. In an extended use of the term *edition*, a reference to the "one-volume edition" of Chaucer's works edited by F. N. Robinson indicates its format; the "Robinson edition" of Chaucer, on the other hand, indicates any printed form of the text as edited by Robinson.

eglogue: See **eclogue.**

elegiac couplet: See **elegiac meter.**

elegiac meter: The meter used in Greek and Roman prosody for the elegiac couplet, a dactylic hexameter followed by a dactylic pentameter or a hexameter in which the unaccented parts of the third and sixth feet have been dropped. The elegiac couplet, which was Greek in origin, was widely used by Catullus and other Latin poets.

elegiac stanza: See **heroic quatrain.**

elegy: From Greek: *elegeia*, "lament." In Greek and Roman literature, any poem using the **elegiac couplet,** often on such subjects as love and war as well as death. Since the sixteenth century, however, the term has designated a dignified poem mourning the death of an individual (Auden's "In Memory of W. B. Yeats") or of all men (Gray's "Elegy Written in a Country Churchyard"). A specific subtype is the pastoral elegy, originated by the Sicilian Greek poets Theocritus, Bion, and Moschus, and exemplified in English by such poems as Milton's "Lycidas" and Shelley's "Adonais." The poet and his subjects are spoken of as shepherds or goatherds, and the setting is the Classical pastoral world. The nymphs, shepherds, and other inhabitants of this world join in mourning, but the poem usually ends peacefully or even joyfully. See **pastoral.**

See Patricia Sacks, *The English Elegy: Studies in the Genre from Spenser to Yeats* (1985).

elision: In verse, the slurring or omission of an unstressed syllable so that the line may conform to the metrical pattern, as in the second and fourth lines of this quatrain by Michael Drayton:

> Calling to mind since first my love begun,
> Th'incertain times oft varying in their course,
> How things still unexpectedly have run,
> As't please the Fates, by their resistless force. . . .

When one of two adjacent vowels is omitted, as in the second line above, the phenomenon is called "synalepha," though the term *elision* is sometimes restricted to this sense. See **syncope.**

emblem: See **emblem book.**

emblem book: A book of symbolic pictures called "emblems," each of which is accompanied by a motto and occasionally by exposition. Popular in the late Middle Ages and the Renaissance, the emblem book was moral and **didactic.** William Blake revived the form in *The Gates of Paradise* (1793).

emendation: The alteration of a text where it appears to be corrupt.

emotive language: Language designed to evoke or express emotional reactions toward its subject, as opposed to referential language —such as the language of science—designed to carry only denotative meanings. The distinction between emotive and referential language was stressed by C. K. Ogden and I. A. Richards in *The Meaning of Meaning* (1923).

encomiastic verse: Poems which praise or glorify people, objects, or abstract ideas. In his odes, Pindar, for example, praises the winners of the Olympic games, and Wordsworth in his "Ode to Duty" glorifies the notion of duty.

end rhyme: See **rhyme.**

end-stopped line: One in which a grammatical pause—such as the end of a phrase, clause, or sentence—coincides with the end of the line. Most eighteenth-century verse, such as this passage from Pope, was end-stopped:

> Meanwhile, declining from the noon of day,
> The sun obliquely shoots his burning ray;
> The hungry Judges soon the Sentence sign,
> And wretches hang that jurymen may dine.
>   *The Rape of the Lock*

English sonnet: See **Shakespearean sonnet.**

enjambement: See **run-on line.**

Enlightenment, the: An intellectual movement in the late seventeenth and eighteenth centuries uniting the concepts of God, nature, reason, and man in the belief that "right reason" could achieve for man a perfect society by freeing him from the oppressive restraints of unexamined authority, superstition, and prejudice. Kant's famous essay "What Is Enlightenment?" (1784) gave wide currency to the name of the movement, which he characterized as "the liberation of mankind."

During this period many thinkers accepted the postulate that reason, combined with man's observations, could reveal truth. Newton's discovery in 1686 of the law of universal gravitation gave impetus to the possibility of extending scientific inquiry to all areas of human activity. Therefore, it was widely believed that politics, society, and religion should be subjected to rational examination in order to eliminate dogmatic authority. Those who called themselves "Deists" (though they frequently remained professing Christians) believed that God, the supreme Architect, had constructed an ordered cosmos on mathematical principles which man could understand with his reason. By denying a God who participated in human history (the traditional theism of Christianity), the Deists rejected the possibility of miracles and mysteries, since such "irrational" occurrences and beliefs were a denial of natural law and hence offensive to God's very nature. In France, Voltaire and other *philosophes* used the rational bias of Deism to attack the entrenched political power of the Church; in England, where Deism first achieved prominence, the movement away from traditional Christian concerns with the mysterious nature of God was expressed by Alexander Pope, himself a Catholic, in *An Essay on Man* (1734):

Know then thyself, presume not God to scan,
The proper study of mankind is man. . . .

A graver danger to traditional Christian belief, however, lay in the rational skepticism of the philosopher David Hume, who cast doubt on such ideas as cause and effect, the existence of the soul, and even God. During the period of the Enlightenment, there were attempts to exclude spiritual realities from the reach of skepticism: Kant contended that God was discoverable through non-rational means, and others, such as John Wesley, whose evangelical Christianity stressed personal salvation through Christ, and Rousseau, whose so-called "religion of the heart" anticipated **Romanticism**, attempted to provide alternatives to the dehumanized, rational theology of the Deists.

The early rationalists of the Enlightenment, in their attempt to free mankind from the burden of original sin, asserted that man was basically good. If, on occasion, he was wicked, the fault lay not in his nature but in his environment. In *An Essay Concerning Human Understanding* (1690), John Locke stated that reason, rightly exercised without interference, would result in right conduct. Yet even among the rationalists there were disagreements concerning the relationship between reason, knowledge, and virtue: for example, the Earl of Shaftesbury believed that human nature contained an instinctive benevolence, not at odds with reason, that led to virtuous behavior and natural piety.

In their political theorizing, the Enlightenment thinkers assumed that because human society was clearly falling short of what natural law seemed to dictate as an ideal, it must be radically reorganized. Oppressive authority in church and state was to be eliminated, and, indeed, as Adam Smith argued in his *Wealth of Nations* (1776), trade must also be free to follow natural law (the idea of laissez-faire). By transforming society, man would be able to realize his full potentialities as a rational creature in an ordered cosmos. In Locke's *Two Treatises of Government* (1689), man's natural rights were duly proclaimed: only by the consent of the governed was a government legitimate; the ultimate right to rebel was likewise reserved to the governed.

The idea of progress was, for the Enlightenment, a major concern. Diderot and other *philosophes* published the *Encyclopédie* (1751–72), which proposed that the primary task of mankind was moral and social progress in all areas of human activity; and Condorcet, in his *Sketch for a Historical Picture of the Progress of the Human Mind* (1794), saw all of human history as a march toward the perfection of society and man. By the late eighteenth century, however, the "Age of Reason" was already disintegrating, for other forces, such as Romanticism, evangelical Christianity, skepticism, and perhaps the excesses of the French Revolution, were casting strong doubt on "right reason" as the key to man's salvation.

See Ernst Cassirer, *The Philosophy of the Enlightenment* (English trans., 1951); Peter Gay, *The Enlightenment*, 2 vols. (1966–69).

entr'acte: A brief performance, usually musical, to entertain the audience between the acts of a drama.

enumerative bibliography: See **bibliography.**

envoy (envoi): From French: "a sending on the way." A concluding stanza, shorter than the preceding ones. See **ballade.**

épater le bourgeois: See **Philistine.**

epic: An extended narrative poem, exalted in style and heroic in theme. Early or "primary" epics, such as the *Iliad*, the *Odyssey*, and the Anglo-Saxon *Beowulf*, are written versions, often anonymous, of the oral legends of a tribe or nation. "Literary" epics, such as Vergil's *Aeneid*, are later imitations of early epics. The term *epic* is also applied to a number of poems—Dante's *Divine Comedy*, Tasso's *Gerusalemme Liberata*, and Spenser's *Faerie Queene*, for example—which do not observe all the conventions established by Homer.

These conventions, only some of which can be mentioned here, are followed by writers of epic with varying degrees of strictness. The poet begins by announcing his theme, invoking the aid of a muse, and asking her an epic question, with the reply to which the story begins. He then launches his action *in medias res*, in the middle of things. (The preceding events are narrated at some appropriate point later on.) This action concerns a hero, a man of stature and significance; Odysseus, for example, is King of Ithaca, and Aeneas is the founder of the Roman Empire. In the course of the story, the hero performs many notable deeds, one of which is to descend into the underworld. The major characters are catalogued and described, many of them having dignified set speeches that reveal their characters. There are usually great battles in which the gods themselves, who are regularly involved in epic stories, take part. Finally, the epic poet adopts a style, dignified, elaborate, and exalted, suitable to his theme.

Byron satirizes the epic apparatus in the following stanza from *Don Juan*:

> My poem's epic, and is meant to be
>   Divided in twelve books; each book containing,
> With love, and war, a heavy gale at sea,
>   A list of ships, and captains, and kings reigning,
> New characters; the episodes are three:
>   A panoramic view of hell's in training,
> After the style of Virgil and of Homer,
> So that my name of Epic's no misnomer.

See C. M. Bowra, *From Virgil to Milton* (1945); E. M. W. Tillyard, *The English Epic and Its Background* (1954); Paul Merchant, *The Epic* (1971).

epic (or **Homeric**) **simile:** An extended simile in which one or both of the objects compared are elaborately described. This device is regular in epic poetry but appears in other types as well.

> Thus Satan talking to his nearest mate
> With head uplift above the wave, and eyes
> That sparkling blazed; his other parts besides,
> Prone on the flood extended, long and large
> Lay floating many a rood, in bulk as huge
> As whom the fables name of monstrous size,
> Titanian, or Earth-born, that warred on Jove,
> Briareos or Typhon, whom the den
> By ancient Tarsus held, or that sea-beast
> Leviathan, which God of all his works
> Created hugest that swim the ocean stream:
> Him haply slumbering on the Norway foam
> The pilot of some small night-foundered skiff,
> Deeming some island, oft, as seamen tell,
> With fixèd anchor in his scaly rind
> Moors by his side under lee, while night

Invests the sea, and wishëd morn delays:
So stretched out huge in length the Arch-Fiend lay
Chained on the burning lake . . .
       Milton, *Paradise Lost*

Epic Theater: The theory and, to some extent, the practice of the modern German dramatist Bertolt Brecht. Wishing to avoid the characteristics of what he called the Aristotelian drama—a creation of the illusion of reality, a sense that the action is occurring in the present, an identification with the central figure of the play, and a cathartic emotional release—Brecht tried to create a "non-Aristotelian" drama in which the audience would sense the action as already in the past and would view it with the calm detachment supposedly evoked by the original singers of epic. The aim of the Epic Theater was to lead the audience not to feel intensely but to judge critically, to see the characters' actions as determined not by fate and human nature but by social circumstances, to leave the theater not emotionally drained but intellectually stimulated and determined to bring about Marxist reforms. To achieve this effect of emotional distance between audience and action, called the "Alienation Effect" (*Verfremdungseffekt*), Brecht made use of short, self-contained scenes instead of building action to a climax, used songs to comment on the action rather than to heighten its intensity, and encouraged his actors to avoid emotional identification with their roles and to play in a relaxed, unrhetorical style.

See John Willett, ed. and trans., *Brecht on Theatre* (1964); Martin Esslin, *Brecht: The Man and His Work* (rev. ed., 1971).

epigram: A short, usually witty statement, graceful in style and ingenious in thought.

> Man is a rational animal who always loses his temper when he is called upon to act in accordance with the dictates of reason.
>   Oscar Wilde, "The Critic as Artist"

Originally referring to an inscription on a monument, the term came to be associated with short satirical poems, such as those of Martial (first century A.D.). In English literature, such poets as Jonson, Herrick, and Byron have carried on the epigrammatic tradition.

epigraph: A quotation preceding a book, chapter, or poem, often intended to evoke something of its theme or atmosphere. For example, the quotation from the "Inferno" of Dante's *Divine Comedy* which precedes T. S. Eliot's "The Love Song of J. Alfred Prufrock" suggests much about the timid Prufrock, who lives in his private hell.

epilogue: 1. The final section of a **speech,** also called the "peroration." 2. The conclusion of a fable where the moral is pointed out. 3. A speech by an actor at the end of a play in which the indulgence of the critics and the applause of the audience are requested.

epiphany: From Greek: "a showing forth." A term used by James Joyce in *Stephen Hero* to refer to "a sudden spiritual manifestation" which an object or action achieves as a result of the observer's apprehension of its significance. Sometimes, when observing a trivial incident or listening to a fragment of conversation, Stephen perceives it as a symbol of a spiritual state; the action achieves an epiphany as a result of his awareness of its meaning. In the novel, Stephen plans to gather such epiphanies. In Joyce's *A Portrait of the Artist as a Young Man*, a rewriting of the uncompleted *Stephen Hero*, a number of these "insights" appear; one is described in the following passage:

> . . . he felt that the augury he had sought in the wheeling darting birds and in the pale space of sky above him had come forth from his heart like a bird from a turret quietly and swiftly. Symbol of departure or loneliness?

The device of the epiphany may be traced to Wordsworth, who, in *The Prelude* (1805), refers to recalled "spots of time" that reveal moments of significance; in modern literature, Virginia Woolf's "moments of Being" suggest a similar experience.
    See Morris Beha, *Epiphany in the Modern Novel* (1971); Zack Bowen, "Joyce and the Epiphany Concept: A New Approach," *Journal of Modern Literature*, 9 (1981–82).

episode: An incident within a longer narrative, sometimes closely related to the plot, sometimes a digression.

epistle: 1. A verse letter. This form has been used by many English poets, such as Jonson, Burns, Shelley, Byron, and Donne, whose "To the Countesse of Bedford" is an example:

> Madame,
> Reason is our Soules left hand, Faith her right,
> By these wee reach divinity, that's you;
> Their loves, who have the blessings of your light,
> Grew from their reason, mine from faire faith grew.

2. From the Renaissance through the eighteenth century, dedications of books and poems were usually cast in the form of a letter, and the word *epistle* sometimes carried the sense of preface.

epistolary novel: A narrative in the form of letters. Popular in the eighteenth century, the epistolary device was notably successful in Samuel Richardson's *Pamela* (1740) and *Clarissa Harlowe* (1747–48). The form enabled Richardson conveniently to reveal his heroine's private thoughts and feelings while advancing the plot. The reader, in the role of literary voyeur, could then see the shifting points of view without the intrusion of the author. The artificiality of the method, however, soon led to the demise of the genre as a popular form, though later writers have employed its technique from time to time.

See Frank G. Black, *The Epistolary Novel in the Late Eighteenth Century* (1940; rpt. 1969); Godfrey F. Singer, *The Epistolary Novel* (1963); Natascha Wurzbach, *The Novel in Letters: Epistolary Fiction in the Early English Novel, 1678–1740* (1969).

epitaph: Originally referring to an inscription in verse on a tombstone, the term has also been used to designate a poem or a part of a long poem which expresses respect (see the epitaph from Gray's "Elegy Written in a Country Churchyard"), and occasionally disrespect, for the dead. Some epitaphs, perhaps unintentionally, are humorous:

> Here lie I, Martin Elginbrodde:
> Have mercy on my soul, Lord God,
> As I wad do, were I Lord God,
> And ye were Martin Elginbrodde.
> Anonymous

epithalamion: Greek: "at the bridal chamber" (or Latin *epithalamium*). A poem or song, solemn or ribald, to be recited or sung outside the bridal chamber. Derived from the Greek poets and perfected by the Roman poet Catullus, the epithalamion was widely used in sixteenth- and seventeenth-century England by such poets as Donne, Jonson, and Herrick. However, Edmund Spenser's "Epithalamion" (1595), a celebration of his own marriage, is often held to be the greatest such poem in English. Rich in symbolism and in classical allusions, the poem opens with an invocation to the muse to praise the bride and closes with a request for Juno's blessing. The events of the day—from the assembling of the guests to the marriage feast—organize the poem.

Later writers, such as Shelley, have used the form, as have Tennyson (at the conclusion of *In Memoriam*) and Auden.

See Virginia Tufte, *The Poetry of Marriage: The Epithalamium in Europe and Its Development in England* (1970).

epithet: An adjective or other term used to characterize a person or thing, as in Ethelred *the Unready* or Jack *the Ripper*. Homer tended to link certain adjectives and nouns which are called "Homeric epithets": swift-footed Achilles; rosy-fingered dawn; Odysseus, sacker of cities.

epode: Greek: "additional song." 1. A poem in which a long verse is followed by a shorter one, as in the *Epodes* of Horace. 2. A section of the Pindaric ode. See **ode.**

equivalence: In **quantitative verse,** the rule that two short syllables equal one long. See **substitution.**

Erziehungsroman: See *Bildungsroman.*

essay: A short composition which is usually in prose (Pope's *An Essay on Man* and *An Essay on Criticism* are exceptions) and which discusses, either formally or informally, one or more topics. Such essays as those in the *Characters* of Theophrastus or in the *Meditations* of Marcus Aurelius were well known in the ancient world, but the term *essai* (attempt) was first applied to the form by Montaigne when he published a volume of informal pieces in 1580. Seventeen years later, Francis Bacon used the English word *essay* to describe his brief philosophic discourses.

Montaigne, intimate, informal, and graceful, and Bacon, dogmatic, formal, and expository, illustrate the range of the essay. With the development of periodicals, the essay became a popular form, and such writers as Addison, Steele, Lamb, Hazlitt, Pater, and Beerbohm made it their major concern.

euphony: Agreeable sounds which are perhaps as much the result of ease of articulation and a sequence of attractive images as of the inherently pleasing nature of the sounds, as in the following lines from Tennyson's "Lotos-Eaters":

> Dark faces pale against that rosy flame,
> The mild-eyed melancholy Lotos-eaters came.

euphuism: A convoluted and highly colored style, popular in the late sixteenth century, which takes its name from John Lyly's prose romances, *Euphues: The Anatomy of Wit* (1578) and *Euphues and His England* (1580). The style, with its heavy alliteration, elaborate antitheses, and extended comparisons, was condemned by some and imitated by others, but it helped to demonstrate the capabilities of English prose as an instrument of expression:

> You see what love is, begon with griefe, continued with sorrowe, ended with death. A paine full of pleasure, a joye replenished with misery, a Heaven, a Hell, a God, a Divell, and what not, that either hath in it solace or sorrowe? Where the days are spent in thoughts, the nights in dreames, both in daunger, either beguylying us of that we had, or promising us that we had not. Full of jealousie without cause, and voyde of feare when there is a cause: and so many inconveniences hanging upon it, as to recken them all were infinite, and to taste but one of them, intollerable.

The style is reflected in some of Shakespeare's early plays, especially in *Love's Labour's Lost*.

exegesis: An explanation or interpretation, especially of the Bible. In literature, an exegesis is an analysis and, it is presumed, a clarification of a difficult text.

exemplum: A story told to illustrate a moral point. The telling of exempla was a common practice of preachers in the Middle Ages, and from the sermon the form passed into literature. In Chaucer's *Canterbury Tales*, the "Pardoner's Tale" and the "Nun's

Priest's Tale" are both exempla. Unlike the **parable,** the exemplum was usually presumed to be true and the moral placed at the beginning rather than at the end.

Existentialism: Though Existentialism has been called a philosophical "school," the Existentialists themselves differ markedly in doctrine and attitude. Since World War II, there have been two major developments of Existentialist thinking. One, Christian Existentialism, influenced by Kierkegaard, has stressed the idea that in God man may find freedom from tension, for in Him the finite and infinite are one. Some of the leading exponents of this general orientation are Karl Barth, Paul Tillich, and Gabriel Marcel. Karl Jaspers, though a believer in some transcendent reality in the universe, does not accept the restrictions of any formal theology. The other major development is attributable to Jean-Paul Sartre and Martin Heidegger, who posit the idea that man is alone in a godless universe; in this atheistic philosophy, man has no reality if he unthinkingly follows social law or convention. Suffering anguish and despair in his loneliness, he may, nevertheless, become what he wishes by the exercise of free will.

Both groups of Existentialists, however, hold certain elements in common: the concern with man's being; the feeling that reason is insufficient to understand the mysteries of the universe; the awareness that anguish is a universal phenomenon; and the idea that morality has validity only when there is positive participation.

As a basis for literary expression, Existentialism has provided an orientation for such writers as Albert Camus and Simone de Beauvoir, as well as for Sartre himself. Many of the Existentialist writers look to Dostoevsky and Kafka, often considered analogous in their philosophical outlook, for literary inspiration.

See William Barrett, *Irrational Man: A Study in Existentialist Philosophy* (1958); Frederick H. Heinemann, *Existentialism and the Modern Predicament* (2nd ed., 1958); Marjorie G. Grene, *Introduction to Existentialism* (1968); John Macquarrie, *Existentialism* (1972).

exodos: See **Greek tragedy, structure of.**

exordium: See **speech, divisions of a.**

experimental novel: See **naturalism.**

explication de texte: A detailed analysis of a passage of prose or verse. In the *explication,* as practiced in the study of French literature, where it is one of the basic pedagogic devices, the student is presented with a scene from a play, a passage of prose, a short poem, or a section from a long one. The writing is then analyzed in detail, with consideration being given both to the style and the significance of the content. In English, the term *explication* denotes any detailed explanation of a text.

exposition: That part of a play in which the audience is given the background information which it needs to know. Shakespeare, like many dramatists before him, sometimes begins with a section of undisguised exposition, as in *Richard III* and *Henry V,* but, as in *Hamlet* and *Othello,* he can also introduce expository material with great subtlety. In a modern realistic drama the exposition presents a particularly difficult problem, for the playwright often finds himself with a great deal of information which must somehow be conveyed with an appearance of ease and naturalness. The maid and butler of nineteenth-century drama, who began the play by discussing the affairs of their employers, eventually became such familiar stage figures as to be, in later times, objects of satire. (See the beginning of Thornton Wilder's *The Skin of Our Teeth.*) Ibsen, a master of exposition, developed the technique of gradually revealing the past as the play developed. The exposition remains one of the tests of a playwright's technical skill.

Expressionism: An anti-realistic mode of artistic expression that flourished in Germany from about 1910 through the 1920's. Such German Expressionist painters as Oskar Kokoschka and Wassily Kandinsky were inspired by Van Gogh, Gauguin, and Edvard Munch to employ expressive devices—for example, sharply angular lines unknown in nature and objects endowed with unnatural color—in an attempt to suggest a new perception of reality.

Such German Expressionist dramatists as Georg Kaiser, Ernst Toller, and the early Bertolt Brecht, inspired by the Swedish playwright August Strindberg, avoided depictions of individualized characters in realistic settings; Strindberg's *Dream Play*

(1902), with its fragmented, stylized action and its flowering castle, had shown the way to a new theatrical symbolism. In general, Expressionists rejected the imitation of external reality in order to express either a private, inner vision or a wider political one of a world often depicted as bizarre and violent. In American drama, some of Eugene O'Neill's plays, particularly *The Emperor Jones* (1920), *The Hairy Ape* (1922), and *The Great God Brown* (1926), with its use of masks, were influenced by Expressionism in their departures from certain realistic conventions of drama.

The term *Expressionism* is problematic since it can be used to describe virtually any of the deliberate distortions of or departures from reality that pervade modern literature and art. Thus, the fragmentary construction of T. S. Eliot's *The Waste Land*, the symbolic metamorphoses of the characters in Joyce's *Finnegans Wake*, and Kafka's *Metamorphosis* (in which a nightmarish metaphor becomes literal fact) can be regarded as examples of Expressionism, but such an imprecise designation, embracing so many disparate works, casts doubt on its usefulness as a literary description.

See Richard Samuel and R. H. Thomas, *Expressionism in German Life, Literature and the Theater, 1910–1924* (1939); John Willett, *Expressionism* (1970); R. S. Furness, *Expressionism* (1973).

extension: See **meaning.**

extrametrical verse: See **acatalectic.**

extravaganza: In nineteenth-century English drama, a fairy tale or other fanciful subject in an elaborate production with song and dance. In current usage, the term refers to a theatrical presentation, usually musical, characterized by exuberant staging, decorative costumes, and a notable irregularity of form. The Ziegfeld Follies is a well-known example of the extravaganza.

eye rhyme: Rhyme which is apparent to the eye but not to the ear, usually the result of a change in pronunciation. In the first and third lines of the following quatrain by the seventeenth-century poet William Habington, the words *spread* and *read* constitute an eye rhyme:

My soul her wings doth spread
  And heavenward flies,
Th'Almighty's Mysteries to read
In the large volumes of the skies.
      "Nox Nocti Indicat Scientiam (David)"

F

fable: 1. A brief narrative, in either verse or prose, which illustrates some moral truth. The characters are often animals, as in the fables attributed to the Greek slave Aesop, but are not invariably so. Animal fables are sometimes distinguished by being called "apologues," but this term is also used as a general synonym for fable. For recent examples of this form, see James Thurber's *Fables for Our Time* and George Orwell's extended political fable, *Animal Farm.* 2. Also used synonymously with **plot.**

fabliau: A type of short verse tale popular in the Middle Ages. The *fabliaux* were comic, often ribald, accounts of ordinary life, satirizing such matters as the sanctity of the clergy and the chastity of women. Although the form is primarily French, there are examples, such as Chaucer's "Miller's Tale" in *The Canterbury Tales*, in English.

fairy tale: A short narrative derived from the oral tradition of the **folk tale,** involving such figures as witches, giants, fairies, voracious wolves and clever foxes (who speak with marvelous tongues), princes (sometimes miraculously transformed from frogs), princesses (usually in distress), and stepmothers (regularly cruel). Fairy tales, such as "Little Red Riding Hood," "Cinderella," "Beauty and the Beast," and "Snow White," invariably suggest that good triumphs over evil, an important moral function. They have, moreover, a beneficial psychological effect that may account for their capacity to absorb children. As the psychoanalyst Bruno Bettelheim states:

> fairy tales carry important messages to the conscious, the preconscious, and the unconscious mind, on whatever level each is functioning at the time. By dealing with universal human problems,

particularly those which preoccupy the child's mind, these stories speak to his budding ego and encourage its development, while at the same time relieving preconscious and unconscious pressures.

In the early nineteenth century, the Grimm brothers collected *Märchen* (folk or fairy tales) which had been orally transmitted over the centuries; in the Victorian period, such writers as Rudyard Kipling and Oscar Wilde wrote fairy tales based on some of the conventions of the form.

See Bruno Bettelheim, *The Uses of Enchantment: The Meaning and Importance of Fairy Tales* (1976).

falling action: See **plot.**

falling rhythm: One in which the stress comes on the first syllable of the metrical foot:

> Georgie Porgie, pudding and pie,
> Kissed the girls and made them cry;
> When the boys came out to play,
> Georgie Porgie ran away.
>> Anonymous

See **rising rhythm.**

fancy and imagination: Until the Romantic period, *fancy* and *imagination* were largely synonymous terms, though Dryden suggested that *imagination* was the more significant of the two. However, the Romantics, particularly Wordsworth and Coleridge, made a distinction between them which has influenced critics and theoreticians to the present day. In his preface to the 1815 edition of the *Lyrical Ballads*, Wordsworth, attempting to define fancy more precisely than did Coleridge, who regarded it as an "aggregative and associative power," wrote: "Fancy does not require that the materials which she makes use of should be susceptible to change in their constitution, from her touch; and where they admit of modification, it is enough for her purpose if it be slight, limited and evanescent. Directly the reverse of these, are the desires and demands of the Imagination. She recoils from everything but the plastic, the pliant and the indefinite." In short, fancy is a relatively superficial and mechanical faculty involving memory and association, the ability to correlate images (derived from the senses) without substantively transforming them. As Coleridge states in Chapter XIII of his *Biographia Literaria* (1817): "The Fancy is indeed no other than a mode of Memory emancipated from the order of time and space."

Like Wordsworth, Coleridge believed that the imagination, a vastly superior faculty, was allied to the creative power of the universe, for the poet could create realities hitherto unknown. In the same chapter of the *Biographia*, Coleridge asserts that the imagination "dissolves, diffuses, dissipates, in order to re-create; or where this process is rendered impossible, yet still at all events it struggles to idealize and to unify. It is essentially *vital*, even as all objects (*as* objects) are essentially fixed and dead." In Chapter XIV, the imagination is described by Coleridge as a "synthetic and magical power . . . [which] reveals itself in the balance or reconcilement of opposite or discordant qualities: of sameness, with difference; of the general with the concrete; the idea with the image; the individual with the representative. . . ."

In asserting the primacy of the imagination, the Romantics rejected the Neoclassical insistence on conformity to "rules" by which a literary work was to be created. Instead, they insisted on an organic conception of art, created by what Coleridge, in his poem "Dejection: An Ode," called "My shaping spirit of Imagination"—a concept illustrated by T. S. Eliot in his essay "The Metaphysical Poets" (1921): "When a poet's mind is perfectly equipped for its work, it is constantly amalgamating disparate experience; the ordinary man's experience is chaotic, irregular, fragmentary. The latter falls in love, or reads Spinoza, and these two experiences have nothing to do with each other, or with the noise of the typewriter or the smell of cooking; in the mind of the poet these experiences are always forming new wholes."

See M. H. Abrams, *The Mirror and the Lamp: Romantic Theory and the Critical Tradition* (1953), Chapter VII; R. L. Brett, *Fancy and Imagination* (1969).

fantastic, the: See **fantasy.**

fantasy: In a literary work, a radical departure, sometimes bizarre or grotesque, from our sense of the "real" world or from the literary conventions of **realism.** The term *fantasy* may embrace such a wide variety of works as Swift's *Gulliver's Travels,* Lewis Carroll's *Alice's Adventures in Wonderland,* Oscar Wilde's *The*

Picture of Dorian Gray, and J. R. R. Tolkien's *The Lord of the Rings*. They remain, however, "reality-oriented"—that is, characterization and action are logically consistent and psychologically meaningful though not always subject to rational explanation. Often in fantasies, common everyday activities are included in order to lend credence to the story. To be sure, a **willing suspension of disbelief** is initially required of the reader in order to accept the "counter-structure" of the fantasy world.

The fantastic generally implies a sudden, dramatic incident in a fantasy, such as Gregor Samsa's awakening one morning in Kafka's *Metamorphosis* to discover that he is a monstrous insect or the revelation at the end of Wilde's novel that the youthful, handsome Dorian Gray is in reality a hideous old man. Thus, our perspective is suddenly altered, bewilderment or shock ensues, and we experience a strange, disturbing event that transports us beyond the boundaries of rationality.

See Eric S. Rabkin, *The Fantastic in Literature* (1976); Rosemary Jackson, *Fantasy: The Literature of Subversion* (1981); Roger C. Schlobin, ed., *The Aesthetics of Fantasy: Literature and Art* (1982).

farce: From Latin: *farcire*, "to stuff." Originally any insertion in the church liturgy. Later, farces were the comic scenes interpolated in the early liturgical plays. The word now refers to any play which evokes laughter by such devices of **low comedy** as physical buffoonery, rough wit, or the creation of ridiculous situations, and which is little concerned with subtlety of characterization or probability of plot. Shakespeare's *The Comedy of Errors* is almost entirely farcical, but many plays which are not farces, such as *Twelfth Night*, contain farcical elements, *e.g.*, the mock duel between Viola and Sir Andrew.

See Jessica M. Davis, *Farce* (1978).

feeling: See **four meanings of a poem.**

feminine ending: An extra unstressed syllable at the end of a verse, as in the second and fourth lines of the following quatrain:

> Sigh no more, ladies, sigh no more,
>   Men were deceivers ever,
> One foot in sea and one on shore,

To one thing constant never.
    Shakespeare, *Much Ado about Nothing*

feminine rhyme: See **rhyme.**

feminist criticism: A mode of critical discourse that emphasizes culturally determined gender differences in the interpretation of
literary works. The principal inspirations for the rise of feminist
criticism since the late 1960's have been such works as Simone
de Beauvoir's *The Second Sex* (1949), Mary Ellmann's *Thinking
about Women* (1968), and Kate Millett's *Sexual Politics* (1970).
Their general thrust has been to condemn male attitudes toward
women, charging that men have historically imposed their will
on women in order to convince them of their inherent inferiority.
Such a male view of the world has been called "phallocentrism"
by feminists, who took the term from the British psychoanalyst
Ernest Jones.

    Feminist criticism has generally focused on this history of male
dominance and oppression, observable in every aspect of society,
particularly in literature and language—hence the new coinages
(such as "chairperson" instead of "chairman") to eliminate sexist
implications. In addition, feminist critics have sought to recover
the works of many neglected women writers and to reinterpret
them from a revised perspective.

    In recent years, feminist criticism has been combined with
other current modes of criticism, such as **psychoanalytic criticism, Marxist criticism,** and **post-structuralism.** It has also developed internal divisions, resulting, for example, in a group of
black feminist critics who have added a racial orientation.

    See Josephine Donovan, ed., *Feminist Literary Criticism: Ex-
plorations in Theory* (1975); K. K. Ruthven, *Feminist Literary
Studies: An Introduction* (1984).

Festschrift: German: *Fest*, "celebration"; *schrift*, "writing." A volume of essays written by colleagues and friends in celebration
of such occasions as a noted scholar's retirement or a significant
birthday.

fiction: A narrative, usually in the form of a novel or short tale, that
tells an imaginative story, as distinguished from non-fiction, which
may present historical or biographical fact. Events in a fictional

narration are not therefore "untrue" simply because they cannot be "verified" as having actually existed in the external world. "Truth" in fiction rests on the logic of cause and effect in the plot, the complexity or psychological credibility of characterization—in short, all of the elements that convince the reader of their correspondence to life, albeit in an ordered, symbolic form.

When fiction moves beyond **realism** into a world of unexpected **fantasy,** it necessarily retains some coherent relation to reality in order to hold the reader's interest—that is, character and plot, no matter how strange or fantastic, retain an essential logic, such as the events in Stevenson's *Dr. Jekyll and Mr. Hyde,* in which the evil in Dr. Jekyll is split off into a separate personality, Mr. Hyde. Such a "poetics of fiction" is often called "narratology."

For various forms of fiction, see the listing under "Narrative Types" at the end of this book.

See Wayne Booth, *The Rhetoric of Fiction* (1961); Mark Spilka, ed., *Towards a Poetics of Fiction* (1977); Seymour Chatman, *Story and Discourse: Narrative Structure in Fiction and Film* (1978); James Phelan, *Worlds from Words: A Theory of Language in Fiction* (1981).

figurative language: Language which makes use of certain devices called "figures of speech," most of which are techniques for comparing dissimilar objects, to achieve effects beyond the range of literal language. These devices are by no means limited to poetry; everyone uses them to add color and intensity to his speech. If someone says, "Hotchkiss is as blind as a bat," he is using figurative language. To be precise, he is using the device called **simile** to compare Hotchkiss's eyesight with that of a bat, but he does not intend the comparison to be taken literally. He does not mean that the unfortunate Hotchkiss is nearly blind, but only that he is unobservant. In ordinary speech, these devices are casually employed (the expression "beyond the range" in the first sentence of this paragraph is a metaphor, yet most of us grasp its meaning without recognizing it as such), but the poet uses them not only as ornament but also to express ideas which can be expressed in no other way. Thus, Shakespeare's phrase "bare ruined choirs, where late the sweet birds sang" contains complexities of association beyond the power of literal language to delineate. For a discussion of some of the major figures, see **hyperbole; metaphor; metonymy; personification; synecdoche.**

figure of speech: Any of the devices of figurative language. See above.

fin de siècle: See **Decadence.**

flashback: A scene inserted into a film, novel, story, or play showing events which happened at an earlier time. The device is particularly useful in film (in *Citizen Kane*, for example, Orson Welles employed it with great skill), but it is also effective in literature. See Thornton Wilder's *The Bridge of San Luis Rey* for its use in the novel.

flat and round characters: Terms used by E. M. Forster in *Aspects of the Novel* (1927) to designate different types of characterization. A flat character is one embodying a "single idea or quality." Lacking any complexity, it never surprises. The flat character, Forster states, is sometimes called a "type" or "caricature," for it "can be summed up in a sentence." An advantage of flat characters is that they are immediately recognizable. To the writer, they are convenient, for he may move them about without concerning himself with their development. To the reader, they are easy to remember later. A flat character may be delightful in comedy but dull if he is the central character in tragedy, for complexity is necessary to move our deepest feelings. By creating flat characters, which appear deep if not complex, a writer such as Dickens may achieve vividness and size. An inept writer, on the other hand, may attempt to make his flat characters round and produce, instead, unconvincing portraits.

A round character must, according to Forster, be capable of surprising a reader "in a convincing way." Complexity of characterization, moreover, must be accompanied by an organization of traits or qualities. Forster believes that though Jane Austen's characters, which are usually round, are smaller than Dickens's flat characters, they are "more highly organized." He concludes by saying that serious work often requires a combination of flat and round characters, for the intermingling of both types reflects life as we view it.

Fleshly School of Poetry: See **Pre-Raphaelites.**

folio: 1. Latin: "a leaf" (abbr. F.). A book made by folding the original printer's sheet once to make two leaves or four pages. In general, a folio is a very large book, but in modern publishing, the dimensions of a printer's sheet vary considerably and the term does not designate a precise size. In addition, this subject is complicated by the fact that some publishers use such terms as *folio,* *quarto, octavo,* and *duodecimo* as arbitrary designations of size regardless of the number of leaves to the sheet.

2. In Shakespearean criticism, the term *folios* refers to the collections of his plays published in folio editions some years after his death. The First Folio, one of four, appeared in 1623. The quartos are the editions of separate plays published during and after Shakespeare's lifetime. The texts of a single play often vary widely among the quartos and folios.

folk drama: 1. Plays on folk themes produced by amateurs at popular festivals and religious celebrations. In medieval England, these plays concerned such characters as Robin Hood and St. George. The body of medieval **liturgical drama,** though derived from a highly developed theology, is considered by some as a part of folk drama.

2. Plays written by sophisticated literary craftsmen on folk themes. Such plays are usually performed not by or for the "folk" but by professional actors before a literate, urban audience. Much of the drama of the **Irish Literary Renaissance,** such as the plays of John Millington Synge and Lady Gregory, are folk plays of this sort, as are the peasant plays of Pirandello and García Lorca.

folklore: The songs, stories, myths, and proverbs of a people or "folk" as handed down by word of mouth. Some scholars also consider such things as traditional ceremonies, architectural forms, and agricultural techniques to be parts of folklore. Since the publication of Percy's *Reliques of Ancient English Poetry* in 1765, the study of folklore has developed steadily. The art of the "folk" has influenced such disparate figures as Sir Walter Scott and D. H. Lawrence.

folk tale: A traditional story handed down, in either written or oral form. This term covers a variety of material from primitive myths to **fairy tales,** or *Märchen,* to such literary works as the stories of Hans Christian Andersen. Folk tales had long been recorded in such collections as the *Thousand and One Nights* and the *Gesta Romanorum,* but since the collection of the German philologists Wilhelm and Jacob Grimm early in the nineteenth century, the nature and distribution of the folk tale has been extensively studied.

foot: A group of syllables forming a metrical unit. Most of the feet recognized in English verse contain one accented and one or two unaccented syllables. The most commonly used feet are as follows:

Iamb(us): ◡ ´	Anapest: ◡ ◡ ´
Trochee: ´ ◡	Dactyl: ´ ◡ ◡
Spondee: ´ ´	

See the individual listings of these terms for further discussion and examples. See also **amphibrach; amphimac; choriamb; dibrach; meter.**

foreshadowing: See **atmosphere.**

form: 1. A fixed metrical arrangement, such as the **sonnet** form or the **ballade** form.

  2. The essential structure of a work of art. *Form* is sometimes contrasted with *content* (the terms *expression* and *thought* are often substituted) as if the two were separable entities. We speak of the poet as having "something to say" and saying it in, for example, the sonnet form, as if this form were a decoration inscribed on the outside of the thought. But this artificial separation of form and content is misleading, for it implies that the poet's business is to *say* things rather than to *make* things. A poet makes a poem out of words, which inevitably carry various meanings, but it is only when the complex structure of meanings expresses a particular unity that it achieves aesthetic form. Taken in this sense, form is more than an external scheme; it is, rather, the total structural integration of the work itself. The form of a successful work of art is, as Coleridge said, shaped from within, not imposed from without.

four levels of meaning: In a letter to his patron Can Grande della

Scala, Dante explained the way in which *The Divine Comedy* should be read. The reader, he said, should be aware of four levels of meaning: (1) *the literal or historical*, that which actually occurs; (2) *the moral meaning;* (3) *the allegorical*, the symbolic significance which pertains to mankind; and (4) *the anagogical*, the spiritual or mystical meaning stating an eternal truth. Dante adds that all except the first level may be called "allegorical."

The technique of the fourfold interpretation was widespread in medieval criticism. Cassian (ca. 400) was perhaps the first to interpret the Scriptures according to the levels which Dante later refers to. In his *Moralia on the Book of Job*, Pope Gregory I likewise demonstrated how this device of exegesis could be employed. Later, secular poetry was also subjected to this method.

four meanings of a poem: In *Practical Criticism* (1929), I. A. Richards, discussing the total meaning of a communication, particularly poetry, outlines four different meanings: (1) *Sense:* what is said, or the "items" referred to by a writer; (2) *Feeling:* the emotional attitudes which he has toward these items; (3) *Tone:* the writer's attitude toward his audience (the use of language is determined by the writer's "recognition" of his relation to his readers); (4) *Intention:* the writer's purpose, whether conscious or unconscious—the effect he tries to achieve. A scientist writing a treatise, for example, puts the sense first, subordinates his feeling, establishes his tone by following academic convention, and clearly states his intention. In verse, however, the poet makes statements which function as vehicles for the expression of feelings and attitudes. The perceptive reader, Richards suggests, must be prepared to apprehend the interplay of the four meanings which together comprise the total meaning of the poem.

See David Newton-DeMolina, ed., *On Literary Intention: Critical Essays* (1976).

fourteener: A line of fourteen syllables, usually seven iambs. Though once popular—Chapman's translation of the *Iliad* is in this meter—it has seldom been used in recent verse.

frame story: See **story within a story.**

free verse: Called *vers libre* by the French, free verse lacks regular meter and line length, relying upon the natural speech rhythms of the language, the cadences which result from the alternation of stressed and unstressed syllables. Though free verse has had its vogue particularly in this century, it was employed by French poets of the nineteenth century trying to free themselves from the metrical regularity of the **alexandrine** and by English and American poets seeking greater liberty in verse structure. Earlier, free verse had been used in the King James translation of the Bible, particularly in the Song of Solomon and the Psalms. Whitman's *Leaves of Grass* is, perhaps, the most notable example of the organization of speech patterns into verse cadences:

> A child said *What is the grass?* fetching it
> to me with full hands,
> How could I answer the child? I do not know
> what it is any more than he.
> I guess it must be the flag of my disposition, out
> of hopeful green stuff woven.

See Charles O. Hartman, *Free Verse: An Essay on Prosody* (1980).

French forms: Certain elaborate metrical forms which originated in Provençal troubadour verse and which were later imported into English. They were much used by the Victorians for light verse. For individual definitions and examples, see **ballade; rondeau; rondel; sestina; villanelle; virelay.**

Freytag's Pyramid: In his *The Technique of the Drama* (1863) the German critic Gustav Freytag described the structure of the typical five-act play in terms of rising action, climax, and falling action, as illustrated in the diagram below. This pattern has been widely used, though it is not appropriate to all plays.

a. Introduction
a¹. Inciting moment
b. Rising action
c. Climax
d. Falling action
e. Catastrophe

Fugitives and Agrarians: The Fugitives were a group of sixteen Southern writers (chiefly poets) who met frequently in Nashville, Tennessee, between 1915 and 1921 to read their own work and to discuss philosophical and literary questions. These writers, most of them teachers and students at Vanderbilt University, included John Crowe Ransom, Donald Davidson, Allen Tate, Laura Riding, Merrill Moore, and Robert Penn Warren. Without a manifesto or aesthetic, the Fugitives agreed, as Davidson wrote, on the need "to flee from the extremes of conventionalism, whether new or old. They hope to keep in touch with and to utilize in their works the best qualities of modern poetry, without at the same time casting aside as unworthy all that is established as good in the past." The group published *The Fugitive* between the years 1922 and 1925 as well as *The Fugitives: An Anthology of Verse* (1928), their final joint effort.

After 1928, four of the leading Fugitives—Ransom, Tate, Davidson, and Warren—joined eight others (mostly scholars, including the critic Stark Young and the poet John Gould Fletcher) to form a new group calling themselves "Agrarians," who, until 1935, communicated by letter and essay in continuing discussions of politics and philosophy, unlike the Fugitives, who were primarily concerned with literature. The Agrarians published an anthology of essays, *I'll Take My Stand* (1930), which supported, as its preface stated, "a southern way of life against what may be called the American prevailing way, and all as much as agree that the best terms in which to represent the distinction are contained in the phrase Agrarian versus Industrial." Tate, Warren, and Ransom were later leading critics and theorists of the **New Criticism.**

See John L. Stewart, *The Burden of Time: The Fugitives and the Agrarians* (1965).

fustian: Referring to thick cotton cloth, the term *fustian* has also come to mean bombastic or pompously ornate language. In "Epistle to Dr. Arbuthnot," Pope makes reference to a writer

> . . . whose fustian's so sublimely bad,
> It is not poetry, but prose run mad.

Futurism: A literary and artistic movement which flourished chiefly in Italy and France between 1908 and the 1920's. Early in 1909, Futurism was officially launched with the publication in *Le Figaro* of a manifesto by the Italian poet F. T. Marinetti, who announced: "We shall sing the love of danger, the habit of energy and boldness. . . . We wish to glorify War—the only health giver of the world. . . . The foundations of our poetry shall be courage, audacity, and revolt." Futurist art, he declared, would thenceforth be concerned with "the beauty of Speed" ("a speeding automobile is more beautiful than the *Victory of Samothrace*"). In subsequent manifestos, some Italian artists insisted that Futuristic painting must destroy "the materiality of bodies" to effect a fusion of objects with their surroundings.

Between 1912 and 1914, the flamboyant Marinetti visited England, where he lectured frequently and caused a sensation with his poetry readings (on occasion, he imitated the sound of a machine gun or had a drum offstage beating to his verse). In his writings and lectures, Marinetti outlined his aesthetic for Futurist poetry: it abandons conventional syntax and verb forms; transforms or deforms words "at liberty"; introduces total freedom in the use of images; expresses a "most rapid, brutal and immediate lyricism . . . a telegraphic lyricism"; renders "all the sounds and even the most cacophonous noises of modern life"; and employs a typography (*e.g.*, twenty kinds of type on a single page) that suggests the "bursts of style." Soon the term *Futurism* was used by journalists for anything new or bizarre, including clothing.

At first Wyndham Lewis (and certain other writers), attracted by Marinetti's energy, acknowledged Futurism as a major development in twentieth-century poetry, but later he rejected its "automobilism" and "romantic rebellion" in favor of the static stability of **Vorticism.** In its rejection of all literary and artistic traditions and in its noisy public displays, Futurism anticipated not only Vorticism but also **Dadaism.**

See *Marinetti: Selected Writings*, ed. R. W. Flint (1972); Marianne W. Martin, *Futurist Art and Theory, 1909–1915* (1968); Caroline Tisdall and Angelo Bozzolla, *Futurism* (1978).

G

gallows humor: See **black humor.**

gathering: The group of leaves in a book cut from a single printer's sheet. See **folio.**

genetic fallacy: See **intentional fallacy.**

genius and talent: As we use the word today, *genius* designates an extraordinary, innate intellectual capacity, especially for imaginative creation or for original speculation or invention. It is often contrasted with *talent*, a lesser order of ability or artistic gift.

Originally, a genius was a spirit (in this sense, we now use *genii* as the plural and usually *jinn* or *jinni* as the singular), then one of the two spirits—good and bad—supposed to attend on every man. By extension, it became a person's natural bent or inclination and then his capacity or quality of mind. By the late eighteenth century, it designated a man's inborn ability as contrasted with a skill which could be acquired. Probably reinforced by the original sense of *genius* as spirit, the word took on its modern connotations of transcendent power in the Romantic period. In this sense, it was much used in Germany, where the epoch of **Sturm und Drang** is sometimes called the *Genieperiode*, but the usage seems to have originated in England. In an autobiographical sketch, Thomas De Quincey wrote, "Talent and genius . . . are not merely different, they are in polar opposition to each other. Talent is intellectual power of every kind, which acts and manifests itself . . . through the will and the active forces. Genius . . . is that much rarer species of intellectual power which is derived from the genial nature—from the spirit of suffering and enjoying—from the spirit of pleasure and pain. . . . It is a function of the passive nature."

genre: 1. A literary type or class. Works are sometimes classified by subject—thus **carpe diem** poems may be said to constitute a genre—but the more usual classification is by form and treatment. Some of the recognized genres are **epic, tragedy, comedy,** and **lyric.** From the Renaissance through the eighteenth century, the various genres were rigorously distinguished and were governed by sets of rules which a writer was expected to follow. Recently, however, criticism has become less directly prescriptive and less concerned with distinctions among the genres, though they are still considered useful.

2. A "genre painting" is one which takes its subject from ordinary life rather than mythology or history. By analogy, a

literary work which portrays ordinary people or scenes may be called a "genre piece."

See Heather Dubrow, *Genre* (1982).

genre criticism: A critical approach to literature that focuses on definitions that distinguish one **genre,** or literary type, from another. Frequently, such criticism employs a historical approach in order to account for a genre's development. In the 1950's, the **Chicago critics,** who were influenced by Aristotle's method of analysis, and Northrop Frye, who employed **archetypes** and **myths,** attempted to redefine and distinguish various genres.

See Northrop Frye, *Anatomy of Criticism* (1957); Paul Hernadi, *Beyond Genre: New Directions in Literary Classification* (1972).

Georgian poetry: Verse which appeared in five anthologies titled *Georgian Poetry* (after George V, then king), edited by Edward Marsh between 1912 and 1922. Reacting against Victorian discursiveness, *fin de siècle* **Decadence**, and the prevailing urban realism in literature, the Georgians wished to return to earlier nineteenth-century traditions associated with Wordsworth. Consequently, their principal subject was nature in its gentler aspects, but, in the final analysis, their poetry suffered from the absence of passion or vision. As Robert H. Ross has written in *The Georgian Revolt: Rise and Fall of a Poetic Ideal, 1910–1922* (1965): "They attempted to preserve the Wordsworthian tradition divorced from the thoughtful aspects of Wordsworth." The anthologies presented the work of such poets as John Drinkwater, John Masefield, Walter de la Mare, Rupert Brooke, and W. H. Davies; D. H. Lawrence and Robert Graves were occasional contributors.

See Myron Simon, *The Georgian Poetic* (1975).

georgic: From Latin: *georgicus,* "agricultural." A poem didactic in purpose and precise in its description of rustic life. The most important work in this tradition is Vergil's *Georgics.* In the eighteenth century, the English country tradition was expressed by James Thomson, "the English Vergil," in *The Seasons* (1730) and by William Cowper in *The Task* (1785).

The two primary subjects of georgic poems are descriptions of rustic occupations and of nature. Generally, these poems instruct readers in such occupations as farming, sheep shearing, or hunting. Addison, in "Essay on the Georgic" (1697), states that such a poem "consists in giving plain and direct instructions." Sometimes, however, georgics digress into such subjects as folklore and mythology. Whereas traditional **pastoral** poetry depicts a stylized, artificial world of singing and dancing shepherds, the georgic depicts the dignity of rustic labor. See **eclogue; idyl(l)**.

See John Chalker, *The English Georgic* (1970); Anthony Low, *The Georgic Revolution* (1985).

gesta: Deeds or tales of adventure, as in the fourteenth-century *Gest Historiale of the Destruction of Troy*. One of the most famous medieval collections of tales was the *Gesta Romanorum* (*Deeds of the Romans*). See **chanson de geste**.

gloss: 1. Originally a marginal or interlinear explanation of a difficult word or phrase. Many Greek manuscripts, when copied, were given Latin glosses. E.K.'s gloss to Spenser's *Shepheardes Calender* contains general comment on the poem as well as explanations of difficult words. Coleridge's gloss to *The Rime of the Ancient Mariner* consists of marginal paragraphs which sometimes summarize the story.

2. A deliberately misleading interpretation.

gnomic verse: Verse made up of or largely characterized by gnomes, or aphorisms. Gnomic verse has been common since early Greek poetry. There are many ancient and medieval collections of gnomes, and they appear in innumerable works from Homer to *Beowulf*. Among the best-known gnomic verses in English are the following:

> He that is in the battle slain
> Will never rise to fight again:
> But he that fights and runs away
> Will live to fight another day.
> Anonymous

Goliardic verse: Verse, primarily Latin, of the twelfth and thirteenth centuries attributed to the Goliards, or wandering scholars. Much of it was ribald and satiric, devoted to the praise of love and wine. The most notable collection of such verse is the famous *Carmina Burana*, a thirteenth-century songbook originally in the Benedictbeuern Monastery in Bavaria.

Gongorism: An intricate and affected style, so called from the work of the Spanish poet Luis de Gongora y Argote (1561–1627). In an effort to add polish to the language of his day, Gongora began introducing new words coined from Greek, Latin, and Italian, along with puns, paradoxes, conceits, and inversions of word order. Because this controversial style was designed to appeal to the cultivated, it was also called *cultismo* or *culteranismo*. See **Marinism.**

Gothic novel: A type of romance popular in the late eighteenth and early nineteenth centuries. The form was inaugurated by Horace Walpole's *Castle of Otranto* (1764), whose popularity attracted many imitations, among the best known of which were Ann Radcliffe's *The Mysteries of Udolfo* and Matthew Lewis's *The Monk*. These stories, usually set in medieval castles complete with secret passageways, mysterious dungeons, peripatetic ghosts, and much gloom and supernatural paraphernalia, were thrillers designed to evoke genteel shudders, although Mary Shelley's *Frankenstein* (1817), one of the most original of the Gothic novels, had a more serious purpose. The influence of this genre extended to such works as Coleridge's "Christabel," the novels of the Brontës, the mysteries of Edgar Allan Poe, and the writings of innumerable imitators. Recent critics have interpreted the Gothic elements not only as melodramatic devices calculated to evoke terror in the reader but also as symbolic manifestations of the characters' own unconscious fears or spiritual confusion.

See Edith Birkhead, *The Tale of Terror: A Study of the Gothic Romance* (1963); "Sources of Terror to the American Imagination," essays edited by Robert D. Jacobs, *Studies in the Literary Imagination*, 7 (Spring 1974); Linda Bayer-Berenbaum, *The Gothic Imagination* (1982).

Graveyard School of Poetry: A group of English poets of the mid-eighteenth century who, unlike the contemporary Neoclassicists, cultivated the mysterious and the melancholy. The members of this group, which included Thomas Parnell, Robert Blair, and

Edward Young, were much attracted to death and gloomy scenery, anticipating some of the melancholy of the Romantics. The most famous of the "Graveyard" poems is Gray's "Elegy Written in a Country Churchyard."

Great Chain of Being: See **Chain of Being.**

Greek tragedy, structure of: In general, the structure of Greek tragedy is as follows: (1) *Prologus* or *Prologue:* the introductory scene, containing either a monologue or dialogue which is devoted to exposition, though portrayal of character is often important. (In Sophocles' *Oedipus Rex,* the first scene finds Oedipus and a priest in a conversation that both presents the problem of the play and characterizes its hero.) (2) *Parodos:* the entrance of the chorus which, in song, usually presents further exposition or foreshadows the tragedy of the play. (3) *Episodes:* frequently four or five which contain the action of the play. Episodes are separated by choral odes, or *stasimons.* In some plays, part of an episode may be a *Kommos,* a lamentation involving actors and chorus. (4) *Exodos:* the final section following the last ode sung and danced by the chorus. In this part, two characteristic features recur in Greek tragedy: the messenger's speech—though sometimes occurring in earlier sections of the play—and the **deus ex machina.** (In *Oedipus Rex* a messenger reports Jocasta's suicide and Oedipus blinds himself.) The device of the *deus ex machina* is characteristic only of the plays of Euripides.

Grub Street: Once the name of a London street (now Milton Street) much inhabited by indigent writers whose hack work resulted in their earning no more than a meager living. Since many critics found even this result insufficient justification for their scribblings, the term *Grub Street* has come to be applied to any inept commercial writing.

Grundyism: An excessive conformity to conventional morality. The term is derived from the name of Mrs. Grundy, a character who is alluded to but who never appears in Thomas Morton's play *Speed the Plough* (1798), in which another character, concerned with the slightest departure from convention, inevitably asks the question: "What will Mrs. Grundy say?"

Guignol: Originally a puppet character created in Lyons around the end of the eighteenth century, the witty and audacious Guignol achieved great popularity. He was brought from Lyons to Paris, where he gave his name to a theater, the Grand Guignol, which eventually came to produce plays, performed by live actors, dealing with the horrifying and the macabre. The term *Grand Guignol* is now applied to any such play.

H

hagiography: The writing or study of saints' lives, widespread in the Middle Ages and the Renaissance. See John Foxe's *Book of Martyrs* (1559) and William Roper's *Life of Sir Thomas More* (1626).

hagiology: See **hagiography.**

haiku: An unrhymed Japanese poem, usually consisting of seventeen *jion* (Japanese symbol-sounds), which records the essence of a moment keenly perceived, usually linking nature to human nature. Though there is no fixed form for Japanese haiku, foreign adaptations, particularly those developed by American poets, have usually consisted of three lines of five, seven, and five syllables. Seventeen syllables is the norm in an English-language haiku, but it frequently contains fewer than this number though rarely more. The following haiku by Taniguchi Buson (1715–83), translated by Harold G. Henderson, is characteristic of the genre, but in translation does not correspond precisely to the seventeen *jion:*

> The short night is through:
>   on the hairy caterpillar,
>   little beads of dew.

Hokku, an old Japanese word applicable to more than one kind of verse, included what is now called haiku (the latter term proposed around 1890 by the Japanese poet Masaoka Shiki). Today, *hokku*, as a synonym for haiku, is obsolete in Japan as well as in the United States. In the early twentieth century, poets of the movement called **Imagism**, inspired by Ezra Pound, tried to achieve the effects of haiku, though they made no attempt to imitate its verse structure.

See Harold G. Henderson, *Haiku in English* (1967).

half rhyme: See **rhyme.**

hamartia: See **tragedy.**

Harlem Renaissance: An outpouring of artistic energy in the arts after World War I, when Harlem became "the international capital of black culture." As Langston Hughes wrote: "Harlem was in vogue." Though precise dates are difficult to assign to the period, the years 1919 to 1929 are most often cited; some critics have extended it to the 1930's.

The most prominent of those associated with the Harlem Renaissance were, besides Langston Hughes, the poets Countee Cullen, Claude McKay, and Jean Toomer; the novelists Eric Waldron, Zora Neale Hurston, and Arna Bontemps. Less well known are such sculptors and painters as Meta Warrick Fuller, William H. Johnson, Palmer Hayden, and, in the 1930's, Aaron Douglas. Though there was no uniform aesthetic that united these artists and writers, there was a major influence that gave their work direction: Alain Locke's anthology *New Negro: An Interpretation* (1925), which envisioned a new black presence in American culture and a "spiritual emancipation" for blacks in general. In addition, Locke urged American blacks to regard African art as their legacy and to give expression to it in their works. (Indeed, African art had already made its impact on **Modernism,** as in the work of Picasso.) Thus, much painting, sculpture, and jazz reflected African influences, both in subject matter and in technique.

The Harlem Renaissance, associated with the New Negro Movement, was regarded by some of its critics as elitist (focusing on the arts as a means of raising the status of American blacks and establishing better relations with whites). Wallace Thurman's novel *The Blacker the Berry* (1929), which satirizes the movement as pretentious and derivative, has been credited with ending the Harlem Renaissance, but it is more likely that the economic realities of the Great Depression had the stronger impact.

See Nathan Irvin Huggins, *Harlem Renaissance* (1971); Charles Miers, ed., *Harlem Renaissance: Art of Black America* (1987); Houston A. Baker, Jr., *Modernism and the Harlem Renaissance* (1987).

headless line: See **acatalectic.**

head rhyme: See **alliteration.**

Hebraism—Hellenism: Terms used by Matthew Arnold in Chapter IV of *Culture and Anarchy* (1869) to characterize the two governing forces in man: "The uppermost idea with Hellenism is to see things as they really are; the uppermost idea with Hebraism is conduct and obedience." Arnold, describing the essence of Hellenism as "spontaneity of consciousness" and that of Hebraism as "strictness of conscience," maintained that both forces were necessary for a full, civilized life but that in England Hebraism had been emphasized at the expense of Hellenism and that a corrective emphasis on culture was in order. Since Arnold's day, these terms have been widely used in social and literary criticism.

See David DeLaura, *Hebrew and Hellene in Victorian England: Newman, Arnold, and Pater* (1969).

hemistich: A half line of verse, frequently on one side of a **caesura.**

hendecasyllabic verse: A verse of eleven syllables.

hendiadys: From Greek: "one by means of two." A rhetorical device by which two nouns are joined by a conjunction to express a single complex idea by means of two related images, as in Vergil's *Georgics*: "we drink from cups and gold" (instead of "golden cups"). The term was coined by the Latin grammarian Servius (ca. A.D. 400) to describe such a device in Vergil's *Aeneid*. Shakespeare makes considerable use of it in his tragedies, particularly *Hamlet*, in which such phrases as "slings and arrows of outrageous fortune" and "scourge and minister" suggest not "parallel terms" but an ambiguous structure that enriches the context.

See George T. Wright, "Hendiadys and *Hamlet*," *PMLA*, 96 (March 1981).

heptameter: A line of verse consisting of seven metrical feet, as in Robert Southwell's "The Burning Babe":

As I / in hoar / y win / ter's night / stood
   shi / vering in / the snow,
Surprised I was with sudden heat which made my heart to glow;
And lifting up a fearful eye to view what fire was near,
A pretty babe, all burning bright, did in the air appear. . . .

heptastich: A stanza of seven lines.

Heresy of Paraphrase: A term used by Cleanth Brooks in *The Well-Wrought Urn* (1947) to reject the notion that a poem can be paraphrased without doing violence to it. A paraphrase implies that the "ideas" or "thought" of the poem can be expressed in other words; however, what a poem "says"—that is, the formulation of the "statement" made by the poet—is not the poem. As Brooks states: "The truth of the matter is that all such formulations lead away from the center of the poem—not toward it; that the 'prose-sense' of the poem is not a rack on which the stuff of the poem [*i.e.*, images, metaphors, tensions, rhythms, etc.] is hung; that it does not represent the 'inner' structure or the 'essential' structure or the 'real' structure of the poem." We use formulations for convenience to refer to various parts of the poem, but they are, Brooks says, "scaffoldings thrown about the building, not to be confused with the building itself."

hermeneutic circle: See **hermeneutics**.

hermeneutics: In its most general sense, any theory of interpretation. Originally, the term was limited to Biblical **exegesis**, but since the nineteenth century it has been extended to any theory or procedure in interpreting literary, legal, or social science texts.

The "hermeneutic circle," first described in the early nineteenth century by the German theologian Friedrich Schleiermacher, was so named later in the century by the philosopher Wilhelm Dilthey to describe an approach to understanding: the meaning of constituent parts of a whole can be understood only if the whole has prior meaning, but only when those constituent parts are understood can the full meaning of the whole be grasped. Thus, the interrelationships of words, sentences, paragraphs to whole literary works involve a progressive clarification of mutually conferred meanings.

In *The Validity of Interpretation* (1967) and *The Aims of Interpretation* (1976), the American critic E. D. Hirsch has argued that, in employing the hermeneutic circle, a reader may determine the meaning of a work by progressively testing a hypothesis of interpretation while examining the relationship of the whole to its parts: the result is likely to be a close approximation of the author's intent.

See David Couzens Hoy, *The Critical Circle: Literature and History in Contemporary Hermeneutics* (1978); W. Wolfgang Holdheim, *The Hermeneutic Mode* (1984).

hero: Traditionally, a character who has such admirable traits as courage, idealism, and fortitude. The earliest heroes, as revealed in myth and literature, were frequently favored by the gods or were themselves semi-divine; such were Achilles and Odysseus. The deified hero symbolized the possibility of overcoming human limitations in a hostile universe ruled by the certainty of death. Moreover, the hero embodied the cultural values of his time and functioned as defender of his society.

In time, however, as man's values changed, different concepts of the hero emerged. In the Renaissance, for example, Marlowe's tragic hero Dr. Faustus challenges existing religious doctrine by bartering his soul for divine knowledge. By the nineteenth century, the Romantic values of individualism, aspiration, and inspired creativity transformed such rebels in myth and literature as Prometheus, Cain, Satan, and Faust into idealized heroes (the **Byronic hero**, in particular, was derived from elements in these figures). While the warrior-hero of antiquity offered himself as a noble sacrifice in defense of his culture, the Romantic hero rejected all social ties in his yearning for ultimate truth. The emergence of the **anti-hero** in nineteenth- and twentieth-century literature indicates a further development in the history of the hero and in man's view of himself.

See Joseph Campbell, *The Hero with a Thousand Faces* (1949); Victor Brombert, ed., *The Hero in Literature* (1969); Walter L. Reed, *Meditations on the Hero* (1974).

heroic couplet: A pair of rhymed iambic pentameter lines. The heroic couplet first appeared in English in the verse of Chaucer (*e.g.*, "She was a worthy womman al hir lyve: / Housbondes at chirche dore she hadde fyve") and has, though varying in popularity, remained in continuous use. In the Neoclassic writers, for whom the heroic couplet was the dominant form, there is usually a pause at the end of the first line and the termination of a syntactical unit at the end of the second. Such a unit is called a "closed heroic couplet." The most skillful exponent of this form was Alexander Pope, who used it almost exclusively:

> One science only will one genius fit;
> So vast is art, so narrow human wit:
> Not only bounded to peculiar arts,
> But oft in those confined to single parts.
> *An Essay on Criticism*

See William B. Piper, *The Heroic Couplet* (1969).

heroic drama: A type of play popular for a time in Restoration England (1660–88). Usually written in **heroic couplets**, it was regularly serious, though it might have a happy ending. In a typical heroic drama, a conflict between love and honor was the motivating force. The hero, a paragon of the amorous and military virtues, is forced to choose between the demands of duty and those of love. He may, for example, as commander of his country's army, be forced to conquer the empire ruled by his inamorata's father. The heroine's rival is usually a passionate princess of dubious virtue; the hero's rival may be the villain or his closest friend. The fates of empires regularly hang upon the whims of these improbable personages. Filled with bombast and spectacle, these plays—by such writers as Dryden, Howard, and Otway—pleased the Restoration palate for a while, but their excesses began to cloy; finally, ridicule, like that of Buckingham's satirical play *The Rehearsal* (1671), destroyed such taste for them as remained.

See Eugene M. Waith, *Ideas of Greatness: Heroic Drama in England* (1971).

heroic quatrain (or **stanza**): Four lines of verse in iambic pentameter (see **foot** and **pentameter**), rhyming *abab*. Also known as the elegiac stanza, it is the stanzaic structure of Gray's "Elegy Written in a Country Churchyard" (1751).

hexameter: 1. A line of six metrical feet, as in the last line of this stanza from Shelley's "To a Skylark":

> Hail to thee, blithe Spirit!
>   Bird thou never wert,
> That from Heaven, or near it,
>   Pourest thy full heart
> In pro / fuse strains / of un / premed / ita / ted art.

2. In the classical hexameter, which was the line used for the epic and some other poetry, the first four feet were either **dactylic** or **spondaic**, the fifth was dactylic, the sixth spondaic.

hexastich: A stanza of six lines.

hiatus: A pause or break caused by the occurrence of two vowel sounds unseparated by a consonant in successive words or syllables, as in *cooperate*. Its "repair" by the running together of the two vowels is called **elision.**

high comedy: A term broadly applied to satiric comedy whose appeal is primarily intellectual. There are no precise criteria for distinguishing high from **low comedy,** but where the latter achieves its effect with jokes and buffoonery, high comedy works with intellect and wit. In general, it is graceful, witty, and urbane. George Meredith wrote: "The laughter of comedy is impersonal and of unrivaled politeness, nearer a smile—often no more than a smile. It laughs through the mind, for the mind directs it. . . . The test of true comedy is that it shall awaken thoughtful laughter" *(The Idea of Comedy and the Uses of the Comic Spirit)*. High comedy avoids the excesses of sentimental comedy, but it includes the **comedy of manners.** Although this term is usually used to describe plays such as those of Congreve and Molière, it can be extended to other literary works, such as Pope's *The Rape of the Lock.*

See Maurice Charney, *Comedy High and Low: An Introduction to the Experience of Comedy* (1978).

Higher Criticism: 1. The study of the antecedents, genesis, and historical surroundings of a work, as distinguished from Lower Criticism, which concerns itself with the establishment of a correct text by such means as restitution and emendation. Through consideration of the historical and philosophical aspects of texts, especially the Greek and Roman classics and the Scriptures, the Higher Criticism attempts to interpret a writer's meaning and to delineate the intellectual and cultural climate of a historical period. As a discipline, this critical technique originated in Germany, especially at the University of Göttingen in the latter part of the eighteenth century.

2. When the term *Higher Criticism* is limited to Biblical studies, it then denotes the application of the scientific method, particularly modern historical techniques, to the study of the Scriptures. The books of the Bible, considered as human documents rather than as divine revelations, are studied to determine the time and place of their composition, their authorship, and their relations to each other and to their cultural and historical backgrounds.

historical linguistics: See **linguistics.**

historical novel: A narrative which utilizes history to present an imaginative reconstruction of events, using either fictional or historical personages or both. While considerable latitude is permitted the historical novelist, he generally attempts, sometimes aided by considerable research, to re-create, with some accuracy, the pageantry and drama of the events he deals with. Scott's novels, for example, combine the adventure generally associated with the historical novel with events and characters drawn from history. A modern example of this genre is Thornton Wilder's *The Ides of March*, which deals with Julius Caesar and his time.

See Avrom Fleishman, *The English Historical Novel* (1971).

historic present: The use of the present tense to describe past events. Note the shift from the vivid present tense to the past in the middle of this passage of the player's speech from *Hamlet:*

> Anon, he finds him
> Striking too short at Greeks; his antique sword,
> Rebellious to his arm, lies where it falls,
> Repugnant to command. Unequal match'd,
> Pyrrhus at Priam drives; in rage strikes wide;
> But with the whiff and wind of his fell sword
> The unnerved father falls. Then senseless Ilium,
> Seeming to feel this blow, with flaming top

Stoops to his base, and with a hideous crash
Takes prisoner Pyrrhus' ear: for lo! his sword
Which was declining on the milky head
Of reverend Priam, seem'd i' the air to stick:
So, as a painted tyrant, Pyrrhus stood,
And like a neutral to his will and matter,
Did nothing.

history play: See **chronicle play.**

hokku: See **haiku.**

holograph: A document, such as the original manuscript of a literary
work, wholly written by the author. The holographs of many
early works, such as Shakespeare's plays, are lost and so are
unavailable for study. Many modern holographs, however, such
as the partial holograph of Oscar Wilde's *The Importance of
Being Earnest,* now in the Arents Collection of the New York
Public Library, enable scholars to study the development of a
literary work.

Homeric epithet: See **epithet.**

Homeric simile: See **epic simile.**

homily: 1. A sermon addressed to a congregation. 2. A work which
admonishes its readers and urges them to adopt moral attitudes.

Horatian ode: See **ode.**

Horatian satire: See **satire.**

hornbook: A primer which was popular in England between the
sixteenth and eighteenth centuries. Consisting of a single sheet
of paper or vellum mounted on wood, on which were printed
the alphabet, the Lord's Prayer, and Roman numerals, the hornbook derived its name from the protective covering of horn over
the sheet. The term is used by Thomas Dekker in his *Gull's
Hornbook,* a witty pamphlet for the young men-about-town of
early-seventeenth-century London.

hovering accent: Occurs when it is difficult to determine which of
two consecutive syllables in a verse is to be stressed. This phenomenon, also called "distributed stress," may result from the
poet's clumsiness, but it may also be introduced intentionally to

achieve certain effects. In "The Lotos-Eaters," Tennyson uses hovering accent to evoke a mood of languorous ease:

> There is sweet music here that softer falls
> Than petals from blown roses on the grass
> Or night-dews on still waters between walls
> Of shadowy granite, in a gleaming pass.

hubris (hybris): Greek: "insolence," "pride." The emotion in the Greek tragic hero which leads him to ignore warnings from the gods or to transgress against their moral codes. By extension, the term is applied to tragic pride in the heroes of later dramas. In Sophocles' *Antigone*, Tiresias, the blind prophet, having told Creon of the foreboding signs of death, attempts to persuade him that he has mistakenly condemned Antigone:

> O my son!
> These are no trifles! Think: all men make mistakes,
> But a good man yields when he knows his course is wrong,
> And repairs the evil. The only crime is pride.

Rejecting Tiresias's warnings, Creon must endure not only Antigone's death but also the self-inflicted deaths of his wife and son. At the conclusion of the play, the leader of the chorus, addressing the audience, cautions against the danger of hubris:

> There is no happiness where there is no wisdom;
> No wisdom but in submission to the gods.
> Big words are always punished,
> And proud men in old age learn to be wise.
>   Translated by Dudley Fitts and Robert Fitzgerald

Hudibrastic verse: Octosyllabic couplets consisting of iambic tetrameter verses, frequently satirical—in the manner of Samuel Butler's *Hudibras* (1663–78). For an example, see **burlesque**.

humanists: See **Renaissance**.

humor: The most general of the terms denoting the laughable. Originally, humor had no connection with laughter but was a term in medieval medicine. The **humours** (we retain the British spelling for this sense) were the four bodily fluids, any excess of which distorted the personality. By extension, the term came to mean "disposition" or "mood," then "whim," "fancy," or "personal eccentricity." Finally, something "humorous" was something which made people laugh.

Just what it is that makes us laugh, however, though it has been the subject of much investigation, is still disputed. Aristotle said that the subject of comedy was some defect or ugliness which was not great enough to cause pain. His remark suggests that laughter was directed at some person when he was placed in an inferior position. This idea was developed by Thomas Hobbes, the seventeenth-century British philosopher, who said that "those grimaces called laughter" were the result of self-delight or "sudden glory." Hobbes's leading modern disciple, Anthony Ludovici, replaced "self-glory" with the phrase "superior adaptation," but did not alter Hobbes's primary ideas. The modern French philosopher Henri Bergson, who saw laughter as a weapon which the *élan vital* used to chastise social rigidities, must be placed in the Hobbesian camp. Kant, Schopenhauer, and Herbert Spencer are the most renowned names to be associated with the incongruity theory, the idea that perception of an incongruity, causing our expectations to be disappointed, is the source of our laughter. Spencer advanced the notion that the laughter at the culmination of a joke was a release of energy gathered for a larger purpose. Freud accepted part of this but suggested that the release of suppressed sexual or aggressive tendencies from the control of the psychic censor was the key element in laughter. Research and debate on the sources of humor still continue.

The word *humor* is sometimes limited to gentle and sympathetic laughter and contrasted with **wit**, which evokes intellectual and derisive laughter.

See Martin Grotjahn, *Beyond Laughter: Humor and the Subconscious* (1957); Paul Lauter, ed., *Theories of Comedy* (1964); Robert W. Corrigan, ed., *Comedy: Meaning and Form* (1965); Elder Olson, *The Theory of Comedy* (1968); W. K. Wimsatt, ed., *The Idea of Comedy* (1969); Norman N. Holland, *Laughing: A Psychology of Humor* (1982).

humours: During the Middle Ages and the Renaissance, this term referred to the four fluids of the human body: blood, phlegm, yellow bile, and black bile. According to the theory of the time, physical diseases as well as mental and moral temperaments were the result of the relationship of one humour to another. Since the humours released vapors which rose to the brain, an imbalance would result in the dominance of one humour, affecting the behavior of the person accordingly. Thus, a person's physical, mental, and moral condition was determined by the state of his humours. When they were in balance, an ideal temperament prevailed. But an excess of one of the bodily fluids resulted in the following behavior:

Excess	Type of Personality	Traits
Blood	Sanguine	kindly, joyful, amorous
Phlegm	Phlegmatic	cowardly, unresponsive, lacking intellectual vitality
Yellow bile	Choleric	obstinate, vengeful, impatient, easily aroused to anger
Black bile	Melancholic	excessively contemplative, brooding, affected, gluttonous, satiric

By the beginning of the seventeenth century, the term *humour* meant "mood" or "peculiarity." In the drama, the humours came to be used by writers who designed types based on the theory of the imbalance of the bodily fluids. The comedy of humours, consequently, depicted "humourous" characters whose behavior was determined by a single trait or humour. Ben Jonson utilized the theory of the humours in his comedies, of which *Every Man in His Humour* (1598) is typical. The first play to be written according to a theory of personality, it contains many characters with names suggesting their controlling trait: Brainworm, Downright, Wellbred, Formal. In his "Induction" to the play, Jonson presents his view of the "humourous" character:

> Some one peculiar quality
> Doth so possess a man, that it doth draw
> All his affects, his spirits, and his powers,
> In their confluctions, all to run one way.

Other Elizabethans were influenced by this physiological theory of personality. In Shakespeare's plays, the humours appear with some frequency. The melancholy Jaques in *As You Like It*, for example, describes his own sadness by using the characteristic vocabulary of the theory of humours:

> I have neither the scholar's melancholy, which is emulation; nor the musician's, which is fantastical; nor the courtier's, which is proud; nor the soldier's, which is ambitious; nor the lawyer's, which is politic; nor the lady's, which is nice; nor the lover's, which is all these: but it is a melancholy of mine own, compounded of many simples, extracted from many objects, and indeed the sundry contemplation of my travels, which, by often rumination, wraps me in a most humorous sadness.

See John J. Enck, *Jonson and the Comic Truth* (1957).

hybris: See **hubris.**

hymn: Greek: *hymnos*, a song praising heroes or the gods. In religious practice, any songs in praise of God, except psalms, may be called "hymns." By extension, a literary hymn is any song of praise, either serious, as Shelley's "Hymn to Intellectual Beauty," or humorous, as Ben Jonson's "Hymn to Comus," which begins:

> Room! room! make room for the bouncing belly,
> First father of sauce and deviser of jelly;
> Prime master of arts, and giver of wit,
> That found out that excellent engine the spit.

hymnal stanza: Duplicates the ballad stanza ($a^4b^3c^4b^3$) but retains the exact rhymes and undeviating iambic meter found in the hymnal; also called "common measure." The hymnal stanza sometimes rhymes *abab*.

hyperbole: A figure of speech in which emphasis is achieved by deliberate exaggeration. Like many such figures, it appears in ordinary speech as well as in verse. Such common expressions as "I wouldn't give him the time of day" and "They were packed in the subway like sardines" are examples of hyperbole. Andrew Marvell, in one of the most remarkable hyperboles in English verse, describes the way in which he would adore his mistress had he but time:

> My vegetable love should grow
> Vaster than empires, and more slow,

> An hundred years should go to praise
> Thine eyes, and on thy forehead gaze:
> Two hundred to adore each breast:
> But thirty thousand to the rest;
> An age at least to every part,
> And the last age should show your heart.
> For, lady, you deserve this state,
> Nor would I love at lower rate.
>   "To His Coy Mistress"

hypercatalectic: See **acatalectic**.

hypermetrical: See **acatalectic**.

hypocorism: A diminutive or "pet" name, such as Bobby for Robert. Hypocoristic language is that which makes extensive use of endearing terms or euphemistic expressions.

hysteron-proteron: A figure of speech in which the element which should logically come at the end is put at the beginning. Such a figure may result from the writer's clumsiness or from his desire to achieve a particular rhetorical effect, as in this passage from Matt. 26:26: "And as they were eating, Jesus took the bread, and blessed it, and brake it, and gave it to the disciples, and said, *Take, eat; this is my body.*"

I

iamb(us): A foot of verse consisting of an unstressed syllable followed by a stressed. The following quatrain is in regular iambic meter:

> The Griz / zly Bear / is huge / and wild;
> He has devoured the infant child.
> The infant child is not aware
> It has been eaten by the bear.
>   A. E. Housman, "Infant Innocence"

icon: The delineation of some person or object, usually through figurative language, as in this stanza by Thomas Lodge:

> Her neck like to a stately tower
>   Where Love himself imprison'd lies,

> To watch for glances every hour
>> From her divine and sacred eyes:
>>> Heigh ho, fair Rosaline!
> Her paps are centers of delight,
>> Her breasts are orbs of heavenly frame,
> Where Nature moulds the dew of light
>> To feed perfection with the same:
>>> Heigh ho, would she were mine!
>>>> "Rosaline"

ictus: The stress placed on certain syllables in a line of verse. When a poet wishes to mark the ictus, he usually uses the sign (ʹ) as Gerard Manley Hopkins does in "Spring and Fall," where his stress pattern is not always the one which the reader would normally adopt:

> Margaret, are you grieving
> Over Goldengrove unleaving?
> Leaves, like the things of man, you
> With your fresh thoughts care for, can you?
> Ah! as the heart grows older
> It will come to such sights colder
> By and by, nor spare a sigh
> Though worlds of wanwood leafmeal lie.

ideal spectator: 1. The "ordinary" observer or reader to whom the playwright addresses his work. Sometimes this observer is synonymous with the "average man" who, in theory at least, approaches a work simply and without literary preconceptions.

2. The character in the play who expresses or seems to share the attitudes and emotions of the playwright or of the majority of the audience. The *raisonneur,* who acts as the author's spokesman, and the chorus of Greek tragedy often fulfill this function.

identical rhyme: See **rhyme.**

idyl(l): A short lyrical poem depicting rural or pastoral life. Such verse frequently contains conventional, idealized descriptions of the simple life of the shepherd. Begun by Theocritus and followed by many Classical poets, such as Vergil, poetry of this kind has been called **pastoral.** However, the pastoral idyll differs from the pastoral elegy in that it avoids a mournful tone. In the

Classical writers, the idyll and the eclogue contained similar material, though in the Renaissance and in modern times, the latter is often used for social and political satire. The Renaissance lyricists, in imitation of their Classical models, carried on the tradition of the idyll by writing of the tranquillity of nature, the drowsiness of contented sheep, and the joyousness of gamboling swains. Perhaps the most famous of these idylls is Marlowe's "The Passionate Shepherd to His Love," which begins:

> Come live with me and be my love,
> And we will all the pleasures prove,
> That hills and valleys, dales and fields,
> Or woods or steepy mountain yields.
>
> There we will sit upon the rocks,
> And see the shepherds feed their flocks,
> By shallow rivers to whose falls
> Melodious birds sing madrigals.

Later writers, tiring of the artificiality of the pastoral idyll, attempted to bring other material to the form. Wordsworth, in "The Solitary Reaper," retains the country scene but portrays a working girl in the fields:

> Behold her, single in the field,
> Yon solitary Highland Lass!
> Reaping and singing by herself;
> Stop here, or gently pass!
> Alone she cuts and binds the grain,
> And sings a melancholy strain;
> O listen: for the vale profound
> Is overflowing with the sound.

The idea of work, foreign to the Classical idyll, and the note of melancholy mark a departure from the conventions of the form.

In later usage, the term *idyll* has been extended far beyond the traditional limits. Tennyson's *Idylls of the King*, for example, is not brief, and, though its Arthurian subject matter is remote from modern life, neither it nor Browning's *Dramatic Idyls* presents images of rustic bliss.

illusion: A quality of belief which is evoked by every successful narrative or drama. No matter how intensely a story or play moves a reader, it is never "real" in the way that the actions of his own life are. If, however, the work produces an illusion of reality, he can, by the process which Coleridge called a **willing suspension of disbelief,** accept the work as aesthetically valid. For the most part, the maintenance of illusion is one of the writer's primary tasks, but he may, on occasion, deliberately break the illusion to achieve certain effects. The novelist who stops his story to address the reader in his own person or the playwright who has his actors address the audience directly sacrifices illusion to gain some other end. For an example, see the speeches of the knights immediately after the murder of Becket in T. S. Eliot's *Murder in the Cathedral.*

illusion of the first time: The impression of spontaneity given by a successful actor. Although he has rehearsed his role many times and may have played it for weeks, months, or even years, to be believable the actor must appear to be saying his lines for the first time under the emotional impetus of the dramatic situation.

imagery: In general, the term *imagery* refers to the use of language to represent descriptively things, actions, or even abstract ideas. This word, however, has been so widely used by recent critics that it cannot be said to have a single agreed-upon meaning. In its most common use, *imagery* suggests visual pictures, though many critics insist that words denoting other sensory experiences are, properly speaking, images. Frequently, a writer combines both visual and non-visual images, as in Poe's "The Haunted Palace":

> Along the ramparts plumed and pallid
> A wingèd odour went away.

An example of an auditory image occurs in Coleridge's *Rime of the Ancient Mariner.* Though instruments are referred to, it is the sound, which is compared to that of all instruments, that the reader "hears":

> And now 'twas like all instruments,
> Now like a lonely flute;
> And now it is an angel's song,
> That makes the heavens be mute.

To express abstract ideas, imaginative writers turn to figures of speech, such as metaphors and similes, to give vividness and immediacy to their thought. In Shakespeare's Sonnet 60, for example, the ideas of time and the inevitability of death are visualized in the images of the opening lines:

> Like as the waves make towards the pebbled shore,
> So do our minutes hasten to their end.

Similarly, an abstract idea personified may be presented in an image, as in Keats's "To Autumn":

> Who hath not seen thee oft amid thy store?
> Sometimes whoever seeks abroad may find
> Thee sitting careless on a granary floor,
> Thy hair soft-lifted by the winnowing wind. . . .

At a certain point in our use of the term *image*, we refer not to a single picture but to an abstraction or condensation of a series of pictures. Thus, we speak of the image of autumn in Keats's poem as a symbol for the writer's feelings about the nature of time and its passage. All symbols, in fact, are apprehended through specific images, such as the white whale in *Moby Dick*. In its furthest extension, the term *image* becomes synonymous with *idea* or *vision*, as when we speak of the "Paradiso" in Dante's *Divine Comedy* as the author's image of salvation and bliss. In short, imagery serves as the vehicle for the imaginative thought, the aesthetic experience, which the writer attempts to communicate.

imagination: See fancy.

Imagism: The theory and practice of a group of poets, in England and the United States between 1908 and 1917, who maintained that the precise image was central in verse. In 1908 and 1909, T. E. Hulme established a "School of Images," as Pound later called it, a group of poets, including F. S. Flint, Edward Storer, and Pound himself, who discussed poetic techniques and such foreign verse techniques and forms as the **free verse** of the French Symbolists and Japanese **haiku.** Hulme insisted on accurate, well-defined images and the elimination of verbiage. To his own volume of poems, *Ripostes* (1912), Pound appended "The Complete Poetical Works of T. E. Hulme," consisting of five poems designed to illustrate the work of *Les Imagistes* (though

Pound, in his explanatory note, makes no mention of who they were).

For the next two years, Imagist poems (as they were then called) appeared in such periodicals as *Poetry* in Chicago and *The Egoist* (co-edited by Pound and Richard Aldington) in London. In 1914, Pound edited *Des Imagistes*, containing poems by Pound, Aldington, H.D. (Hilda Doolittle), F. S. Flint, Amy Lowell, William Carlos Williams, and James Joyce. Objecting to Pound's editorial practices in refusing to restrict the anthology to purely Imagist poems, Amy Lowell undertook to publish, between 1915 and 1917, three anthologies titled *Some Imagist Poets* (a translation of Pound's title), which contained four of the poets in Pound's anthology (Aldington, H.D., Flint, and Lowell) in addition to the American poet John Gould Fletcher and D. H. Lawrence. The first anthology, the best of the three, contained a statement of principles guiding the "Amygists," as Pound called them: to (1) use the language of common speech but to employ always the *exact* word; (2) create new rhythms as the expression of new moods; (3) allow absolute freedom in subject matter; (4) present an image: ". . . we believe that poetry should render particulars exactly and not deal in vague generalities, however magnificent and sonorous"; (5) produce hard, clear poetry, never blurred or indefinite; (6) write concisely: ". . . concentration is of the very essence of poetry."

In the preface to the 1916 volume, the contributors clarified their position: " 'Imagism' does not mean merely the presentation of pictures. 'Imagism' refers to the manner of presentation, not to the subject. It means a clear presentation of whatever the author wishes to convey." Among her fellow poets, H.D. was regarded as the "perfect Imagist," whose "Oread" was exemplary:

> Whirl up, sea—
> whirl your pointed pines,
> splash your great pines
> on our rocks,
> hurl your green over us,
> cover us with your pools of fir.

Since 1917, Imagism has been a significant influence on virtually every important poet, for in its elimination of discursiveness, in its concentration on the image as the source of new imaginative experiences, in its loosening of rigid meter, and in its advocacy of freedom in subject matter, it succeeded in breaking with many of the conventions of earlier poetry.

See Stanley K. Coffman, *Imagism: A Chapter for the History of Modern Poetry* (1951); William Pratt, ed., *The Imagist Poem* (1963); John Gage, *In the Arresting Eye: The Rhetoric of Imagism* (1981).

imitation: In our time, imitation is in poor repute, suggesting the secondhand and derivative rather than the original and creative. These pejorative associations are part of our inheritance from Romantic criticism, but to earlier periods such associations were unknown. For most of literary history, in fact, imitation has been not only a respectable practice by which apprentice writers learned their craft but also the way in which later writers sought to achieve the excellence which had been attained by the ancients.

Plato, it is true, attacked the poets for imitating the appearances of nature and ignoring the absolutes, but Aristotle defended them as imitators not of the external or incidental but of the universal, as opposed to the historians, who dealt with particulars. In Rome, such writers as Cicero, Quintilian, and Horace advocated that young writers steep themselves in the traditions of their Greek predecessors in order to develop their own skills. In no sense was the imitation of earlier poets regarded as plagiarism by the Romans or by their medieval and Renaissance successors.

Some critics advocated the strict imitation of earlier models, but the commonest idea was that since the proper rules for the imitation of nature had been discovered by the writers of antiquity, their practices should be followed. Pope expresses this view in the eighteenth century in *An Essay on Criticism*:

> Those RULES of old discovered, not devised,
> Are Nature still, but Nature methodized;
> Nature, like liberty, is but restrained
> By the same laws which first herself ordained.
>
> Hear how learned Greece her useful rules indites,
> When to repress, and when indulge our flights:
> High on Parnassus' top her sons she showed,

And pointed out those arduous paths they trod;
Held from afar, aloft, th'immortal prize,
And urged the rest by equal steps to rise.
Just precepts thus from great examples given
She drew from them what they derived from Heaven.

As the Neoclassic period developed into the Romantic, in which the poet's originality was stressed, the pejorative connotations of the word *imitation* became more prominent.

See M. H. Abrams, *The Mirror and the Lamp: Romantic Theory and the Critical Tradition* (1953).

impression: See **edition.**

Impressionism: In general, literary practice which emphasizes not objective reality as it is but rather the impressions the author or character derives from it. The term comes from the school of mid-nineteenth-century French painting which was in reaction to the academic style of the day. Such painters as Monet and Renoir concerned themselves with the effects of light, sometimes rendering several paintings of the same object or scene to demonstrate that "objective reality" was different to the viewer at different times of day. Developing a technique by which objects were seen not as solids but as fragments of color which the spectator's eye unified, the Impressionists, as they called themselves, made the act of perception the key for the understanding of the structure of reality. The basic premise involved was that "truth" lay in the mental processes, not in the precise representation of external reality.

The literary use of the term *Impressionism* is, however, far less precise. Many of the French Symbolist poets have, at one time or another, been called Impressionists. In England, Walter Pater, concerned with aesthetic matters, used the term *impression* in *The Renaissance* (1873) to indicate that the critic must first examine his own reactions in judging a work of art. The verse of such Aesthetes as Lord Alfred Douglas, Oscar Wilde, and Arthur Symons abounds in poems entitled "Impression" to suggest their indebtedness to the French Impressionists and to indicate that they were painting word pictures. Symons felt that the Impressionist in verse should record his sensitivity to experience, not the experience itself; he should "express the inexpressible." In Wilde's "Impression du Matin," perhaps influenced by Whistler's paintings, the Impressionist technique is apparent in the subjectivity of description and the suggestiveness of the colors:

> The Thames nocturne of blue and gold
> > Changed to a Harmony in grey:
> > A barge with ochre-coloured hay
> Dropt from the wharf: and chill and cold
>
> The yellow fog came creeping down
> > The bridges, till the houses' walls
> > Seemed changed to shadows and St. Paul's
> Loomed like a bubble o'er the town. . . .

In the modern novel, *Impressionism* frequently refers to the technique of centering on the mental life of the chief character rather than on the reality around him. Such writers as Proust, Joyce, and Virginia Woolf dwell on their characters' memories, associations, and inner emotional reactions. In *A Portrait of the Artist as a Young Man*, for example, Joyce presents Stephen Dedalus's unarticulated feelings, but comparatively little of his physical surroundings is described. Consequently, Stephen's environment is shadowy, almost "unreal," but his inner life is vivid. See **stream of consciousness**.

impressionistic criticism: See **criticism.**

incremental repetition: A term coined by Francis B. Gummere in *The Popular Ballad* (1907) to describe one of the important structural devices of the ballad form. Incremental repetition refers not to the use of refrains but to the repetition of succeeding stanzas with increments, changes in certain key words to indicate a development of the situation. One of the commonest accompaniments to this device is the question-and-answer formula, as in this passage from the ballad "Edward":

> "Why dois your brand sae drap wi bluid,
> > Edward, Edward,
> Why dois your brand sae drap wi bluid,
> > And why sae sad gang ye O?"
> "O I hae killed my hauke sae guid,
> > Mither, mither,

> O I hae killed my hauke sae guid,
>   And I had nae mair bot hee O."
>
> "Your haukis bluid was nevir sae reid,
>   Edward, Edward,
> Your haukis bluid was nevir sae reid,
>   My deir son I tell thee O."
> "O I hae killed my reid-roan steid,
>   Mither, mither,
> O I hae killed my reid-roan steid,
>   That erst was sae fair and frie O."

incunabula: Latin: "swaddling clothes." Books printed before the year 1501 are referred to as *incunabula*, or *cradle books*. Many of the estimated eight million incunabula survive and are deposited in libraries or sought after by collectors. Some of them are remarkable examples of workmanship, resembling medieval manuscripts in size and ornamentation. In the United States, there are considerable collections of incunabula in the Library of Congress in Washington, D.C., the Morgan Library in New York City, and the Huntington Library in San Marino, California.

induction: An archaic word for *introduction* or *prologue*. As used in the sixteenth century, the induction sometimes served as the "frame" for the work. In Shakespeare's *Taming of the Shrew*, for example, the opening scene, marked "Induction," precedes Act I. In it, Christopher Sly, a drunken tinker, is made to believe that he is a lord. For his amusement, a play is performed—*The Taming of the Shrew*. *The Mirror for Magistrates* (1563), however, has for an "Induction" a long poem which describes, in the manner of Vergil and Dante, a descent into Hell. There the shades of historic personages are encountered; following this "Induction," each shade tells of the tragic circumstances which led to his fall.

influence, anxiety of: See **anxiety of influence.**

inkhorn term: In Elizabethan times, a phrase applied contemptuously to learned words newly coined or brought into English from other languages, especially Latin but also Greek, French, Italian, and Spanish. Thomas Wilson, whose *Arte of Rhetorique*

(1553) was reprinted several times during the century, wrote, "Among all other lessons this should first be learned, that we never affect any straunge ynkhorne termes, but to speake as is commonly received." As a sample of what he opposed, he adduced a letter to the Lord Chancellor supposed to have been written by a Lincolnshire man requesting a benefice. The first sentence will illustrate Wilson's point: "Pondering, *expending*, and *revoluting* with my selfe, your *ingent affabilitie*, and *ingenious capacity* for *mundane* affaires: I cannot but *celebrate* and *extol* your *magnifical dexteritie* above all other." The italicized words are those unfamiliar in Wilson's day, but it should be noted that several of them have since become accepted in the language.

in medias res: See **epic**.

inscape and instress: Terms coined by Gerard Manley Hopkins and used in his letters and *Journals*. *Inscape* refers to the "individually-distinctive" inner structure, or underlying pattern, of a thing. The essence, or inscape, of an object may be perceived, Hopkins believes, through the senses in a moment of illumination. This experience is possible because the instress, or force, ultimately divine, which determines the inscape and holds it together, impresses the inner design upon the mind. Thus, writing about a bluebell, Hopkins states: "I know the beauty of our Lord by it."

See W. A. M. Peters, *Gerard Manley Hopkins: A Critical Study Towards the Understanding of His Poetry* (1948).

inspiration: Writers, attempting to account for the sources of their own creativity, have sometimes resorted to the term *inspiration*, which suggests suprahuman origins. (The Latin *inspirare*, meaning "to breathe into," implies the infusion of divine power; the Greeks thought of the soul as a "breath.") In older literature, the writer's direct appeal to a god or a muse was traditional, though it is sometimes difficult to determine whether the device was a literary convention or an earnest appeal for aid. In the *Iliad* and *Odyssey*, for example, Homer repeatedly invokes the muse to give him the creative energy to tell his tale.

Convinced that poets were possessed by divine forces which drove them mad, Plato said in the *Ion* that the epic and lyric poets uttered all their beautiful poems not through art but through divine inspiration. A poet, he said, is capable of poetry only when he is inspired by the gods and "out of his mind"—when there is no reason in him. Influenced by Plato, Aristotle wrote in the *Poetics* that poetry implied either a happy gift of nature or a strain of madness. In the latter, the poet is "lifted out of himself," a phrase suggesting the power of the gods. In *Of the Nature of the Gods*, Cicero, following Greek belief, wrote: "No one . . . was ever great without a certain divine afflatus."

In the Renaissance, the Classical view of the poet's madness was popularly believed. Indeed, Plato's discussion of inspiration in the *Ion* was referred to as *de furore poetica*, "concerning poetic madness." In Shakespeare's *Midsummer Night's Dream*, this idea finds expression in the speech in which Theseus, with some levity, suggests the relationship of "divine power" and creativity:

> The lunatic, the lover, and the poet,
> Are of imagination all compact:
> One sees more devils than vast hell can hold,
> That is the madman; the lover, all as frantic,
> Sees Helen's beauty in a brow of Egypt:
> The poet's eye, in a fine frenzy rolling,
> Doth glance from heaven to earth, from earth to heaven;
> And, as imagination bodies forth
> The forms of things unknown, the poet's pen
> Turns them to shapes, and gives to airy nothing
> A local habitation and a name.

Later, Milton, substituting the divine light of Christian inspiration for the pagan notion of poetic frenzy, wrote in *Reason in Church Government* that the poet needs the assistance of the "eternal Spirit . . . who sends out his seraphim with the hallowed fire of his altar."

Modern psychoanalytic theory suggests that inspiration, or creativity, has its source in the unconscious, which is the wellspring of repressed emotions craving expression. Adopting this notion, the Surrealists have theorized that art which is the true image of the creator's soul should be wrought without the interference and control of reason. In short, some Surrealists, at least, have claimed to be possessed by that modern "muse," the force of the unconscious. But whether from the psyche or from the gods, the source of a poet's gift is still called his "inspiration."

See C. M. Bowra, *Inspiration and Poetry* (1955).

instress: See **inscape and instress.**

intention: See **four meanings of a poem.**

intentional fallacy: In *An Essay on Criticism*, Alexander Pope suggested that the critic should "In every work regard the writer's end, / Since none can compass more than they intend." Many modern critics, however, regard a literary work as a public document, complete in itself, and the writer's intention, if he had one other than the invariable intention of writing the work, an external irrelevance. The error of judging a work by the author's success or failure in achieving his intention these critics call the "intentional" or "genetic fallacy." In *The Verbal Icon*, W. K. Wimsatt, Jr., and Monroe C. Beardsley wrote, "The poem is not the critic's own and not the author's (it is detached from the author at birth and goes about the world beyond his power to intend about it or control it). The poem belongs to the public. . . . What is said about the poem [such as the poet's statement of intention] is subject to the same scrutiny as any statement in linguistics or in the general science of psychology." Wimsatt and Beardsley find the source of the intentional fallacy in Romantic subjectivism, in the concern for the artist's psyche rather than his art.

Certain of the New Critics (*e.g.*, J. C. Ransom and Cleanth Brooks) recognize a "total intention," by which they refer to the total meaning or organization of a work. See **affective fallacy; New Criticism.**

interior monologue: See **stream of consciousness.**

interlude: A type of short play, often a farce, popular in fifteenth- and sixteenth-century England. The English interlude resembles such Continental works as the anonymous French farce *Pierre Pathelin (La Farce de Maître Pathelin)* and the comedies of the German mastersinger Hans Sachs. Designed to be played as the entertainment, or part of the entertainment, at the banquets of the aristocracy, the interludes might be serious and moralistic, like Medwall's *Fulgens and Lucres*, but were more

likely to be rough and farcical, like Heywood's *The Foure PP.*
This play, by the master of the singing boys of St. Paul's Cathedral, is simply a lying contest held by a palmer, a pardoner,
a pothecary, and a peddler and won by the palmer, who stuns
his companions by announcing that in all his travels he has never
seen a woman out of patience. Other interludes by Heywood
are *The Play of the Wether* and *A Mery Play betwene Johan
Johan, the Husbande, Tyb, his Wyfe, and Syr Johan, the Preest.*

The term *interlude* is sometimes applied to comic episodes in
the medieval drama, such as the scene in Mak's house in the
Towneley *Second Shepherd's Play.*

See T. W. Craik, *The Tudor Interlude* (1962).

internal rhyme: Occurs within a single verse. It may serve several
functions: giving pleasure in itself, pointing up the rhythmical
structure, or, as in this example from Gilbert and Sullivan's
Iolanthe, breaking a long line into shorter units:

> When you're lying a*wake* with a dismal head*ache*, and repose is
> taboo'd by anxiety,
> I conceive you may *use* any language you *choose* to indulge in,
> without impropriety;
> For your brain is on *fire*—the bedclothes con*spire* of usual slumber
> to plunder you:
> First your counterpane *goes*, and uncovers your *toes*, and your sheet
> slips demurely from under you.
> Then the blanketing *tickles*—you feel like mixed *pickles*—so ter-
> ribly sharp is the pricking,
> And you're hot, and you're *cross*, and you tumble and *toss* till there's
> nothing twixt you and the ticking.

See **leonine rhyme.**

intertextuality: A term used to refer to such matters as influences,
sources, allusions, and **archetypes** in order to suggest how authors echo some elements of other texts in their own works. The
French critic Julia Kristeva, who has made extensive use of the
term, states that "every text builds itself as a mosaic of quotations;
every text is absorption and transformation of another text." T. S.
Eliot expressed a related notion more playfully: "Minor poets
borrow, major poets steal." Such "theft"—involving the "inter-
textual mirror," in which texts reflect each other—occurs most
obviously in Eliot's *The Waste Land.*

See Jeanine P. Plottel and Hanna Charney, eds., *Intertextuality: New Perspectives in Criticism* (1978).

intrigue: The incidents that make up the plot of a play. Although the word *intrigue* may properly be used to refer to any plot in the drama, it is most likely to be applied to one which is elaborate and especially to one in which the schemes of one or more of the characters provide the motivating force. Such intricately plotted works as Congreve's *Love for Love* and *The Way of the World* are sometimes called "comedies of intrigue."

introduction: 1. Usually an essay, though sometimes a poem, which precedes a literary work. The function of the introduction is frequently to state the author's intention and acquaint the reader with some of the material to be found in the work. The term *prolegomena* (sing. *prolegomenon* is rare) designates a series of preliminary remarks on the subject of the book.

2. The first part of a speech. See **speech, divisions of a.**

invective: An attack, on a person or idea, using abusive language to ridicule or denounce. The opening stanza of James Stephens's "A Glass of Beer" is a particularly good example:

> The lanky hank of a she in the inn over there
> Nearly killed me for asking the loan of a glass of beer;
> May the devil grip the whey-faced slut by the hair,
> And beat bad manners out of her skin for a year.

invention: In the modern period, an inventive writer is one whose work is marked by originality, either in form or in material. At first, however, invention, the *inventio* of Classical and medieval rhetoric, referred to the finding of an orator's arguments. By extension, it came to mean the original finding and arranging of material for any literary work. In Renaissance and Neoclassical criticism, *invention* was a word used widely but without any agreed-upon denotation. Generally, it was a synonym for such words as *wit* or *imagination*, and to say of a writer that he possessed invention was merely to say that he had literary ability. The word is little used in Romantic and post-Romantic criticism.

inverted accent, foot, stress: See **substitution.**

invocation: An appeal, usually directed to Calliope, the muse of epic poetry, in which the poet asks for divine assistance at the beginning of an epic or other long work. The invocation remained a literary convention through the Renaissance and Neoclassic periods. At the beginning of *Paradise Lost* occurs the most famous invocation in English, but Milton appeals not to Calliope but to Urania, who is officially the muse of astronomy but is here converted into a holy spirit:

> Sing, Heavenly Muse, that on the secret top
> Of Oreb, or of Sinai, didst inspire
> That Shepherd, who first taught the chosen seed,
> In the beginning how the Heavens and Earth
> Rose out of Chaos; or if Sion Hill
> Delight thee more, and Siloa's brook that flowed
> Fast by the oracle of God, I thence
> Invoke thy aid to my adventurous song,
> That with no middle flight intends to soar
> Above the Aonian mount.

See **inspiration.**

Irish Literary Renaissance: In 1878, the publication of Standish O'Grady's *History of Ireland: Heroic Period* marked the beginning of the Irish Literary Renaissance. The work, an account of the heroic exploits of such mythological figures as Finn MacCool and Cuchulain, stirred a new spirit of nationalism among Irish intellectuals and writers who looked forward to an art within the Celtic tradition and to the restoration of Ireland's cultural position. Attempting to divorce themselves from the dominance of British literature, Irish writers turned to their own heritage and wrote of past heroes and of the glories of Ireland's Golden Age. Yeats, for example, deals with a mythic odyssey in the legendary "The Wanderings of Oisin" (1889); other poems are populated by Fergus, Cuchulain, and other figures of Irish folklore. Though some Irishmen, such as Douglas Hyde, championed the use of Gaelic as appropriate for verse, others felt that English was a suitable instrument for expression provided Irish material was used.

In 1891, feeling that Ireland was ready for a "new literary consciousness," Yeats, with other prominent poets, founded the Irish Literary Society in London, and in the following year the Irish National Literary Society in Dublin. Now that the Irish leader Parnell was dead and resistance to British rule was split into factions, many Irish writers turned their energies to the cultural revival and supported the two societies. The two organizations established libraries, published books on Irish subjects, sponsored lectures, and attempted to stimulate the public's interest in the movement.

In 1899, encouraged by the revival, Yeats, George Moore, and Edward Martyn founded the Irish Literary Theatre, which lasted for three seasons. It was later discontinued because of disagreement over the repertory. Martyn and Moore preferred modern realistic drama; Yeats wanted verse and legend.

Determined to have a national drama, Frank and William Fay established another Irish theater in 1901, which was later known as the Abbey or the National Theatre Society. Under the direction of Yeats and Lady Gregory, the theater presented plays depicting peasant life as well as the legendary deeds of past heroes. Such plays as A.E.'s *Deirdre* and Yeats's *Cathleen Ni Houlihan*, acted by native performers, established an indigenous Irish theater. Perhaps the greatest playwright of the group was John Millington Synge. His *Playboy of the Western World* (1907), which provoked riots in the theater for an entire week because of its unorthodox view of Irish life, is often considered the most significant play to emerge from the Irish Renaissance.

The early plays of Sean O'Casey, though produced at the Abbey Theatre in the 1920's, are outside the Irish literary revival, since they are concerned with social and political problems in urban, realistic settings rather than with folklore and rustic characters.

See Phillip L. Marcus, *Yeats and the Beginning of the Irish Renaissance* (1970); Ulick O'Connor, *All the Olympians: A Biographical Portrait of the Irish Literary Renaissance* (1984).

Irish literary revival: See **Irish Literary Renaissance.**

irony: A device by which a writer expresses a meaning contradictory to the stated or ostensible one. There are many techniques for achieving irony. The writer may, for example, make it clear that the meaning he intends is the opposite of his literal one, or he may construct a discrepancy between an expectation and its fulfillment or between the appearance of a situation and the reality that underlies it. Whatever his technique, the writer demands that the reader perceive the concealed meaning that lies beneath his surface statement.

It is this element of concealment or dissimulation from which irony developed. *Eironeia*, or "dissembling," was what characterized the *eiron*, a stock character of Greek comedy. Though small and weak, the *eiron*, by means of his wit and resourcefulness, was always able to prevail over the *alazon*, the bullying braggart.

The success of the *eiron* in defeating his opponent by seeming to retreat parallels that of Socrates, who, in the Platonic dialogues, pretends to be ignorant and willing to adopt his opponents' views but does so only to display their flaws. This technique of apparent self-denigration is called "Socratic irony."

Of the various types of irony, probably the simplest and the most commonly used is verbal irony, also called "rhetorical irony." It occurs when the attitude of the writer or speaker is the opposite to that which is literally stated. When Horatio mentions that the marriage of Hamlet's mother followed closely the funeral of his father, Hamlet replies: "Thrift, thrift, Horatio! the funeral bak'd meats / Did coldly furnish forth the marriage tables." Hamlet offers a ridiculous explanation of his mother's hasty marriage so that the irony will intensify his expression of revulsion at the lust which he and Horatio both recognize as the real explanation. Again, when Hamlet, feigning madness, says that his father has been dead for less than two hours, Ophelia corrects him: "Nay, 'tis twice two months, my lord."

> Hamlet: So long? . . . O heavens! die two months ago and not forgotten yet? Then there's hope a great man's memory may outlive his life half a year.

Hamlet's ironical delight is more expressive of his grief than any outburst of anger.

Dramatic or tragic irony depends on the structure of the play more than on the actual words of the characters. An extraordinary example of sustained dramatic irony is Sophocles' *Oedipus Rex*, in which Oedipus seeks throughout the play for the murderer of Laius, the former king of Thebes, only to find that he himself is the guilty one. The term *dramatic irony* is also used to describe the situation which arises when a character in a play speaks lines which are understood in a double sense by the audience though not by the characters onstage. When Brabantio warns Othello against being betrayed by Desdemona, the Moor replies, "My life upon her faith." For an audience which knows the story, Othello's remark presages the tragedy to come.

We speak of irony of situation when a set of circumstances turns out to be the reverse of those anticipated or considered appropriate. In Shelley's "Ozymandias," a traveler describes a shattered statue lying in a desert:

> And on the pedestal these words appear:
> "My name is Ozymandias, king of kings;
> Look on my works, ye Mighty, and despair!"
> Nothing beside remains. Round the decay
> Of that colossal wreck, boundless and bare
> The lone and level sands stretch far away.

Romantic irony occurs when a writer builds up a serious emotional tone and then deliberately breaks it and laughs at his own solemnity. Byron, the most noted practitioner of romantic irony in English, does so in this stanza from Canto IV of *Don Juan:*

> If in the course of such a life as was
>   At once adventurous and contemplative,
> Men, who partake all passions as they pass,
>   Acquire the deep and bitter power to give
> Their images again as in a glass,
>   And in such colors that they seem to live;
> You may do right forbidding them to show 'em,
>   But spoil (I think) a very pretty poem.

Several of the New Critics, especially Brooks and Warren, use the term *irony* in a more general sense to describe the way in which, in a complex poem, the total context qualifies the various elements which enter into it. A poem is "ironic" if it takes account of the complexities and incongruities of experience. Even in **New Criticism**, however, this usage is not universal.

See Bert States, *Irony and Drama: A Poetics* (1971); Wayne Booth, *A Rhetoric of Irony* (1974); D. C. Muecke, *Irony and the Ironic* (2nd ed., 1982); Frederick Garber, *Self, Text, and Romantic Irony: The Example of Byron* (1988).

irregular ode: See **ode.**

issue: See **edition.**

Italian sonnet: See **Petrarchan sonnet.**

ivory tower: A term possibly derived from the Song of Solomon ("Thy neck is as a tower of ivory"—7:4) and used by the French poet and critic Sainte-Beuve in his poem "A. M. Villemain," which appeared in *Pensées d'août (Thoughts of August),* published in 1837. Sainte-Beuve used the phrase, suggesting the detachment and aloofness of the artist or philosopher from the mundane preoccupations of mankind, in association with the Romantic writer Alfred de Vigny. The tower alone, as it appears, for example, in Milton's "Il Penseroso" and Yeats's "The Tower," suggests contemplation; the ivory tower, however, generally connotes isolation from life. As such, the term frequently has pejorative meaning, since it suggests a devitalization of the spirit.

J

jabberwocky: Derived from a poem in Lewis Carroll's *Through the Looking Glass,* the term *jabberwocky* refers, by extension, to any unintelligible speech or writing. In the story, Alice, discovering a poem called "Jabberwocky" printed backward in a looking-glass book, holds it up to a mirror so that she may read it and finds this:

> 'Twas brillig, and the slithy toves
> Did gyre and gimble in the wabe:
> All mimsy were the borogoves,
> And the mome raths outgrabe.

Explicating what appears to Alice as nonsense verse, Humpty Dumpty says that "brillig" means "four o'clock in the afternoon—the time when you begin *broiling* things for dinner." While some of his explanation of the poem is persuasive, part of it is very odd. "Wabe," a grass plot around a sundial, is referred to by that name because "it goes a long way before it, and a long way behind it . . . and a long way beyond it on each side."

In constructing the dream language of *Finnegans Wake,* in

which Carroll is mentioned several times, James Joyce is partly indebted to the technique of jabberwocky.

jargon: A term of contempt applied to speech or writing considered ugly-sounding, unintelligible, or meaningless. Often the language of a trade or profession seems full of unnecessarily complex or inflated terminology, which is called "jargon." Thus, we speak of medical jargon or the jargon of the **New Criticism.**

jeremiad: A literary work or speech which expresses a mood of grief or mourning similar to that of the Lamentations of Jeremiah in the Old Testament or which denounces transgressions and prophesies destruction in the manner of the Book of the Prophet Jeremiah. Generally, jeremiads conclude with hope for the future if reforms are instituted.

See Sacvan Bercovitch, *The American Jeremiad* (1978); George P. Landow, *Elegant Jeremiahs: The Sage from Carlyle to Mailer* (1986).

jest books: Collections of witty and satirical anecdotes, widely read in England and on the Continent during and after the sixteenth century. Influenced by the medieval *fabliau* and other genres which were designed to instruct while they amused, the jests are short, frequently ending didactically. The stories, epigrams, and **exempla**—satiric, ribald, sometimes coarse—are populated by characters who are the dupes of practical jokes or the targets of witty remarks. *A Hundred Merry Tales* (ca. 1526) is the earliest example that exists in English.

jeu d'esprit: French: "play of the mind." A witticism or flight of fancy characterized by graceful expression and urbane wit. In Oscar Wilde's *The Picture of Dorian Gray*, Lord Henry Wotton recalls an acquaintance:

> "She is still *décolletée*," he answered, taking an olive in his long fingers; "and when she is in a very smart gown she looks like an *édition de luxe* of a bad French novel. She is really wonderful, and full of surprises. Her capacity for family affection is extraordinary. When her third husband died, her hair turned quite gold from grief."

jongleur: In medieval France, a minstrel or wandering entertainer. As a singer (jongleurs also entertained by juggling or performing tricks), he might present his own material, but he often served merely as the interpreter for the verses of the *trouvère* or **troubadour** poet.

journal: See **autobiography.**

journalese: A cliché-ridden or elaborately pretentious style once used widely by journalists. In the past, newspapers were not always able to maintain a high stylistic standard in their staffs; as a result, newspaper writing was often marked by affectations and the use of hackneyed phrases. A suicide, for example, was regularly converted into "the desperate act." As standards of style rose, newspapermen removed worn-out expressions and strove for simplicity and directness. Nowadays, the word *journalese* is often extended to the sort of semaphore style adopted by space-conscious headline writers who convert the fact that a police commissioner has declined to attend a conference into "TOP COP NIXES CHAT."

Juvenalian satire: See **satire.**

K

Kabuki: In Japan, *Kabuki* began, according to tradition, early in the seventeenth century when a former priestess named O-Kuni gave dance performances, accompanied by the ringing of a little bell, and sang religious songs. Previously, the popular theater had consisted of public recitations of legends accompanied by a guitar and rhythmic tappings of a fan. With another actor, who also functioned as her manager and lover, O-Kuni organized a troupe which included men who were female impersonators. The extraordinary popularity of *Kabuki* as popular entertainment resulted in numerous companies of male and female prostitutes, who created such scandals that *Onna* (woman) *Kabuki* was suppressed in 1629. By the middle of the nineteenth century, the law against women performers was relaxed, but female impersonators continued to perform in *Kabuki* plays.

Unlike the performers of aristocratic *Nō* **drama**, *Kabuki* actors wear no masks. Moreover, in staging, instead of the bridge of the Nō play leading from the actors' dressing room, the *Kabuki* theater has a flowered runway leading from the rear of the audience to the stage so that actors make their appearances not from the side of the stage but directly from the rear of the theater.

Characteristically violent and melodramatic, the elaborately plotted *Kabuki* drama may be shorter or longer than the Western three-act play. Performances frequently continue throughout an entire day, and if spectators remain in the theater, meals are served to them.

See Adolphe Scott, *The Kabuki Theatre of Japan* (1966); Yasuji Toita, *Kabuki: The Popular Theater* (1970).

katharsis: See **tragedy.**

kenning: A standard phrase or metaphor used in Anglo-Saxon and other Germanic verse, such as "the leavings of hammers" for swords or "the whale-road" for the sea. It is analogous to the Homeric **epithet.**

King's English: Correct usage, that of the royal family being presumably beyond question.

kitchen sink drama: Plays, particularly those of the **Angry Young Men** in Great Britain during the 1950's and 1960's, depicting in the style of **naturalism** the daily concerns of working-class life. Among the plays of Arnold Wesker, which are representative of the genre, are works called *The Kitchen* and *Chicken Soup with Barley.*

Kitsch: German: "trash," "trumpery finery." A quality of coy and pretentious sentimentality that at once prettifies and vulgarizes ostensibly artistic productions. *Kitsch* is often the result of the exploitation of culture for a mass audience (*e.g.*, the image of the Mona Lisa on a package of cheese; the use—and consequent distortion—of a Chopin melody in a popular song). Such commercialization of art is, says Gillo Dorfles in *Kitsch: The World of Bad Taste* (1969), the result of an "industrialization of culture" that caters to affluent bourgeois society.

Literary *Kitsch* frequently stems from an author's sentimental evasion of human problems to achieve wide appeal. As Roy Pascal writes in *From Naturalism to Expressionism* (1974): "The trick of *Kitsch* is not to obliterate social reality, but to charm away its conflicts. . . . *Kitsch* is often the cause of the success of a best-seller, though usually it is not calculated but springs from the same sort of earnestness and conviction as good literature." Such abidingly popular successes as Kahlil Gibran's *The Prophet* and the volume of verse *This Is My Beloved* are examples of literary *Kitsch*.

Künstlerroman: A novel which traces the development of the artist (German: *Künstler*, "artist"; *roman*, "novel"), usually from childhood to his maturity. Generally, the pattern of these novels is similar: a sensitive young man, artistically inclined, finds that he must struggle against the misunderstandings and bourgeois attitudes of his family, which is unsympathetic toward his creative desires. Attempting to preserve his "artistic integrity," he leaves home, determined, like Stephen Dedalus in James Joyce's *A Portrait of the Artist as a Young Man*, to fulfill his destiny as a creative artist. In England, Samuel Butler's *The Way of All Flesh* (written in the late nineteenth century but published posthumously in 1903) provided the model for the twentieth-century *Künstlerroman*.

See Maurice Beebe, *Ivory Towers and Sacred Founts: The Artist as Hero in Fiction from Goethe to Joyce* (1964).

L

lai: See lay.

Lake Poets: Wordsworth, Coleridge, and Southey, so called because, at one time or another, each lived in the Lake District of northwestern England. Wordsworth settled in that district in 1799, Southey in 1803; both spent the rest of their lives there. Coleridge lived at Greta Hall, Keswick, from 1800 to 1804, and in 1809–10 stayed with the Wordsworths at Grasmere but then left the Lake Country and never returned. With its lakes and pleasant valleys, the area gave to the poets an example of the serene and gentle nature which they admired.

lament: A work, usually a poem, expressing intense grief or mourning. Among the most famous is the Lamentations of Jeremiah in the Old Testament. A literary work is sometimes called a **jeremiad** when it contains such lamentations. In English, there are several laments in Anglo-Saxon literature, such as "The Wanderer" and "Deor's Lament." A modern example is Shelley's "Lament":

> O world! O life! O time!
> On whose last steps I climb,
>   Trembling at that where I had stood before;
> When will return the glory of your prime?
>   No more—Oh, never more!

Related to the lament is the **elegy**, which, however, has a prescribed form and which usually ends in an expression of transcendent joy. A **complaint** lacks the intensity of grief associated with the lament and indeed may even be humorous.

lampoon: A satirical attack on a person, usually a malicious character sketch. Lampoons, which can be either prose or verse, were widespread in seventeenth- and eighteenth-century England, but their flowering was cut short by the development of libel laws. In these verses, Alexander Pope lampoons the scholars Richard Bentley and Lewis Theobald:

> Yet ne'er one sprig of laurel graced these ribalds,
> From slashing Bentley down to piddling Tibbalds:
> Each wight, who reads not, and but scans and spells,
> Each word catcher, that lives on syllables,
> Even such small critics some regard may claim,
> Preserved in Milton's or in Shakespeare's name.
> Pretty! in amber to observe the forms
> Of hairs, or straws, or dirt, or grubs, or worms!
>   "Epistle to Dr. Arbuthnot"

l'art pour l'art: See **Aestheticism.**

laureate: See **poet laureate.**

lay: In medieval French literature, tales of romance and adventure composed in octosyllabic couplets. The *lais* of Marie de France, who wrote at the court of Henry II during the latter part of the twelfth century, were said to be based upon Celtic legends as sung by the minstrels of Brittany. Some of these "Breton lays" deal with the characters of Arthurian legend.

The Provençal *lai*, usually a love poem, was designed to be sung to a popular tune of the day and as a result had greater metrical variety. In fourteenth-century England, the term *lay* could be used to describe any short narrative poem resembling the Breton lays. The most famous of these is Chaucer's "Franklin's Tale" from *The Canterbury Tales*; its prologue begins:

> Thise olde gentil Britons in hir dayes
> > Of diverse adventures maden layes,
> > Rymeyed in hir firste Briton tongue;
> > Whiche layes with hir instruments they songe.

The term has since been used to describe any simple song or verse narrative of adventure, such as Macaulay's *Lays of Ancient Rome* and Scott's *Lay of the Last Minstrel*.

leaf: A part of a book comprising two pages, printed or blank, one on each side. See **folio**.

legend: 1. A story, sometimes of a national or folk hero, which has a basis in fact but which also includes imaginative material. The story of Paul Bunyan is regarded as legend, for it is believed that there was an extraordinary lumberjack who served as the model. The story of Casey Jones is in process of becoming a legend, for stories of Casey's devotion have grown up around the historical facts of his death.

2. An account of a life. Chaucer's *Legend of Good Women* contains the stories of both historical and mythological figures, such as Cleopatra and Medea, which are united by a single theme—the praise of faithful women.

3. An account of a saint's deeds. The famous *Legenda Aurea*, or *Golden Legend*, a thirteenth-century collection of saints' lives by Jacobus de Voragine, is the most notable example.

legitimate theater: In current usage, any theatrical presentation by actors in a theater, performed solely for the audience present. The legitimacy, in the most restrictive sense, of such presentations derives ultimately from the Letters Patent issued by Charles II in 1662 to Thomas Killigrew and Sir William Davenant (for Drury Lane and Lincoln's Inn Fields, respectively, the latter patent accruing finally to Covent Garden) confining the production of plays in London to these "patent" theaters. In 1737 the

Licensing Act, passed by Parliament through the efforts of Prime Minister Walpole, confirmed the status of Drury Lane and Covent Garden as the sole legal theaters, although other theaters evaded the law by calling their dramatic presentations "concerts" or pantomimes. The Haymarket also became a Theatre Royal in 1766 when Samuel Foote was granted a patent to produce plays there during the summers. The Act continued in force with some modifications until 1843, when restrictions on the number of "legitimate" theaters were abolished. Because plays presented in the unlicensed houses involved music, the term *legitimate theater* came to be associated with non-musical plays, but as it is used today, it includes both types of theatrical presentation.

leonine rhyme: That type of **internal rhyme** in which the word before the **caesura** rhymes with the concluding word. According to tradition, it is so called from Leoninus, Canon of the Church of St. Victor in Paris, whose Latin verses are marked by this kind of rhyme. Although the term is sometimes limited to pentameters and hexameters (lines of five and six metrical units), as used by Leoninus it can be extended to describe the rhymes in the first, third, fifth, and seventh lines of this stanza from W. S. Gilbert's *The Yeomen of the Guard*:

> Oh! a private *buffoon* is a light-hearted *loon*,
>   If you listen to popular rumor;
> From the morn to the *night* he's so joyous and *bright*,
>   And he bubbles with wit and good humor!
> He's so quaint and so *terse*, both in prose and in *verse*,
>   Yet though people forgive his transgression,
> There are one or two *rules* that all family *fools*
>   Must observe, if they love their profession.

letter: 1. In the plural, a synonym for literature or scholarship: "a man of letters." See **belles-lettres.**

2. The personal letter, though not primarily a literary form, has many relations to literature; in fact, some writers, such as Sydney Smith and Lord Chesterfield, are remembered largely for their letters. A scholar or biographer reads the available letters of a writer and his associates for information about his life and the composition of his works. Letters, moreover, among the most revealing of documents, often display aspects of an

author's psychological makeup not immediately apparent in his more public writings. But it is when the letter, by the force of its style and the importance of its statements, becomes an object of interest in its own right that it may be called a literary work. Some letters of this type, such as the one in which Petrarch describes the ascent of Mount Ventoux to Dionisio da Borgo San Sepolcro, are meant for publication, but many of the greatest letters were meant to be seen only by their recipients. When the letters of a great figure are at once vivid, revealing, and significant, as, for example, those of Keats, Mozart, and Flaubert, they become cultural documents of the first importance. See **epistle; epistolary novel.**

level stress (even accent): Occurs when the stress falls evenly on two syllables in the same word or on two monosyllabic words which are closely linked, as *daybreak*, *girl friend*. For the use of this phenomenon in verse, see **hovering accent.**

libretto: Italian: "little book." A text of an opera, operetta, or other long vocal composition, containing dialogue or narrative. Traditionally opera librettos, with such exceptions as Da Ponte's libretto for *Le Nozze di Figaro* and Boito's for *Otello* and *Falstaff*, have been of limited literary interest, but in the modern operatic theater, there has been an effort to produce texts of such quality that the music and the libretto may form an organic whole. The collaboration between Richard Strauss and Hugo von Hofmannsthal, for example, has resulted in such unified works.

light ending: A term used as a synonym for both **weak** and **feminine endings.**

light rhyme: Occurs when one of a pair of rhyming syllables is unstressed. This type of rhyme is frequent in ballad literature; in the following stanza, the second syllable of the word *also*, which rhymes with *go*, is unstressed:

> "If I was to leave my husband dear,
>   And my two babes also,
> O what have you to take me to,
>   If with you I should go?"
>   "The Demon Lover"

light stress: In verse, a stress on a word not normally accented in speech. In the following stanza, the first *and* in the last line is so stressed:

> My notion was that you had been
>   (Before she had this fit)
> An obstacle that came between
>   Him, and ourselves, and it.
>   Lewis Carroll

light verse: Poetry written to entertain. Light verse may be brief, as in the lyric, epigram, or limerick, or long, as in Lewis Carroll's "The Hunting of the Snark." The use of French fixed forms, such as the **triolet**, the **ballade**, and the **rondeau**, for light verse was common in the nineteenth century in England, but they have since lost favor.

Although light verse is designed principally to entertain, there may also be a serious side to the poet's play of the mind, for the term *light verse* includes parodies, occasional verse, and satire which may, under the appearance of humor, have a serious intention. In such writers as Swift and T. S. Eliot, light verse has intellectual bite.

limerick: A type of light verse. The limerick, one of the few fixed forms to become genuinely popular in English, consists of five anapestic lines rhyming *aabba*. The first, second, and fifth lines are trimeter and the third and fourth dimeter, though these two may be printed as a single line with internal rhyme. Although there have been several explanations for this term, the most common is that the refrain "Will you come up to Limerick?" was sung at parties at which these verses were extemporized; its origin, however, is not definitely known. In an early limerick, the nursery rhyme "Hickory Dickory Dock," the last line and the first lines are the same; in the limericks of Edward Lear, whose *Book of Nonsense* (1846) popularized the form, the last line is usually a variation on the first:

> There was a young lady of Lucca,
> Whose lovers completely forsook her;
> She ran up a tree, and said "Fiddle-de-dee!"
> Which embarrassed the people of Lucca.

The modern limerick reserves the last line for some climactic or surprising twist:

> There was a young lady from Spain,
> Who was exceedingly sick on a train,
> Not once but again,
> And again, and again,
> And again, and again, and again.

Always vigorous and often bawdy, the limerick may be the last surviving folk poetry in the machine age.

linguistics: The scientific study of language. Descriptive linguistics is concerned with classifying the characteristics of a language, and comparative or historical linguistics with its development. Among the major divisions of the field of linguistics are etymology, the history of word forms; semantics, the study of the meanings of words; phonetics, the study of speech sounds; morphology, the study of the forms or inflections of words; syntax, the study of the groupings of words into sentences or units of meaning.

linked rhyme: See **rhyme.**

link sonnet: See **Spenserian sonnet.**

literary ballad: See **ballad.**

literary epic: See **epic.**

literature: Such genres as the novel, the short story, the epic poem, the lyric, and the play clearly fall within the boundaries of literature; as embodiments of some of man's feelings and thoughts, they are experiences shaped into aesthetic forms. The distinction between literature and other forms of communication is often tenuous. A historical work such as Douglas S. Freeman's monumental biography of George Washington presents the facts and conditions of the subject's life, whereas a work such as Lytton Strachey's *Elizabeth and Essex*, while purporting to be history, is in reality a highly imaginative account written in a style which creates the atmosphere of a historical romance. Sometimes, as a work ceases to have scholarly authority in a field, it acquires distinctly literary value. Thus, because of its impressive Neoclassic style and subjective point of view, Gibbon's *Decline and Fall of the Roman Empire* has perhaps come to be read more as literature than as history.

Whatever its form, however, literature has at least four major functions. Many readers go to literary works for entertainment, which may be elevated and intellectual or which may be of a comparatively less exalted nature. For example, the plays of Shaw are witty, cerebral entertainment, whereas an ordinary farce offers a different quality of amusement. The desire to escape from an oppressive or dull environment may impel the reader to seek the fantasy of science fiction, the remoteness of a Western, or the excitement of a detective story. On the other hand, literature may be valued for its capacity to inculcate moral and spiritual values. The didacticism of a literary work may thus be direct, as in Bunyan's *Pilgrim's Progress*, or indirect, as in Shakespeare's *Macbeth*. One of the greatest values which we can attribute to literature is its capacity to acquaint us with the forces which motivate men and the place of man in society and in the universe. In the final analysis, it provides a reader with intense and unique experiences ordered to give him the aesthetic pleasure that accompanies his apprehension of the work.

litotes: A form of **meiosis** in which an idea is expressed by the denial of its opposite. A scholar who wishes to recommend his work while retaining his modesty may remark that during his research he has learned "not a little" to signify that he has in fact learned a great deal. Milton makes use of this device when, at the beginning of *Paradise Lost*, he asks the muse to aid his adventurous song "That with no middle flight intends to soar," indicating that in reality his poem will soar to the highest levels of imagination.

littérateur: One who devotes himself to the study or writing of literature; a man of letters. The term sometimes suggests the amateur or dilettante rather than the professional.

liturgical drama: Plays performed as part of the liturgy of the medieval Church. When these were merely tropes, or brief interpolations in the service, they were in Latin and chanted by members of the clergy. As these plays became popular, they were expanded, and the vernacular was introduced. After they were moved out of the church buildings, their production was placed in the hands of the laity, and although the plays still dealt with religious themes, they ceased to be liturgical in character. See **miracle** and **mystery plays.**

living newspaper: A type of didactic play produced by the Federal Theater project in the 1930's. These plays dramatized social and economic problems of the time in productions that were elaborate and often experimental in theatrical technique. Episodically constructed and peopled by symbolic characters, the plays made their points not only through acting but also through such devices as dance, mime, film, and the use of extracts from newspapers and political speeches. *One Third of a Nation* and *Triple-A Plowed Under* were among the best-known living newspapers.

l.m.: The abbreviation for **long measure.**

local color: The use of regional detail to add interest to a narrative. Local color, as the term implies, is generally not of crucial importance to the plot or for an understanding of motivation; it is, rather, in descriptions of locale, dress, and customs, concerned with the quaint and the picturesque. In this sense, local color is mere decoration. When, however, description of a region becomes an intrinsic and necessary part of the work, the emphasis on the relationship of region to the action is characteristic of what is called **regionalism.**

logaoedic: In Greek and Latin prosody, a meter composed of anapests and iambs or of dactyls and trochees. The term is sometimes extended to refer to any mixed meter. The following lines of Edward Lear's "The Jumblies" are logaoedic:

> Far and few, far and few,
>   Are the lands where the Jumblies live;
> Their heads are green, and their hands are blue,
>   And they went to sea in a Sieve.

logical stress: Also called "rhetorical stress" and "rhetorical accent." See **accent.**

long measure (l.m.): A **hymnal stanza** in which all four lines are tetrameters.

loose and periodic sentences: A loose sentence is one in which a main clause comes first, followed by further dependent grammatical units: "Hotchkiss rose slowly from his seat with a shy smile, determined to show the class that he could, for once, answer the instructor's question." A periodic sentence is one in which the main clause is withheld until the end: "Delighted by Hotchkiss's resolve, the class and the instructor burst into applause." In formal writing, the periodic sentence is used for structural variety and rhetorical emphasis. The loose sentence, however, a more relaxed construction, is more frequently used in informal writing and in conversation.

Lost Generation: In the presence of Ernest Hemingway, Gertrude Stein made the remark: "You are all a lost generation," echoing and amplifying the comment of her garage proprietor, who had rebuked a young mechanic as a member of a *"génération perdue"* (see Hemingway's memoir, *A Moveable Feast*, 1964). Though Hemingway here claimed to have disputed the general applicability of the remark, he used it as an **epigraph** for his first novel, *The Sun Also Rises* (1926). The emasculation of the hero, Jake Barnes, as a result of a war wound, became symbolic of the loss of energy and idealism, of the sense of betrayal, felt by those who experienced the vast destructiveness of World War I. The phrase *Lost Generation* came to distinguish especially the group of then younger American writers, including Hemingway and Fitzgerald, disillusioned and alienated by the war and the circumstances of the postwar world.

See Malcolm Cowley, *A Second Flowering: Works and Days of the Lost Generation* (1974).

low comedy: In a play, the coarse elements designed to arouse the audience's laughter. Frequently, low comedy consists of off-color jokes or physical action, such as slapstick. In medieval English drama, low comedy commonly made its appearance as added stage business. The character of Vice, for example, often the object of practical jokes, himself engaged in clownish behavior to relieve the solemnity of the play. The Elizabethan playwrights inherited the traditions of medieval drama. In Shakespeare's *The Merry Wives of Windsor*, for instance, Falstaff, getting into a basket to hide from a suspicious husband, has "foul linen" piled atop him. The basket is then carried offstage to be dumped into the Thames. See **high comedy.**

Lucilian satire: See **satire.**

lyric: In Greek poetry, a lyric was a poem sung to the accompaniment of a lyre. We still refer to the words of a song as "the lyrics," but in general the term *lyric* denotes a poem of limited length expressing the thoughts and especially the feelings of a single speaker. Such a poem usually avoids a narrative structure, such as one encounters in an **epic,** in which a linear development is the driving force; instead, the speaker in a lyric may contemplate an image, such as the urn in Keats's meditative "Ode on a Grecian Urn," and reveal complex emotional and intellectual attitudes aroused by it; many lyrics, to be sure, involve a speaker (not necessarily the poet) addressing his or her loved one, as in Christina Rossetti's "Song," which begins:

> When I am dead, my dearest,
>   Sing no sad songs for me;
> Plant thou no roses at my head,
>   Nor shady cypress tree.

The lyric form in English has rarely been prescribed, except when literary forms from other languages have been adapted. For example, such French forms as the **villanelle** and the **triolet** (used by some nineteenth-century English poets) have fixed rhyme schemes and stanzaic structures. For discussions of other lyric forms, see *aube;* **dramatic monologue; elegy; epithalamion; haiku; ode; sonnet.**

See William E. Rogers, *The Three Genres and the Interpretation of Lyric* (1983); W. R. Johnson, *The Idea of Lyric* (1985).

M

macaronic verse: Light verse written in two or more languages. Macaronics are usually made by mixing a modern language with Latin or Greek. English is most commonly mixed with Latin, often to the extent of giving English words Latinate endings, as in the following:

> Qui nunc dancere vult modo,
> Wants to dance in the fashion, oh!
> Discere debet ought to know,
> Kickere floor cum heel and toe.
> One, two, three,
> Hop with me,
> Whirligig, twirligig, rapidee.
> G. A. à Beckett, "A Polka Lyric"

madrigal: A song designed for several voices, the madrigal may be pastoral, satiric, or concerned with love. Italian in origin and influenced by the Tudor court song cultivated during the reigns of Henry VII and Henry VIII, the English madrigal flourished for less than a quarter of a century, reaching its height around 1600. Some of the great English madrigal composers were Thomas Morley, John Wilbye, and Thomas Weelkes. The madrigal is used in a number of Gilbert and Sullivan operas, such as *The Mikado* and *Ruddigore*.

magnum opus: Latin: "a great work." A major literary work, a writer's masterpiece. Today the term often carries ironic connotations.

malapropism: A blunder in speech or writing caused by the substitution of a word for another similar in sound but different in meaning. Shakespeare's Dogberry of *Much Ado about Nothing* is greatly addicted to malapropisms ("O villain! thou wilt be condemned into everlasting redemption for this"), but it is from Mrs. Malaprop of Sheridan's *The Rivals* (1775) that the term derives. In this speech, she explains to Sir Anthony Absolute her ideas on the education of women:

> Observe me, Sir Anthony, I would by no means wish a daughter of mine to be a progeny of learning. . . . But, Sir Anthony, I would send her at nine years old to a boarding school, in order to let her learn a little ingenuity and artifice. Then, sir, she should have a supercilious knowledge in accounts;—and as she grew up, I would have her instructed in geometry, that she might know something of the contagious countries;—but above all, Sir Anthony, she should be mistress of orthodoxy, that she might not mis-spell and mis-pronounce words so shamefully as girls usually do; and likewise that she might reprehend the true meaning of what she is saying.

mannerism: A term in art history that refers primarily to the styles of painting prominent in Rome and Florence between the High Renaissance and the Baroque—from about 1525 through the remainder of the sixteenth century—but that has also been applied to the work of Tintoretto and El Greco. Since the term embraces a considerable range of styles, from the hieratic formalism of Bronzino, for example, to the intensely spiritualized elongations of El Greco's style, its precise meaning, even its usefulness, has been disputed. Beyond a certain self-awareness in the quest for an individual *bella maniera*, or beautiful style, deriving perhaps from an uneasy sense of being successors to the great masters of the preceding age, the artists of the mannerist epoch can hardly be said to embody a clearly definable sensibility.

The attempt to extend this term to literary practice has made it even more vexing. The general sense of affected or "mannered" in style is too vague to mean much. Characterizing the work of John Donne or the Jacobean dramatists as "mannerist" probably stretches the term beyond useful limits. But the convoluted prose of Lyly's *Euphues*, the elegant artifices of those who adopted the pastoral mode, or the self-conscious echoings of the lyricists who perpetuated the Petrarchan tradition might more appropriately be designated by this term. Thus, for instance, Shakespeare's "My mistress' eyes are nothing like the sun," with its parodic undercutting of the Petrarchan catalogue of feminine beauty, could well be seen as a mannerist poem.

See James V. Mirollo, *Mannerism and Renaissance Poetry* (1984).

Märchen: See **fairy tale**; **folk tale**.

marginalia: Notes written in the margin by a reader as a commentary on the text. Sometimes marginalia may be of significance, if the reader is a distinguished author or scholar.

Marinism: A style named after the Italian poet Giambattista Marino (1569–1625), whose writing is notable for its excessive verbal ornament and its daring **conceits** designed to astonish the reader by its witty presentation of the marvelous and the unusual. Marino's themes and images exploit minutely and hyperbolically such diverse traditional sources as Classical mythology, the conventions of the love lyric, New Testament scenes and characters, all of the arts, and physical nature. These elements abound in his extraordinary mythological romance, *L'Adone* (1623), a poem of over forty thousand lines to which he devoted more than thirty years.

Though Marino has been generally considered a **baroque** poet, his style, according to James V. Mirollo, in *The Poet of the Marvelous: Giambattista Marino* (1963), may be easily distinguished from other, more complex seventeenth-century styles: "It has a specific thematic range, an arsenal of well-known devices, a plainly discernible repertoire of metaphor, and a resultant imagery whose characteristics are capable of description." The Marinesque style had a considerable European-wide influence in the seventeenth century; in England, some of the Metaphysical poets, notably Marvell, Herbert, and Crashaw, were touched by it.

Marivaudage: Writing characterized by psychological subtlety and stylistic elegance approaching affectation, in the manner of the eighteenth-century French playwright and novelist Pierre de Marivaux. In the refined and subtle world of Marivaux's plays, his characters, elegant and graceful, take part in an elaborate courtship during which Marivaux analyzes with great subtlety the conflicting impulses and hesitations of his lovers. Among the best of his plays, which have influenced such dramatists as Musset and Giraudoux, are *Arlequin poli par l'amour* (1720), *La Surprise de l'amour* (1722), and *Le Jeu de l'amour et du hasard* (1734).

See Kenneth N. McKee, *The Theater of Marivaux* (1958); E. J. H. Greene, *Marivaux* (1965).

Marxist criticism: See **criticism; New Historicism.**

masculine ending: Occurs when the final syllable in a line of verse is stressed.

masculine rhyme: See **rhyme.**

masked comedy: See *commedia dell'arte.*

masque: During the first half of the seventeenth century in England, a courtly form of entertainment characterized by song, dance, lavish costumes, and extraordinary spectacle. Introduced into England from Italy, the masque flourished in the latter part of Elizabeth's reign, continued at the court of James I, and reached its highest development in the time of Charles I, who was its most devoted admirer. Astonishing sums were spent on the productions of masques for the entertainment of nobility and distinguished foreign visitors.

Elaborate stage machinery designed by Inigo Jones (1573–1652), the great theatrical architect, produced such effects as splitting mountains, growing trees, clouds in motion, through which a *deus ex machina* could descend. The masques themselves usually had only slight dramatic interest. Dealing largely with mythological and pastoral figures, the action served as a vehicle for spectacle and for the appearance of masked dancers who joined the actors. Except for the dancers of the anti-masque, a light or grotesque interlude often featuring bawdy humor (an innovation introduced by Ben Jonson, the greatest of the masque writers), all the performers were from the nobility and even, on occasion, from royalty. As an allegorical entertainment, the masque was frequently presented in order to praise the monarch. In *Inigo Jones: The Theatre of the Stuart Court* (1973), Stephen Orgel states: "Every masque is a ritual in which the society affirms its destiny. The glories of the transformation scene express the power of princes, bringing order to human and elemental nature, partaking thereby of the divine."

In the popular theater of the time, many Elizabethan playwrights incorporated elements from the courtly masque into their plays. In Act IV of Shakespeare's *The Tempest*, for example, Prospero provides a masque for Ferdinand and Miranda in which mythological and pastoral figures appear accompanied by song and dance celebrating marriage. A later masque, Milton's *Comus* (1634), depends more on poetry than on spectacle for its effects. The final masque was presented at court in 1640, two years before the Puritans closed the theaters.

See Sarah P. Sutherland, *Masques in Jacobean Tragedy* (1983).

maxim: See **aphorism.**

meaning: Two types of meaning, emotive and cognitive (or referential), are usually distinguished. The emotive meaning of the word *thug*, for example, is its tendency to induce fear or anger; its cognitive meaning is a thought process, namely its suggestion of a man who perpetrates crimes of violence.

Cognitive meaning may be further considered under the headings *extension* and *intension*. In formal logic, the extension of a word is the aggregate of all the individual objects or concepts to which it may be applied. Thus, the extension of the word *chair* is the chair on which the reader is sitting and all other particular chairs. The intension of a word is the group of attributes comprised by it. Thus, the intension of *chair* is the sum of its attributes, such as "being inanimate, having four legs, a back, and a seat," etc. The extension and intension of a word are sometimes called the denotation and connotation, respectively, but the former set of terms so used are technical terms in logic and are not to be confused with the usual senses of denotation and connotation as given under those entries in this book.

meaning, four levels of: See **four levels of meaning.**

medieval drama: In the ninth century, when words were added to the elaborate Hallelujahs chanted during church services, medieval drama began. Soon these words took the form of playlets performed in Latin by members of the clergy. As these plays grew in popularity and in length, the vernacular was introduced to make them more readily comprehensible. When the performances were moved out of the church and placed in the hands of the laity, a secular drama came into existence. Under the sponsorship of the guilds, cycles of plays arose in which Scriptural history from the fall of Lucifer to the Last Judgment was dramatized. There were also plays dealing with the lives of the saints and the miracles they performed. Morality plays, moral allegories, were given as community performances, as, on a different level, were folk plays about such figures as Robin Hood and St. George. From these plays and from the rediscovery of the Classical theater, the modern drama developed. See **liturgical drama; miracle play; morality play; mystery play.**

See Karl Young, *The Drama of the Medieval Church* (1933); Arnold Williams, *The Drama of Medieval England* (1961); Clifford Davidson, C. J. Gianakaris, and John H. Stroupe, eds., *Drama in the Middle Ages* (1982).

medieval romance: See **romance**.

meiosis: Understatement, the device of presenting something as less significant than it really is, as in a description of *Hamlet* as "a play of some interest."

melic poetry: Greek: *melos*, "song." Verse written for musical accompaniment on the lyre or flute. Greek melic poetry, which flourished particularly between the seventh and fifth centuries B.C., was composed by such poets as Sappho, Anacreon, and Pindar.

melodrama: Greek: *melos*, "song," + *drama*. During the Italian Renaissance, there was no distinction between opera and melodrama. The fusion of music and drama was, in intention, a revival of the Classical theater. In the eighteenth century, Handel referred to some of his works with both terms, *opera* and *melodrama*. During this time, French playwrights wrote plays which emphasized music, sensationalism, spectacle, and the happy ending. In time, melodrama depicted the conflict of despicable evil and extraordinary good, as personified in the hero (or heroine), who was always a model of magnanimous virtue, and the villain, who existed in the play for the express purpose of making other people's lives wretched. The broad, forceful style of acting employed emphasized this conflict with perhaps excessive clarity. In nineteenth-century England, melodrama flourished in a variety of plays which ranged in subject from the supernatural to domestic life. While disappearing skeletons, conjuring wizards, or horrid demons furnished the playgoer with suitable thrills, his moral indignation was pleasurably aroused by improbable spectacles of the evils of drunkenness, the cruelties of a foreclosed mortgage, or the machinations of a fiendish murderer. Such well-known plays as *Sweeney Todd, the Demon Barber of Fleet Street* (1842) and *Ten Nights in a Bar-room* (1858) are characteristic of the popular melodramas of the day.

At the end of the nineteenth century, Shaw incorporated melodramatic elements in *The Devil's Disciple*, which, in fact, he subtitled "A Melodrama." In the last act of the play, as Dick Dudgeon is about to be hanged by General Burgoyne, Pastor Anderson appears at the crucial moment and saves Dudgeon. Witty and urbane, Shaw uses the action for his own comic purposes.

In the modern theater, melodrama has given way to more sophisticated treatments of character and situation, though melodramatic elements are still found, on occasion, to be theatrically effective.

See Michael R. Booth, *English Melodrama* (1965).

memoir: An account of a person's life and experiences written by himself. Where the autobiography is concerned primarily with the writer, his personal experiences, and the delineation of his character, the memoir centers more on the world in which he has lived. Sometimes the writer of a memoir is a person of no great significance but one who has come into contact with noteworthy people and events; he himself may play a relatively minor part in his book. Since World War II, innumerable memoirs have appeared in which high-ranking officers describe their roles in that conflict.

Menippean satire: See **satire.**

mesostich: See **acrostic.**

metafiction: Novels or stories manifesting a playful awareness of their own status as fictions, such as, for example, some of the work of John Barth, Vladimir Nabokov, and Kurt Vonnegut among recent American writers.

See Robert Scholes, *Fabulation and Metafiction* (1979).

metaphor: A figure of speech in which two unlike objects are compared by identification or by the substitution of one for the other. Metaphors, like many other figures of speech, are common in everyday conversation. We say, for instance, "Hotchkiss is a dead duck," fully aware that he is nothing of the kind, but for rhetorical force we compare him and the dead duck by identifying them. Wordsworth, in one of his sonnets, says of England, ". . . she is a fen of stagnant waters." The comparison, however, is not always so direct. In the following stanza, Blake also speaks about the state of England:

> And did the Countenance Divine
> Shine forth upon our clouded hills?
> And was Jerusalem builded here
> Among these dark Satanic Mills?

Here only half a metaphor is directly expressed. Jerusalem is substituted for a state of godly peace supposed to have once existed. Another metaphor is concealed in the word *clouded*. Not only are the hills covered by cloudlike gusts of smoke from the Satanic Mills, the instruments of industrialism blighting the English countryside, but the squalor and evil which they cause shut off from the land the light of the Countenance Divine as clouds shut it off from the sun.

When a metaphor serves to illustrate an idea which can be expressed in other ways, it is merely decorative, as when we speak of the "ship of State." When, however, a metaphor expresses a complex of thought and feeling that is so subtle or precise that it cannot be expressed in any other way, it is called a "functional," "organic," or "structural metaphor." In the octet of Sonnet 146, Shakespeare portrays the relationship between the soul and the body in a series of such metaphors. First, the body is the earth, of which the soul is the center; then it is a rebel army surrounding a rightful king; and finally a house upon which the owner wastes his substance:

> Poor soul, the centre of my sinful earth,
> Thrall to these rebel pow'rs that thee array,
> Why dost thou pine within and suffer dearth,
> Painting thy outward walls so costly gay?
> Why so large cost, having so short a lease,
> Dost thou upon thy fading mansion spend?
> Shall worms, inheritors of this excess,
> Eat up thy charge? Is this thy body's end?

When a metaphor, such as "the arm of a chair," has become so common that it is no longer recognized as such, it is called a "dead metaphor." If the two elements in a metaphor are startlingly disparate, we call it a mixed metaphor. This is usually a fault, as in the following instance: "The long arm of the law has two strikes against it." Under extraordinary circumstances, however, it may be highly effective, as in Milton's famous description of the corrupt clergy in "Lycidas": "Blind mouths! that scarce themselves know how to hold a sheep-hook."

In *The Philosophy of Rhetoric* (1936), I. A. Richards distinguished the two parts of a metaphor by the terms *tenor* and *vehicle*. The tenor is an idea with which another idea (the vehicle) is identified. It is in the vehicle that the force of such a comparison lies. When Macbeth says that life is but a walking shadow, *life* is the tenor of a metaphor in which *walking shadow* is the vehicle. See **simile**.

See Isabel C. Hungerland, *Poetic Discourse* (1958); Weller Embler, *Metaphor and Meaning* (1966); Sheldon Sacks, ed., *On Metaphor* (1979).

Metaphysical conceit: See **conceit**.

Metaphysical poetry: Although the term *metaphysical* may be applied to any poetry dealing with spiritual or philosophical matters, it is usually limited to the work of a group of seventeenth-century poets, of whom John Donne is the most notable. Other so-called Metaphysical poets (in no sense a "school") were Marvell, Cleveland, Cowley, Crashaw, Herbert, and Vaughan.

The work of these poets is characterized by the use of ordinary speech ("For God's sake hold your tongue, and let me love"), combined with puns, paradoxes, elaborate and startling **conceits,** and abstruse terminology, often drawn from the science of the day. The poems sometimes take the form of arguments, for the Metaphysicals characteristically link intense emotion with intellectual ingenuity. In their amorous verse, some of the Metaphysical poets, particularly Donne and Marvell, utilize ideas drawn from Renaissance **Neo-Platonism** to depict the relationship of soul to body and the union of lovers' souls; at the same time, these poets sought to express a more realistic view of the psychological tensions of sexual love. The range, however, of Metaphysical poetry is extensive: from Marvell's "To His Coy Mistress," a poem about the brevity of life and the desirability of sexual consummation, to Herbert's "Easter Wings," a poem of yearning for the resurrection of the poet's spirit.

In the seventeenth century, John Dryden, in his "Discourse on the Origin and Progress of Satire" (1693), said that Donne "affects the metaphysics," meaning that he was too much given to intellectual analysis (Donne's "A Valediction: Forbidding Mourning," for example, compares a pair of lovers to the legs of a drawing compass). Extending the term *metaphysical* to designate the group of poets who wrote in this style, Dr. Johnson, in his "Life of Cowley" (1779), complained: "The most heterogeneous ideas are yoked by violence together; nature and art are ransacked for illustrations, comparisons, and allusions; their learning instructs and their subtlety surprises; but the reader commonly thinks his improvements dearly bought, and, though he sometimes admires, is seldom pleased." In the late nineteenth century, a new interest in Donne arose (particularly on the part of such critics as Edmund Gosse and Arthur Symons) after long neglect (the Romantics, understandably, saw little to admire in Metaphysical poetry); the Grierson edition of Donne's poetry in 1912 stimulated further interest, as did T. S. Eliot's famous essay "The Metaphysical Poets" (1921).

See Helen C. White, *The Metaphysical Poets* (1936); Alfred Alvarez, *The School of Donne* (1962); Earl Miner, *The Metaphysical Mode from Donne to Cowley* (1969); Judah Stampfer, *John Donne and the Metaphysical Gesture* (1970).

meter: In English verse, which is based on accent rather than **quantity**, the term *meter* refers to the pattern of stressed and unstressed syllables. The number of syllables in a line may be fixed while the number of stresses varies, or the stresses may be fixed with variation in the number of unstressed syllables. In the most frequent form of meter in English, the number of both stresses and syllables is fixed. In actuality, a meter, while retaining its basic pattern, frequently varies in a poem so that the sequence of stressed and unstressed syllables does not resemble the ticking of a metronome. In much modern verse, the regularity of meter is abandoned; instead, **cadences** approximating the flow of speech are employed.

In English verse, the following meters are the most commonly used:

Iambic:	contról	Anapestic:	contradíct
Trochaic:	stúpid	Dactylic:	clúmsiness
	Spondaic:	snów stórm	

These meters are illustrated in a poem by Coleridge:

Tróchee tríps frŏm lóng tŏ shórt.
From long to long in solemn sort
Slów Spóndee stálks; stróng fóot! yĕt ill áble
Éverĕ tŏ cóme ŭp wĭth Dáctyl trĭsylláble.

Iambics march from short to long.
With a leap and a bound the swift Anapests throng.

When a line is divided into metrical units, or feet, the following terms are used to indicate the number of feet to a line:

Monometer (one)	Pentameter (five)
Dimeter (two)	Hexameter (six)
Trimeter (three)	Heptameter (seven)
Tetrameter (four)	Octometer (eight)

For further discussion and illustrations, see individual entries,
as well as **foot; free verse; quantitative verse; sprung rhythm.**
See Paul Fussell, Jr., *Poetic Meter and Poetic Form* (rev. ed.,
1979).

metonymy: Greek: "a change of name." A figure of speech in which
the name of some object or idea is substituted for another to
which it has some relation, as a cause for its effect, a writer for
his work ("Hotchkiss has never read Browning"), etc. Milton
makes use of the device in the line "When I consider how my
light is spent," where he substitutes *light* for the related word
vision. See **synecdoche.**

metre: See **meter.**

metrical accent: See **accent.**

metrical foot: See **meter; foot.**

Middle Comedy: The Athenian comedy which flourished during the
last three quarters of the fourth century B.C. It avoided the
political satire of the Aristophanic **Old Comedy** and concentrated
on love intrigues and burlesques of mythological stories. No
examples of this form are extant.

miles gloriosus: Latin: "braggart soldier." A stock character who
derives his name from Plautus's Roman comedy *Miles Gloriosus,*
which was based on the anonymous Greek play *Alazon (The
Braggart).* The braggart soldier is a swaggerer and coward who
is regularly duped and made the butt of the other characters'
laughter. In English drama, he first appears as the title character
of Nicholas Udall's *Ralph Roister Doister* (ca. 1550) and later as
Bobadil in Ben Jonson's *Every Man in His Humour* (1598).

Shakespeare's Falstaff is at once a *miles gloriosus* and an example of how the limitations of a type may be transcended and an individualized character created.

Miltonic sonnet: A form, introduced by Milton, which retains the octave rhyme scheme of the Petrarchan sonnet, *abbaabba*, but which does not have any pause or turn in the meaning at the beginning of the sestet or an invariable rhyme scheme within it:

> Avenge, O Lord, thy slaughtered saints, whose bones
> Lie scattered on the Alpine mountains cold;
> Ev'n them who kept thy truth so pure of old,
> When all our fathers worshipped stocks and stones,
> Forget not: in thy book record their groans,
> Who were thy sheep, and in their ancient fold
> Slain by the bloody Piedmontese, that rolled
> Mother with infant down the rocks. Their moans
> The vales redoubled to the hills, and they
> To Heav'n. Their martyred blood and ashes sow
> O'er all th'Italian fields, where still doth sway
> The triple Tyrant; that from these may grow
> A hundredfold, who, having learnt thy way,
> Early may fly the Babylonian woe.
>   "On the Late Massacre in Piedmont"

See **Petrarchan, Shakespearean,** and **Spenserian sonnets** under individual listings.

mime: A type of short **comedy** which originated in Sicily and southern Italy about the fifth century B.C. It dealt with events from ordinary life or burlesqued the gods and heroes. The actors, who wore grotesque masks and the padded *phalli* of ancient comedy, indulged in slapstick and coarse dialogue. Although performances of the mimes were frowned on by the Church, they survived into the Dark Ages. Many of the traditions of the mime appear in the *commedia dell'arte* and have been characteristic of **low comedy** ever since.

mimesis: Greek: "imitation." In the *Poetics*, Aristotle states that tragedy is an imitation of an action. Such a statement, however, does not imply that art and life are synonymous. In his discussion, Aristotle makes it clear that the imitation is achieved not through simple mimicry but by the careful construction of the play; selection and arrangement, consequently, are the primary tasks of the playwright.

In acting, the concept of mimesis has also been used to characterize the relationship of art to life. Hamlet's speech to the players advises them concerning the "purpose of playing, whose end, both at first and now, was and is, to hold, as 'twere the mirror up to nature; to show virtue her own feature, scorn her own image, and the very age and body of the time his form and pressure."

See Erich Auerbach, *Mimesis: The Representation of Reality in Western Literature* (1946; English trans., 1953).

minnesinger: In the Middle Ages, especially in the twelfth and thirteenth centuries, the lyric poet in Germany who wrote of **courtly love.** In subject matter, the songs of the German poets were similar to those of the **troubadours.** The most notable minnesinger of his time was Walther von der Vogelweide.

minstrel: A wandering poet or musician of the later Middle Ages. See **jongleur.**

miracle play: In English, the term *miracle play* has generally referred to the medieval religious drama which dramatized saints' lives and divine miracles as well as stories from the Scriptures. Sometimes, however, the term **mystery play,** as it was used in France, is employed to designate those plays containing Biblical stories, as distinct from those about lives of the saints. English medieval writers referred to all of these plays as "Corpus Christi plays," "Whitsuntide plays," "pageants," and occasionally "miracle plays."

The miracle plays, to use the inclusive term, were first presented in connection with saints' days and religious processions, the most notable being the festival of Corpus Christi held in the spring. At first, these plays were given in Latin as part of the church services. Later, as secular and ribald material entered into the performances, they were moved out into the streets. In France, the plays became the property of the town, which continued to present them in more elaborate form on various religious occasions. In England, the trade guilds of each town assumed the responsibility for presenting one play each so that a series of performances could present the story of the creation of the world through the fall of man, or some other "cycle." These so-called "craft cycles" became enormously popular. Combining serious themes with farce, buffoonery, and coarse humor, medieval religious drama flourished for over four hundred years. A major theatrical entertainment of the time, it reached its highest development in the fifteenth and sixteenth centuries. In England, the cycles grew to considerable size, the Wakefield cycle, for example, having thirty-two plays; the other important groups were the York, Chester, and Coventry cycles.

The cycle was presented with each play mounted on a wagon with a high curtained scaffold, the lower part of the wagon serving as a dressing room. After the play was performed at a stated time in a prearranged place, the wagon moved on to follow another play in another street; thus, a series of wagons moved through the city so that the entire population might see the complete cycle.

The settings of the plays were elaborate. Heaven, where God the Father made his appearance, was designed to be awe-inspiring, whereas "Hell-mouth," shaped to resemble a dragon's mouth, contained costumed devils whose principal function was to entertain. Trapdoors, pulleys, and other mechanical devices served to create ingenious theatrical effects. Costuming was frequently ornate, and lighting effects highly imaginative. A nativity scene might thus be brilliantly illuminated in an evening performance to create the proper effect. As many as three hundred actors, members of the guilds, might be used for one cycle of plays.

See Arnold Williams, *The Drama of Medieval England* (1961).

miscellanies, poetical: Collections of poems by various authors. In 1557, Richard Tottel published a collection called *Songs and Sonnets*, usually known as *Tottel's Miscellany*, which contained the work of Wyatt and Surrey, among others. The publishing of poetical miscellanies, begun by Tottel, was extremely popular in the Elizabethan period and has continued ever since. The Elizabethan miscellanies often have elaborate titles, such as *The Paradise of Dainty Devices* or *A Gorgeous Gallery of Gallant Inventions*. The authors of the various poems are sometimes unnamed, sometimes identified by initials. When a poem is ascribed to a particular author, the ascription is not always accurate. Nevertheless, it was through the miscellanies that some of the best Elizabethan verse was published.

mise en scène: French: "placing on stage." The scenery, costumes, properties, etc., of a theatrical production.

mixed metaphor: See **metaphor.**

mock epic: See **burlesque.**

mock heroic: The style of the **mock epic** and other works which satirize their subjects by inflating them with false dignity. Many works besides strict mock epics make use of the mock heroic style. Fielding's *Tom Thumb*, for example, is a mock heroic play. Byron has mock heroic passages in *Don Juan*, and Wilde uses the style in *The Importance of Being Earnest*, where the characters discuss ridiculous events, such as being born "or at any rate, bred" in a handbag, with portentous solemnity.

Modernism: The term *Modernism* refers to the literature and general culture of, roughly, the first part of the twentieth century, but two qualifications should be borne in mind when it is used. First of all, since historical epochs do not proceed conveniently in successive blocks but overlap and blur into each other, the limits of the Modernist period, like those of other eras, are extremely difficult to determine. At its narrowest the period covers about thirty-five years from approximately 1910 to the end of World War II; at its broadest it embraces the period from the mid-1870's to the present. In any case, it is widely assumed that Modernism as a distinctive cultural phenomenon has ended or is ending and that a "Post-Modern" or "Contemporary" period is succeeding it. At this point, however, the second qualification must be considered. Many critics do not grant the existence of Modernism at all. They argue, rather, that no major cultural shift has occurred since the beginning of the nineteenth century and that the literature of the past is, therefore, a natural extension of **Romanticism.**

Those who oppose this view, however, maintain that Modernism exists and that to a considerable extent it is defined by its rejection of the literary diction and techniques of the previous period and by its opposition to the social and economic values of bourgeois society. As Irving Howe has said in his essay "The Idea of the Modern" (1967), to the Modernist sensibility "the usual morality seems counterfeit; taste, a genteel indulgence; tradition, a wearisome fetter." Certainly a fascination with fresh, experimental techniques marks the work of many Modernist writers; in such figures as Joyce and Eliot, for example, the use of **myth** as a formal organizing device rather than as a means for enforcing belief marks a departure from previous practice. But other qualities that have been claimed as special to Modernism —the **Existential** vision of an absurdly meaningless universe, the sense of man as trapped at an end-point in history, the intense subjectivism of a post-Freudian ethos, the conflict between the need for individualism and the longing for communality—may arguably be traced back at least to the Romantics. It remains still to be seen whether these and other concerns as they have been reflected in recent literature serve to distinguish a distinct Modernist movement or a natural extension and intensification of the past.

See Joseph Wood Krutch, *The Modern Temper* (1929); Richard Ellmann and Charles Feidelson, Jr., eds., *The Modern Tradition* (1965); Irving Howe, ed., *Literary Modernism* (1967); Malcolm Bradley and James McFarlane, eds., *Modernism, 1890–1930* (1976); Robert Kiely, ed., *Modernism Reconsidered* (1983).

monodrama: A theatrical presentation featuring only one character. The term *monodrama* was also used by Tennyson to characterize his poem "Maud."

monody: In Greek poetry, a poem, especially of mourning, presented by one singer. Matthew Arnold called his elegy on Arthur Hugh Clough "Thyrsis, a Monody," and "Lycidas" is so referred to in Milton's introduction, added to the poem in 1645.

monograph: A lengthy essay, usually on a scientific subject or of a scholarly nature.

monologue: An extended speech by one person. A remarkable use of the monologue occurs in Strindberg's one-act play *The Stronger*, which consists entirely of the speech of one character. For subtypes of the monologue, see **dramatic monologue; soliloquy; stream of consciousness.**

monometer: A line of verse consisting of one foot; also called "monopody." See **amphimac** for an example.

monopody: See **monometer.**

monostich: 1. A line of verse. 2. A poem of one line.

mood: See **atmosphere.**

mora: A unit of measure in **quantitative verse.** A mora is the time taken up by a short syllable. A long syllable is equal to two morae. In quantitative verse, a metrical foot can be substituted for another without changing the speed of the verse only if the two feet have equal numbers of morae. Iambs and trochees, for example, each having three morae, can be readily substituted for each other. A spondee may replace a dactyl or an anapest, since each of these feet has four morae.

moral, the: The "teaching" or "lesson" in a literary work which is either implied or specifically stated. Many critics avoid discussing "the moral" since the value of a literary work, a complex aesthetic experience, does not depend on the "lesson" which may be extracted from it. See **didactic.**

morality play: A form of late medieval and Renaissance drama containing allegorical figures who are frequently involved in the struggle over a man's soul. The term *morality play* was not used at the time; usually the terms *moral, pithy,* or *goodly Interlude* referred to this type of theatrical presentation. The moralities developed from a combination of the medieval religious drama and such allegories as the *Roman de la Rose.*

The first known moralities, called the *Paternoster* plays, performed in York and elsewhere in the latter part of the fourteenth century, dealt with the conflict between the Seven Moral Virtues and the Seven Deadly Sins, which try to lead Man astray. The most notable morality play is *Everyman* (early sixteenth century), which, instead of the vices and virtues, contains the characters of God, Death, Good Fellowship, Good Deeds, etc., who are concerned with the future of Everyman's soul.

Unlike the **mystery** and **miracle plays**, the morality play, instead of being mounted on wagons, was staged on simple platforms. Moreover, it lacked the elaborateness of production and ingenuity of staging that characterized the miracle plays.

In the sixteenth century, the morality play served as a vehicle for religious and political propaganda. By the middle of the century, the popularity of the morality play had waned. However, the survival of elements of the form may be seen in Marlowe's *Dr. Faustus* (ca. 1588), which contains a procession of the Seven Deadly Sins as well as the recurring appearances of the Good and Evil Angels, who struggle over Faustus's soul.

See David M. Bevington, *From Mankind to Marlowe: Growth of Structure in the Popular Drama of Tudor England* (1962).

morphology: In linguistics, the study of the form and structure of words, including their derivation and inflection. See **Russian Formalism.**

motif: A theme, character, or verbal pattern which recurs in literature or folklore. The reveler who blasphemes upon a grave and is later dragged to damnation by the ghost of the man who was buried there is a widespread folklore motif which later becomes part of the Don Juan legend. A motif may be a theme which runs through a number of different works. The motif of the imperishability of art, for example, appears in Shakespeare, Keats, Yeats, and many other writers. A recurring element within a single work is also called a motif. Among the many motifs that appear and reappear in Joyce's *Ulysses*, for example, are Plumtree's Potted Meat, the man in the brown mackintosh, and the one-legged sailor.

motivation: The combination of circumstance and temperament which determines the actions of a character. If this combination is inadequate to account for these actions—if, for example, a timid and diffident soul suddenly and without apparent reason attacks the town bully—the character is insufficiently or implausibly motivated. In a work which purports to be psychologically realistic, the behavior of characters must be in keeping with their natures as acted upon by the circumstances of the plot.

movement: A literary trend or development. The term may be used very broadly to describe a general literary tendency, as the Romantic Movement, or precisely to denote the work of a few writers, as the Imagist Movement.

Movement, the: A group of British poets and novelists in the 1950's who believed that the social consciousness of the 1930's and the "loose, fashionable writing" of the 1940's were inappropriate in "modern Britain." The group was named in an anonymous article that appeared on October 1, 1954, in the London *Spectator* (written by J. D. Scott, the literary editor), which saw the Movement as opposed to the old order and anti-Modernist in its aesthetic:

> So it's goodbye to all those rather sad little discussions about "how the writer ought to live," and it's goodbye to the Little Magazine and "experimental writing." The Movement, as well as being anti-phoney, is anti-wet; sceptical, robust, ironic, prepared to be as comfortable as possible.

The article named two poets, Donald Davie and Thom Gunn, and the novelists Kingsley Amis, Iris Murdoch, and John Wain. In two anthologies of poetry—D. J. Enright, ed., *Poets of the 1950s* (1955), and Robert Conquest, ed., *New Lines* (1956)— additional poets, such as Philip Larkin and Elizabeth Jennings, as well as Enright and Conquest, were associated with the Movement.

By the late 1950's, when a concurrent phenomenon called the **Angry Young Men** (some of whom were associated with the Movement) began to emerge into brief prominence, the Movement was no longer identifiable, though some of its attitudes lingered on in the works of the Angry Young Men and others as they moved into middle age.

See Blake Morrison, *The Movement: English Poetry and Fiction of the 1950s* (1980).

mummery: In the Middle Ages, celebration of such festive occasions as Christmas and New Year's frequently took the form of mumming, the wearing of masks or grotesque disguises and participation in dances and buffoonery. By extension, the term *mummery* refers to a theatrical presentation in which the actors or dancers are masked or in disguise. In addition, the term may also refer to acting in general.

muses: In Greek mythology, there were nine muses, the daughters of Zeus and Mnemosyne, or Memory. Though at first one was not distinguished from another, they later had their individual provinces to preside over. Clio was the muse of history, Calliope of epic poetry, Erato of love poetry, Euterpe of lyric poetry,

Melpomene of tragedy, Polyhymnia of songs to the gods, Terpsichore of the dance, Thalia of comedy, Urania of astronomy.

Traditionally, poets appealed to a particular muse for aid in assisting them to compose their works. In later literature, writers have used the notion of the muse but without invoking a specific Classical figure. In Shakespeare's *Henry V*, for example, the chorus, in the opening lines of the play, exclaims:

> O! for a Muse of fire, that would ascend
> The brightest heaven of invention . . .

musical comedy: A theatrical form, developed in the United States during the twentieth century, mingling song and spoken dialogue. Deriving from vaudeville and operetta, the earliest musical comedies had conventional romantic plots interspersed with pleasant, if irrelevant, songs. Much of their effect derived from spectacular staging and low comedy. Although there were a few previous experiments, the modern musical comedy dates from the early 1940's. It is marked by a libretto of higher literary and dramatic quality, by the close integration of text and music, and often by the use of ballet in place of more popular dance forms. At its best, the musical comedy, or more precisely the musical play, has approached the status of true opera.

mystery play: As used in France, the term *mystère* referred to the medieval religious plays which dramatized stories taken from the Scriptures. Christ's passion, the fall of man, the story of Noah were some of the subjects used by playwrights. In England, the terms *miracle play* and *mystery play* were used interchangeably. See **miracle play** for a discussion of the form and its theatrical history.

See Rosemary Woolf, *The English Mystery Plays* (1972).

myth: An anonymous tale, ostensibly historical, the origins of which are unknown. A mythology, which is a collection of such tales, may contain the story of the origin of the world, the creation of mankind, the feats of gods or heroes, or the tragedies which befell ancient families. For the primitive mentality, many myths provided explanations of natural phenomena; with an increase in scientific knowledge, however, this function is often supplanted and myths survive simply as stories.

Writers have always been fascinated by the remoteness, mystery, and heroism of myth. Blake, for example, created his own mythology. For him, spiritual realities existed in the apocalyptic visions that he embodied in his verse. Like Blake, other writers, seeking aesthetically satisfying systems, have invented their own myths or have turned to those already established. Yeats, for example, employed Irish myths early in his poetic career, but later developed his own metaphysical system or mythology in *A Vision* (1926), which became the source for many images in his verse.

For other writers, established myth satisfied a metaphysical hunger and provided material for their art. D. H. Lawrence in *The Plumed Serpent* used both elements of Christianity and the myth of the Mexican god Quetzalcoatl to formulate his own vision. In Joyce's novels, elements of Classical, Christian, and Hebraic myth are fused to create a universal myth which, he felt, embodied the experiences of all men. On this point, C. G. Jung has declared that the materials of myths lie in the collective unconscious of the race; the widespread similarity between myths, he has stated, results from a common inheritance.

In *Moby Dick*, Melville created a significant story which, by extension, we may call a myth. The novel, to be fully understood, must be apprehended as a symbol of a primal conflict; the story emerges as myth, for it evokes, as Jung might say, responses from the unconscious which we regard as universal.

See Philip Wheelwright, *The Burning Fountain* (1954; rev. ed., 1968); Northrop Frye, *Anatomy of Criticism* (1957); John B. Vickery, ed., *Myth and Literature: Contemporary Theory and Practice* (1966); K. K. Ruthven, *Myth* (1976); John B. Vickery, *Myths and Texts: Strategies of Incorporation and Displacement* (1983).

N

naïve and sentimental writing: A distinction developed by Schiller in his essay *Über naive und sentimentalische Dichtung* (1795). He felt that such writers as the ancient Greeks, Shakespeare, and Goethe were in harmony with nature and had produced a certain kind of literature which he called "naïve" as opposed to the "sentimental" writing of himself and most of his contemporaries, who, out of touch with nature, saw it as an ideal to which they sought to return. Schiller's concept of the instinctive, realistic, "naïve" poet continued to be influential in the nineteenth century, as did the idea of the "naïve" poet's complementary relationship with the idealistic "sentimental" writer. In Schiller's usage, neither of these terms has the pejorative connotations that they carry in English.

narrative verse: Non-dramatic verse that tells a story. *The Canterbury Tales* is a notable example in English. Verse narratives, of such disparate types and quality as Marlowe's *Hero and Leander* and Kipling's *Ballad of East and West*, were common in English literature up to the twentieth century. Today, such factors as the popularity of the novel and the disinclination of poets to use verse for subjects that can be adequately treated in prose have made narrative verse a rarity.

narratology: See **fiction.**

naturalism: 1. A literary movement related to and sometimes described as an extreme form of **realism** but which may be more appropriately considered as a parallel to philosophic naturalism. This doctrine holds that all existent phenomena are in nature and thus within the sphere of scientific knowledge; it maintains that no supernatural realities exist. In the first half of the nineteenth century, Comte applied the ideas of science to the study of society, and soon after, Taine applied them to literature, maintaining that psychological states as well as human actions were the results of material causes.

Carefully documenting their work, the Goncourt brothers produced *Germinie Lacerteux* (1865), a novel which examines in clinical detail the sordid life of a servant girl. This novel was admired by Emile Zola, the great theorist of naturalism. In his essay "Le Roman expérimental" ("The Experimental Novel"), dated 1880, Zola said that the novelist should be, like the scientist performing an experiment, independent of moral conventions or preconceived theories. In his novel, which is based on careful documentation, he should examine dispassionately certain phenomena and draw indisputable conclusions. Among the things that his experiments will confirm is the law that the actions of men are determined by heredity and environment. Zola carried out his theories in such novels as *Thérèse Raquin* (1868) and *L'Assommoir* (1877). To distinguish his work from the realism of Balzac and Flaubert, Zola called his novels "naturalistic." Although he wished by this term to characterize his theories and methods, it has often served only to denote his usual subject matter and that of his followers. Theoretically, there is no reason why the experimental or naturalistic method could not be applied to an investigation of the highest levels of society, but in fact naturalistic novels have usually concerned themselves with slums, poverty, disease, and dirt.

It was this preoccupation with ugliness that brought forth such comments as this by Tennyson in "Locksley Hall Sixty Years After" (1886):

> Feed the budding rose of boyhood with the drainage of your sewer;
> Send the drain into the fountain, lest the stream should issue pure.
> Set the maiden fancies wallowing in the troughs of Zolaism,—
> Forward, forward, ay, and backward, downward too into the abysm!

In these lines, Tennyson may have been referring to Zola's English disciple George Moore, who, along with such writers as Gissing, Maupassant, and the early Huysmans, carried on the naturalistic tradition. Among the American naturalistic novelists were Frank Norris, Theodore Dreiser, and James T. Farrell. In the drama, naturalistic plays were written by such playwrights as Gorky and Hauptmann.

2. The term *naturalism* is sometimes used to describe the work of a "nature" poet, such as Wordsworth, who deals sympathetically with the beauties of the countryside.

For further discussion and bibliography, see **realism.**

near rhyme: See **rhyme.**

Negative Capability: An expression used by Keats in his letter of December 21, 1817, to his brothers, George and Thomas. While talking with a friend, Keats wrote, "several things dovetailed in my mind, & at once it struck me, what quality went to form a Man of Achievement especially in Literature & which Shakespeare possessed so enormously—I mean *Negative Capability*, that is when a man is capable of being in uncertainties, Mysteries, doubts, without any irritable reaching after fact & reason—Coleridge, for instance, would let go by a fine isolated verisimilitude caught from the Penetralium of mystery, from being incapable of remaining content with half knowledge. This pursued through Volumes would perhaps take us no further than this, that with a great poet the sense of Beauty overcomes every other consideration, or rather obliterates all consideration." *Negative Capability*, a highly ambiguous term, has been much discussed and commented on. A great poet, Keats seems to be suggesting, does not assert his own ego but remains objective, open to all experience regardless of its nature, identifying with the object of his contemplation. The "poetical Character," Keats wrote in another letter (October 27, 1818), "has as much delight in conceiving an Iago as an Imogen [the virtuous heroine of *Cymbeline*]. . . . A Poet is the most unpoetical of any thing in existence; because he has no identity—."

See Walter Jackson Bate, *John Keats* (1963); Aileen Ward, *John Keats: The Making of a Poet* (1963).

Neo-Aristotelians: See **Chicago critics.**

Neoclassicism: In its widest sense, *Neoclassicism* refers to the revival of the style and attitudes of a former literature. More specifically, however, in English literature the term designates the theories and practices of most writers from the latter part of the seventeenth century through the eighteenth. As with all terms covering broad cultural phenomena, *Neoclassicism* cannot without gross distortion be limited in its reference to a single quality that adequately characterizes the art of an age. Nevertheless, though Neoclassic writers such as Dryden, Pope, Swift, Addison, and Johnson differ in practice as well as temperament, some general principles underlying Neoclassicism can be distinguished in their work and that of their contemporaries.

The Neoclassicists generally regarded man as a limited creature whose understanding was not adequate to an exploration of the infinite. In his *Essay Concerning Human Understanding* (1690), the philosopher John Locke expressed the hope that his "inquiry into the nature of understanding" would lead "the busy mind of man to be more cautious in meddling with things exceeding its comprehension. . . . Our business here is not to know all things, but those which concern our conduct." This acceptance of human limitations and this emphasis on "conduct," on the behavior proper to men in society, was congenial to an age in which many of the greatest literary productions were satires of human pretensions. Commonly, the enlightened minds of the age believed that the orderly laws of the physical universe (as Newton and others were revealing them) demonstrated that a beneficent creator existed and that human efforts were to be directed toward understanding man's position in that physical universe and in the social world. "The proper study of mankind," Pope wrote, "is man."

For the writer, the proper goal was, as the Roman poet Horace had said, to instruct and to delight. Through the embellishments of language the poet was to please his reader and thus lead him to see his characters as individuals who were yet general representatives of mankind. Recognizing in the actions of these characters what was virtuous as well as what was foolish, the reader learned, presumably, to admire the former and avoid the latter. To achieve his goal the poet had to do more than merely trust his inspiration; he had to study his craft, particularly as it had been practiced by the great writers of the Classical ages of Greece and Rome. For in their works and in the "rules" that the best critics of the past had devised he would find reflected those general laws governing man and the world that are the true source of knowledge—in short, "Nature." Such, Pope said, had been the experience of Vergil himself when planning the *Aeneid:*

> Perhaps he seemed above the critic's law,
> And but from Nature's fountains scorned to draw;
> But when to examine every part he came,
> Nature and Homer were, he found, the same.
> *An Essay on Criticism*

Essential to the Neoclassic writer was the principle of decorum, the idea that a rich and elevated language was appropriate to the great genres of epic and tragedy and that a simpler language was to be used for comedy and other genres that dealt with ordinary life. In general, then, the Neoclassicists admired—even if they did not always achieve—restraint, clarity, order, balance, proportion.

See **Enlightenment; imitation;** and, for a discussion of the most famous of the "rules," **unities.**

See also Basil Willey, *The Seventeenth-Century Background* (1934) and *The Eighteenth-Century Background* (1940); James Sutherland, *A Preface to Eighteenth-Century Poetry* (1948); John Butt, *The Augustan Age* (1950).

neologism: A new word or a new meaning assigned to an old word. Frequently, the neologism is a word taken from a foreign language, such as the word *sputnik*, which became part of the English vocabulary. In fact, it is a neologism even in Russia, for the term, which means "fellow traveler," now refers to a satellite.

New Comedy: Greek comedy of the third and fourth centuries B.C. With the decline of Greek power and the rise of Macedonia, the biting personal and political satire of Aristophanic **Old Comedy** disappeared. Its place was taken by the New Comedy, which utilized stereotyped plots and characters. Courtesans, young lovers, parsimonious elders, and scheming servants were played off against each other in various combinations. After many complications, the love intrigues, which formed the bases of these plays, regularly ended in a happy marriage. Menander, Philemon, and Diphilus were the most famous writers of this genre. The Romans Plautus and Terence were much influenced by the New Comedy, which has, in fact, supplied the materials of much of the comedy created since its day.

See R. L. Hunter, *The New Comedy of Greece and Rome* (1985).

New Criticism: A movement, largely American, in literary criticism which dates from the 1920's, though it did not receive a name until John Crowe Ransom, one of its practitioners and theoreticians, published a book called *The New Criticism* in 1941. Although this term is sometimes limited to the work of a dozen or so leading modern critics, it is often extended to describe the tendency in recent criticism to emphasize the close reading and the explication of a text rather than biographical or historical study. Despite their common orientation toward textual analysis, the major New Critics have at no time agreed upon a single methodology or set of principles. They do, however, accept the idea that a poem should be considered as such and not as something else, an ornamented form of sociology, philosophy, or ethics, for example. In general, the New Critics, who have excelled in the interpretation of complex, highly intellectual poems, have been essentially formalist in orientation, centering their attention on the linguistic organization of poetry, though some have made use of such disciplines as psychology and anthropology.

The early semantic studies of I. A. Richards, which emphasized the nature of symbolic language, have been influential in the New Criticism, as has the work of Richards's disciple, William Empson. (See **ambiguity**.) Other major figures are Allen Tate, R. P. Blackmur, Yvor Winters, and Kenneth Burke. Through their book *Understanding Poetry* (1938), Cleanth Brooks and Robert Penn Warren spread the doctrines of the New Criticism into American colleges. T. S. Eliot, though not strictly a New Critic, has been important in showing the value of subtle textual study.

See Frank Lentricchia, *After the New Criticism* (1980).

New Historicism: A term applied to what is essentially political criticism (rather than historical scholarship) as practiced by certain American and British leftist, usually Marxist, critics since the 1960's. It designates the work of those who have attempted to transcend the limitations of propagandistic, party-line discourse and to incorporate into their writing some of the intellectual sophistication of postwar literary studies. Such critics argue that literature is always "political" in that it expresses the social values and economic circumstances that make possible or inhibit particular kinds of writing. From the New Historicist point of view, in fact, literary history is likely to be seen as the record of the producing, distributing, and consuming of a certain cultural product.

In contemplating this output, such a critic is less likely to advocate a special methodology—and may well accept any that offers useful insights—than to insist that a commentator must be self-conscious in regard to the forces determining his choice of methodology and shaping not only literature but its professional study as well. The New Historicist critic sees as inherently meaningful the fragments of social experience presented in the literary work and takes it as a function of criticism to strip away the "censorship" imposed by differing historical and cultural perspectives and by the very nature of language to reveal the way the social system inevitably imposes itself upon that experience. Thus such a critic, although he may recognize the "differential" view of language put forth by the theorists of **deconstruction** and accept the fact that history cannot be a coherent rendering of events absolutely known, nonetheless maintains that the literary historian can suggest the flux of historical forces that come together at certain times to shape what is then acceptable as literary discourse.

See Fredric Jameson, *The Political Unconscious: Narrative as a Socially Symbolic Act* (1971); Hayden White, *Metahistory: The Historical Imagination in Nineteenth-Century Europe* (1973); Terry Eagleton, *Marxism and Literary Criticism* (1976); Raymond Williams, *Marxism and Literature* (1977).

New Humanism: A movement in letters and philosophy, primarily American, in the 1920's. Reacting against the excesses of Romantic individualism and realistic naturalism, such men as Irving Babbitt, Paul Elmer More, and Norman Foerster advocated a concern with "human" values. They insisted that man stood apart from nature and possessed free will. They advocated restraint, self-control, and the imitation of a model of typical human excellence. In both life and art, the nearest approach to their ideas of excellence had come, they felt, in the great epochs of the past and especially in the Classical age of Greece. In general, the New Humanists were scholarly and, in both art and politics, conservative.

See J. David Hoeveler, *The New Humanism* (1977).

new journalism: A type of reportage and commentary developed in the United States in the middle 1960's. Writers such as Tom Wolfe in *The Kandy-Kolored Tangerine-Flake Streamline Baby* (1965) and Norman Mailer in his "informal history" of the 1968 political conventions, *Miami and the Siege of Chicago* (1968), used the narrative techniques of fiction, including a lively and personal style, in dramatizing and reporting fact and showed a more open sympathy with popular culture and with radical social and political attitudes than was acceptable in traditional journalism. When a work of the new journalism treats a single subject at considerable length, as does Truman Capote's *In Cold Blood*, it may be called a "non-fiction novel."

See Michael L. Johnson, *The New Journalism* (1971); Tom Wolfe, *The New Journalism: With an Anthology Edited by Tom Wolfe and E. W. Johnson* (1973).

New Novel: From the French: *nouveau roman*. A kind of anti-realistic novel developed by a group of French writers in the mid-1950's. Rejecting such elements of the traditional novel as its social concerns, coherent plot construction, and psychological analysis of character by an omniscient author, the creators of the New Novel function in the experimental tradition of Joyce, Kafka, and Faulkner. Unlike the Existential thinkers Sartre and Camus, who remained conventional stylists in their fiction, these novelists wanted the form of the work itself to express the postwar Existential vision of a world without order or ultimate destiny peopled by characters without innate psychological identity. Alain Robbe-Grillet and others, therefore, broke up the familiar narrative sequence of the conventional novel and substituted for clear moral and thematic elements rigorously detailed descriptions of material objects. In this inanimate world of things, characters—who often appear without such basic identifying elements as descriptions, occupations, or addresses—are presented as fragments of consciousness; the single person at a single moment is, the New Novelists hold, all that can be known. The name of Samuel Beckett, whose novels have been linked with the work of this group, can be added to those of such practitioners of the *nouveau roman* as Marguerite Duras, Michel Butor, and Nathalie Sarraute. The connection between this experimental form and the cinema are evident in the screenplays by Robbe-Grillet (*Last Year at Marienbad*) and Marguerite Duras (*Hiroshima mon amour*).

The New Novel is sometimes known as the *anti-novel*, a term Sartre coined to describe a work by Nathalie Sarraute. This term, however, has upon occasion been extended to refer to any contemporary fiction which works against the familiar conventions of the novel.

See Laurent LeSage, *The French New Novel* (1962); Vivian Mercier, *A Reader's Guide to the New Novel* (1971).

Nine Worthies, the: In his preface to Malory's *Morte d'Arthur*, Caxton lists the Nine Worthies, or heroes, of late medieval and Renaissance literature: Hector, Alexander, and Julius Caesar are the pagan heroes; the Jewish are Joshua, David, and Judas Maccabaeus; and Arthur, Charlemagne, and Godfrey of Boulogne are cited as the Christian worthies. The clowns in Shakespeare's *Love's Labour's Lost*, who set out to play the Nine Worthies, include among them Hercules and Pompey the Great.

Noble Savage: See **primitivism**.

Nō (Noh) **drama:** A type of drama which developed in fourteenth-century Japan from a ritual dance associated with ancient Shinto worship. The plays, unlike those of the *Kabuki* drama, were designed for aristocratic audiences, who welcomed the restraint and subtlety of the form.

Characteristically, the *Nō* play is mysterious and gloomy. The first character, or *shite*, generally meets a ghost (the *waki*, or second character) while on a journey to a shrine; recalling his past life in a stylized dance, the shade dramatizes his earthly struggles. The ghost frequently turns out to be the one to whose shrine the traveler is bound. The general theme, which is stated at the beginning of the play, is the illusion of life.

The actors of the *Nō* drama make their entrances by way of a bridge, actually a corridor with railings, leading from the actors' dressing rooms. Three symbolic trees, signifying heaven, earth, and humanity, are situated in front of the bridge; when playing on it, the performer stands at the appropriate tree. A pebble path separates the audience from the actors.

Performers employ a highly unrealistic style of acting, moving to the rhythmical thumping of feet on a wooden floor. Wearing masks, they speak or chant with high- or low-pitched voices to a musical accompaniment. Since women never act in *Nō* drama, male performers take their roles. During the performance, elaborate costume changes occur on stage; assisting the actors is the property man, who, dressed in black, moves about the stage unobtrusively.

In such plays of W. B. Yeats as *At the Hawk's Well* (1917) and *The Only Jealousy of Emer* (1919), the influence of *Nō* drama is apparent.

See Donald Keene, *Nō: The Classical Theatre of Japan* (1966); Yasuo Nakamura, *Nōh: The Classical Theatre* (English trans. 1971).

nom de guerre: See *nom de plume*.

nom de plume: French: "pen name." A term used in English, but not in French, to indicate a fictitious name employed by a writer. "George Orwell," for example, is the *nom de plume* of Eric Blair. In French, *nom de guerre* is the term used for a pen name, especially that of a journalist.

nonce word: A word invented for a particular occasion. Lewis Carroll's "Jabberwocky," for example, employs a number of nonce words. In *Finnegans Wake*, James Joyce made the nonce word a central element in his style.

non-fiction novel: See **new journalism**.

nonsense verse: A type of **light verse** in which sense is subordinate to sound and absurdity is sought for its own sake. Among the most famous practitioners of nonsense verse are Lewis Carroll and Edward Lear, the author of the following lines:

> On the Coast of Coromandel
> > Where the early pumpkins blow,
> > In the middle of the woods,
> Lived the Yonghy-Bonghy-Bò.
> > > "The Courtship of the Yonghy-Bonghy-Bò"

novel: A fictional prose narrative of considerable length. A description of the novel is necessarily general, for this form is characterized by an extraordinary range of styles and types. The novel has developed so variously not only because it is an inherently flexible form, unrestricted by such things as the limitations of the physical theater, but also because, being the dominant literary genre of the nineteenth and twentieth centuries, it has tempted writers to pursue its possibilities. As a mass entertainment the novel has been supplanted by film and television (though it continues to furnish material to these media), but it remains a viable, if threatened, literary form.

Although there were extended prose narratives in the Classical and medieval periods, these lacked, to various degrees, the re-

alism, the coherently unified plots, and the psychological consideration of character that are usually—though not all of them
invariably—characteristic of the modern novel. In the late Middle Ages and the Renaissance, collections of brief tales were
popular; in sixteenth-century Spain there developed a type of
narrative that recounted, usually for satirical purposes, a loosely
structured series of adventures centering on a clever rascal (*picaro* in Spanish) who lives by his wits. (See **romance, novella,**
and **picaresque narrative.**) Heroic and chivalric ideas were subjected to a rich and subtle criticism when Cervantes's *Don Quixote* appeared in 1605, further pointing the way toward the realism
of the novel. In addition, such other progenitors as travel books,
diaries, and "characters" (in the seventeenth and eighteenth
centuries, sketches of representative social or personality types)
further turned the novel toward the portrayal of contemporary
life.

In *Robinson Crusoe* (1719) and *Moll Flanders* (1722), Defoe
created settings so detailed and convincing and central figures
so credible that, though his plots are loose, he is often credited
with launching the English novel. Around the middle of the
century Samuel Richardson in his epistolary novel *Pamela* (1740)
and especially in his second novel, *Clarissa* (1748), further developed the analysis of character and motive. Henry Fielding,
whose *Joseph Andrews* began as a parody of *Pamela*, revealed
in *Tom Jones* a genial, sophisticated humor and a penetrating
social observation that reflected both his own personality and
the temper of an age that valued balance and sound judgment.

As the novel entered the nineteenth century, exoticism and
adventure returned in the work of Sir Walter Scott and his
followers. (The novel of historical romance remains popular to
the present, and even the Hollywood costume epic of recent
years owes a vast debt to Scott.) But though elements of romance
appear in the work of such American writers as Hawthorne and
Melville and a reflection of the picaresque is discernible in Dickens's *Pickwick Papers*, the novel concerned itself essentially with
the depiction of the contemporary world and the analysis of
character. Such great French realists as Balzac and Flaubert
developed sophisticated analyses of man in society; Zola even
attempted to claim for the novelist the role of scientific exper-

imenter whose novel merely presented the result of his researches (see **naturalism**). Meanwhile, such English writers as George Eliot and Joseph Conrad enriched the novel's ability to present subtle moral analysis. In the twentieth century the novel's technical range has been extended by such experimenters as James Joyce and Franz Kafka, its psychological depth by such analysts of the self as Proust and Virginia Woolf.

For comment on specific types of novels see, in addition to the references in the discussion above: *Bildungsroman;* detective story; historical novel; *Künstlerroman;* New Novel; sentimental novel.

See also E. M. Forster, *Aspects of the Novel* (1927); William Van O'Connor, ed., *Forms of Modern Fiction* (1948); Arnold Kettle, *An Introduction to the Modern Novel* (1951); Dorothy Van Ghent, *The English Novel: Form and Function* (1953); Wayne C. Booth, *The Rhetoric of Fiction* (1961); Mark Spilka, ed., *Towards a Poetics of Fiction* (1977).

novelette: See **short novel**.

novella: Italian: "a story," "a little new thing." A brief prose tale. (Though the English word *novel* designates an extended narrative, it derives from this term.) In Italy collections of *novelle*, such as Boccaccio's *Decameron*, were popular in the late fourteenth century. Shakespeare and other Elizabethan writers drew upon these *novellè* for some of their plots. Occasionally, the term *novella* is used as a synonym for the **short novel**.

See Doyle Springer, *Forms of the Modern Novella* (1976).

nouvelle: See **short novel**.

numbers: Refers to either meter, feet, or verse. In Wordsworth's "The Solitary Reaper," for example, the term designates verses:

> Will no one tell me what she sings?—
> Perhaps the plaintive numbers flow
> For old, unhappy, far-off things,
> And battles long ago. . . .

O

objective correlative: In his essay "Hamlet and His Problems" (1919), T. S. Eliot wrote that "the only way of expressing emotion in the form of art is by finding an 'objective correlative'; in other words, a set of objects; a situation, a chain of events which shall be the formula of that *particular* emotion; such that when the general facts, which must terminate in sensory experience, are given, the emotion is immediately evoked." Regarding *Hamlet* as an artistic failure, Eliot feels that the emotions which dominate Hamlet are in excess of the chain of events which he experiences. Eliot's dictum, disputed by many, has nevertheless had wide popularity, especially among the **New Critics.**

objectivity: A quality assigned to a work in which the author seems to be presenting his characters in an impersonal, noncommittal fashion without offering any judgment of them or their actions. Much modern poetry, reacting against the intensely personal writing of the Romantics, seeks to be impersonal and objective. In "Sweeney Among the Nightingales," for example, T. S. Eliot makes little comment on the sinister scene that he presents. The term *objectivity*, if handled with discretion, can be useful, although it is doubtful if strict objectivity exists in literature. Flaubert makes no comment on Madame Bovary, but the intensity of his feeling for her is as apparent as the intensity of Eliot's revulsion from the world of Apeneck Sweeney. See **subjectivity.**

obligatory scene: French: *scène à faire*. An episode, usually highly emotional, which the audience so strongly anticipates that the dramatist is obliged to write it. In Ibsen's *Ghosts*, for example, the audience, aware that Oswald and Regina are half brother and sister, sees the sexual interest developing between them and anticipates the scene in which they are confronted with their relationship.

oblique rhyme: See **rhyme.**

occasional verse: Poetry written in commemoration of an event. Though much occasional verse succumbs to time, a number of examples have survived the occasions for which they were written. Among the most notable instances are Marvell's "An Horatian Ode upon Cromwell's Return from Ireland" and Milton's "On the Late Massacre in Piedmont." Modern examples are Yeats's "Easter 1916" and Hopkins's "The Wreck of the Deutschland." Occasional verse sometimes takes the form of *vers de société* when the sentiments are witty or satiric.

octameter: See **octometer.**

octastich: A stanza of eight lines.

octave (octet): 1. The first section of a **Petrarchan sonnet.** In this verse form, the octave (eight lines) is contrasted with the sestet (six lines) by a change in the rhyme scheme and some important turn of thought.

    2. An eight-line poem or stanza, especially *ottava rima.*

octavo (abbr. 8vo or 8°): A book in the manufacture of which the printer's sheets have been folded three times, making eight leaves or sixteen pages. As a rough indicator of the dimensions of a volume, this term designates a book of average size.

octet: See **octave.**

octometer: A verse made up of eight metrical feet. The length of this line, which is often broken into two tetrameters, makes it rare. Tennyson, however, uses it in *Frater Ave Atque Vale:*

> Row us out from Desenzano, to your Sirmione row!
> So they rowed, and there we landed—"O venusta Sirmio!"

octosyllable: A verse containing eight syllables.

ode: In English, a lyric poem of some length, serious in subject and dignified in style. The term, now loosely used, has lost any necessary reference to the odes of the Greek poet Pindar, to whom the form is usually traced. Originally an ode was a choral song to be sung and danced at a public occasion, such as the celebration of a victory in the Olympic games. The stanzas were arranged in groups of three. The strophe was sung while the chorus moved in one direction, the antistrophe, which had the same metrical form, while it moved in another, and the epode, which had a different form, as it stood still. Pindaric odes in

English are rare; an example is Thomas Gray's "The Progress of Poesy."

An ode in which the stanzas, or verse paragraphs, are irregular in rhyme scheme and in the number and length of the lines is called a "Cowleyan" or "irregular" ode. The type was established by Abraham Cowley (1618–67) and has been widely used since. Examples are Dryden's "A Song for St. Cecilia's Day," Wordsworth's "Ode: Intimations of Immortality," and Allen Tate's "Ode to the Confederate Dead." The Horatian ode, so called from the Roman poet Horace, is one in which each stanza follows the same metrical pattern. (Horace's odes were also more personal and reflective than those of Pindar.) Marvell's "An Horatian Ode upon Cromwell's Return from Ireland" is an example, as is Keats's "Ode to a Nightingale." These two poems also reflect the range of the English ode, from weighty public proclamation to the private, emotive meditation especially characteristic of the Romantics.

See George N. Shuster, *The English Ode from Milton to Keats* (1940); Carol Maddison, *Apollo and the Nine: A History of the Ode* (1960); John D. Jump, *Ode* (1974).

Old Comedy: Greek comedy of the fifth century B.C. The Old Comedy, which derives from the fertility festivals in honor of the god Dionysus, combines Rabelaisian humor, lyric beauty, and biting personal and political satire. The chorus, which disappears by the period of the **New Comedy,** takes an important part in the action and delivers the long speech called the **parabasis,** which expresses the views of the playwright. The works of such writers of Old Comedy as Crates and Eupolis have been lost; only the plays of Aristophanes survive.

omnibus: A volume of works, usually reprints, by one author or on related subjects.

one-act play: In the history of the drama, there have been many short, unified dramatic works which may properly be called one-act plays, but the term is usually reserved for those written since the late nineteenth century. Interest in the genre grew as part of the development of the modern, experimental (often noncommercial) theater. Such major modern dramatists as Strindberg, Shaw, Synge, O'Neill, Beckett, and Pinter have all written notable one-act plays.

In the current professional theater, "curtain raisers," one-act plays presented prior to longer productions, are rare.

onomatopoeia: The use of words whose sounds seem to express or reinforce their meanings. Certain words, such as *hiss, bang, bowwow,* imitate the sounds they represent. In the strictest sense, onomatopoeia can occur only when the writer is imitating sounds, as in "Hotchkiss dropped to the carpet with a dull thud," or more subtly, as in this line from Alfred Noyes's "The Highwayman," where the explosive *k*'s and *t*'s suggest the sound of a horse's hoofs on cobblestones: "Over the cobbles he clattered and clashed in the dark innyard." It has been suggested that certain sounds bring to mind, perhaps by the process of pronunciation, certain qualities and thus tend to be associated with them, as, for example, the short "i" sound with smallness (*little, slit, midget,* etc.). However, this theory is still unproven.

ontology: See **structure.**

open couplet: A couplet of which the second line is not complete in meaning but depends upon the first line of the following one, as in the second of these couplets from Milton's "L'Allegro":

> And ever against eating cares,
> Lap me in soft Lydian airs,
> Married to immortal verse,
> Such as the meeting soul may pierce
> In notes with many a winding bout
> Of linkèd sweetness long drawn out.

oration: A formal address delivered on a special occasion. Perhaps the most famous oration in literature is Mark Antony's speech to the crowd in Shakespeare's *Julius Caesar.*

organic form: That which is derived from the nature of a literary work's subject and materials rather than from rules externally imposed. In the theory of organic form, the work is said to grow from its inspiration like a plant from its seed, as opposed to a work which, governed by mechanical form, is fitted arbitrarily into a preconceived mold. The concept of organic form originated with Coleridge, who used it to reply to the Neoclassical critics of Shakespeare, whose plays, these critics contended, lacked "form."

ottava rima: In English, a stanza consisting of eight lines in iambic pentameter rhymed *ababbcc.* Used by such noted writers as Boccaccio, Pulci, and Tasso, it was a favored stanza for narrative and epic verse. Adopting the form for his mock epic, Byron uses *ottava rima* in *Don Juan,* which opens:

> I want a hero: an uncommon want,
>   When every year and month sends forth a new one,
> Till, after cloying the gazettes with cant,
>   The age discovers he is not the true one:
> Of such as these I should not care to vaunt,
>   I'll therefore take our ancient friend Don Juan—
> We all have seen him, in the pantomime,
> Sent to the devil somewhat ere his time.

In modern verse, W. B. Yeats uses *ottava rima* in "Sailing to Byzantium" and "Among School Children."

Oxford Movement: Generally considered to have begun with a sermon on "National Apostasy" preached at Oxford by the cleric-poet John Keble in July 1833, the Oxford Movement was a conservative High Church reaction to what was perceived as the encroaching liberalism of the age (the Whigs had just pushed through the Reform Bill of 1832, extending the franchise) as well as to long-standing abuses in the Anglican Church (sinecures, nepotism, and the holding of multiple livings) and, perhaps most significant, to the Church's complacent acceptance of its social role and consequent failure to be a source of religious regeneration.

Led by such men as John Henry Newman, R. H. Froude, and E. B. Pusey, from whom it derived the denigratory name of "Puseyism," the movement succeeded in making theology a vital issue at Oxford and among the educated persons who constituted its followers. However, the ninety *Tracts for the Times* (1833–41), written by Newman and others, through which its ideas were in large part disseminated and which led it also to be called the "Tractarian Movement," did not arouse universal approbation. Not surprisingly, many Anglican bishops responded less than enthusiastically to Newman's assertion in the first *Tract* that, as successors to the holy Apostles, they could hope for no more blessed end than "the spoiling of their goods, and martyrdom."

Behind such dubious enthusiasm lay a genuine concern with the doctrine of the Apostolic Succession as the justification for the rituals of High Anglicanism. Although this idea was part of a wider spiritual revival, it seemed to such men as Dr. Thomas Arnold to lead religion away from an engagement with the great social concerns of the age. As early as 1841 Newman had argued, in the last of the *Tracts*, that the Thirty-nine Articles of the Anglican Church were consistent with Roman Catholicism. With his conversion in 1845 (he later became a priest and ultimately a cardinal) the Oxford Movement lost much of its force, although, under the leadership of Pusey, it remained influential in such areas as the beautification of church buildings, the elaboration of ritual, and the development of lay orders. See **Victorianism.**

See Marvin R. O'Connell, *The Oxford Conspirators: A History of the Oxford Movement, 1833–1845* (1969); G. B. Tennyson, *Victorian Devotional Poetry: The Tractarian Mode* (1981).

oxymoron: Greek: *oxymoros*, "pointedly foolish." A figure of speech consisting generally of two apparently contradictory terms that express a startling paradox. The oxymoron is sometimes used in everyday speech, as in the phrase "conspicuous by his absence." In literature, a remarkable use of the oxymoron occurs in Shakespeare's *Romeo and Juliet*, Act I, in which Romeo, declaring that he is out of favor with Rosalind, jests about the nature of love:

> Why then, O brawling love! O loving hate!
> O any thing! of nothing first create.
> O heavy lightness! serious vanity!
> Mis-shapen chaos of well-seeming forms!
> Feather of lead, bright smoke, cold fire, sick health!
> Still-waking sleep, that is not what it is!
> This love feel I, that feel no love in this!

P

paean: Any song or hymn of joy, praise, or triumph. It is probably so called from Paian, the physician of the Greek gods, who was later identified with Apollo. The paean, sung in gratitude for Apollo's aid, was later used to honor other gods and then sung on various appropriate occasions. An example of the paean can be found in Sophocles' *Antigone*.

paeon: In Classical prosody, a foot of one long and three short syllables, called the first, second, third, or fourth paeon, depending on the position of the long syllable.

pageant: The movable stage or platform upon which the medieval **mystery plays** were presented. The pageant was built on wheels and consisted of two rooms, the lower used as a dressing room, and the upper, which was open, used as a stage. The mystery play itself was also called a pageant. In modern times the term is applied to any elaborate outdoor performance or procession.

palimpsest: A parchment or papyrus from which the original text has been removed and upon which a second (and sometimes a third) text has been imposed. Before the introduction of paper made good writing surfaces inexpensive, a parchment or papyrus was often used more than once. Sometimes, the original text can still be read because it was incompletely erased or has become visible with age. Upon occasion, modern chemical methods can restore the original text.

palindrome: A word, sentence, or verse which reads the same either backward or forward. Common palindromes are "Madam, I'm Adam" and "Able was I ere I saw Elba."

palinode: A poem in which the writer recants a statement made in a previous poem. The practice of writing palinodes was common in Classical and Renaissance literature. The most famous palinode in English is Chaucer's *Legend of Good Women*, written, as Chaucer tells us, to atone for the story of false Cressida.

panegyric: A piece of writing or a formal speech praising someone. See **encomiastic verse.**

pantomime: A type of spectacular theatrical entertainment that developed in England in the early part of the eighteenth century. The story of the pantomime, which was acted out in song and dance, involved characters from both Classical mythology and the *commedia dell'arte*. In production, the pantomime was lavish and elaborate, with much use of theatrical machinery and many changes of scene. The form still survives in England in the spectacular Christmas entertainments designed for children. See **mime**.

pantoum: A Malayan verse form that has been used in French and occasionally in English. There are an indefinite number of stanzas, each consisting of a quatrain rhyming *abab*. The second and fourth lines of each stanza become the first and third lines of the next. In the last stanza, the second and fourth lines are the first and third lines of the opening stanza reversed; thus, the poem ends with the same line with which it began.

parabasis: In the Greek **Old Comedy,** the long speech delivered by the chorus or its leader near the close of the play. In this speech, which was full of witticisms and topical references, often personal, the playwright gave his advice and opinions directly to the audience.

parable: A short, simple story illustrating a moral lesson. In a parable, the story is developed not for its own sake but only insofar as it reinforces the moral, which is always explicit. The parables of Christ, such as those of the Good Samaritan and the Prodigal Son, are the most famous examples of this genre.

paradox: A statement which, though it appears self-contradictory, contains a basis of truth that reconciles the seeming opposites. The apparent contradiction of the paradox often concentrates the reader's attention on a particular point, as here where Pope uses paradoxes to say that a great writer may make a virtue of something that would be a flaw if handled less skillfully:

> Great wits sometimes may gloriously offend,
> And rise to faults true critics dare not mend.
> *An Essay on Criticism*

Sometimes a paradox forms the basis of an entire poem, as in Lovelace's "To Althea, from Prison" (the beginning of which is quoted below), where each stanza describes a different way in which the speaker is free though incarcerated:

> When love with unconfined wings
> Hovers within my gates,
> And my divine Althea brings
> To whisper at the grates:
> When I lie tangled in her hair
> And fettered to her eye,
> The birds that wanton in the air
> Know no such liberty.

Some adherents of the **New Criticism,** especially Cleanth Brooks, have emphasized the importance of paradox, extending its meaning to cover much metaphoric and otherwise striking language and holding it to be not an illustrative device but one of the essential characteristics of poetic speech.

parallelism: The arrangement of equally important ideas in similar grammatical constructions, often reinforced by verbal echoes. Parallelism, which acts as an organizing force directing the reader's attention to the elements that the writer wishes to emphasize, also can help give polish to a piece of writing. It is one of the most persistent rhetorical devices and appears in many types of literature, as these two quotations, one from Psalm 19 of the Bible and the other from Pope's *An Essay on Man*, illustrate:

> The law of the Lord is perfect, converting the soul: the testimony
>   of the Lord is sure, making wise the simple.
> The statutes of the Lord are right, rejoicing the heart: the com-
>   mandment of the Lord is pure, enlightening the eyes.

> All Nature is but art, unknown to thee;
> All chance, direction, which thou canst not see;
> All discord, harmony not understood;
> All partial evil, universal good;
> And, spite of pride, in erring reason's spite,
> One truth is clear: Whatever IS, is RIGHT.

See **anaphora.**

paraphrase: The restatement in different words of the sense of a piece of writing. A paraphrase may be a general statement of the ideas of a work or a clarification of a difficult passage. Usually, it approximates the original in length. Below is a stanza from Donne's "A Valediction: Forbidding Mourning" and a paraphrase of it:

> Moving of th'earth brings harm and fears;
>   Men reckon what it did and meant;
> But trepidation of the spheres,
>   Though greater far, is innocent.

An earthquake causes a great deal of destruction and arouses fear. Men assess the damage it did and speculate about its significance. However, a movement of the heavenly bodies, though a phenomenon far more vast, does not show itself so directly or appear to have such terrible consequences.

See **Heresy of Paraphrase.**

Parnassianism: As a reaction to the earlier Romanticism of Hugo, Vigny, and Lamartine, French Parnassianism emerged under the leadership of Théophile Gautier in the 1830's. Turning their backs on the subjectivism and the social concerns of the Romantics, the Parnassians devoted themselves to objective poetry, from which the personality of the writer was removed, and to poetry which had "hardness" and clarity of outline. "Le poète est le sculpteur"—this statement by Gautier became, for the Parnassians, an emblem for craftsmanship in verse. By emphasizing craft and by using analogies with the other arts, Gautier attempted to place poetry on an equal basis with the plastic arts: the poem, too, should be carved, wrought into a tangible form, for the form was the idea given shape.

Preoccupation with form, among the Parnassians, gave rise to a style which has been called "lapidary." Gems, porcelains, marble statues and tombs, and exquisitely painted miniatures came to be conventional images in their verse.

In limiting their subject matter and by excluding moral and social concerns, the Parnassians declared that they were concerned with art for its own sake—*l'art pour l'art*. In the preface to his novel *Mademoiselle de Maupin* (1835), Gautier advanced the idea that art could not be "used," opposing the dictum held throughout the nineteenth century by political radicals and bourgeois writers that art was a means to an end.

In the 1870's, the doctrines of Parnassianism began to be felt in England through the influence of Théodore de Banville, whose *Petit traité de poésie française* (1872) was read widely. He was in correspondence with Swinburne, Austin Dobson, Edmund Gosse, and Andrew Lang, who all admired his essay on French verse which urged a return to older French fixed forms such as the **ballade,** the **villanelle,** and the **rondeau.** The English Parnassians, notably Dobson, Gosse, and Lang, followed their French colleagues closely in matters of style and form, but the doctrine of *l'art pour l'art* was alien to their temperaments. Essentially moral in their attitudes, they adopted the poetic fashions of Parnassianism and ignored French slogans.

See James K. Robinson, "A Neglected Phase of the Aesthetic Movement: English Parnassianism" *PMLA*, 68 (1953), 733–54; Robert T. Denommé, *The French Parnassian Poets* (1972).

parados: See **Greek tragedy, structure of.**

parody: See **burlesque.**

paronomasia: See **pun.**

pasquinade: A lampoon posted in a public place. The term derives from the name Pasquino, given to an ancient statue which was exhumed in Rome during the Renaissance and to which satirical attacks were customarily affixed.

passion play: A play which depicts the life, in whole or in part, of a god. Passion plays were performed in ancient Egypt and in the Near East. In Western Europe, many of the medieval **mystery plays** presented episodes from the life of Christ and so are called passion plays. A few of these plays, especially the passion play given by the Bavarian town of Oberammergau, are still performed.

pastiche: See **burlesque.**

pastoral: A term that covers a variety of literary forms. The only consistent characteristic of pastoral literature is that it concerns country life. In the third century B.C., the Greek poet Theocritus, writing of Sicilian shepherds, or "pastors," established the conventions of the pastoral world. In this world of trees, flowers, and meadows, it is always summer; no one performs the actual work of farming or sheep raising. Instead, the elegant shepherds and shepherdesses of this golden land occupy themselves with their love affairs or with composing and singing songs, which are usually of three types: the friendly singing contest between two shepherds, the song in which a single shepherd praises his mistress's beauty and laments her cruelty, and the elegy in which a shepherd laments the death of one of his comrades.

Theocritus's pastoral world, though unreal, was at least founded on that of the Sicilian shepherd, but since his time, the pastoral has been based on literary imitation. The most famous Classical writer of pastorals, Vergil, took Theocritus as a model, and subsequent writers of pastoral verse have gone to at least one of these masters (or their imitators) for inspiration. In the Renaissance, two new forms, the pastoral romance and the pastoral drama, developed.

The pastoral romance, of which the *Arcadias* of Sannazaro and Sidney and the *Astrée* of d'Urfé are examples, is a long, complex prose tale of love and adventure set in the pastoral world. Influenced by the pastoral romance, the pastoral drama developed in Italy in the sixteenth century with such plays as Tasso's *Aminta* and Guarini's *Il Pastor Fido*. Elements of the pastoral drama appear in many English plays including Shakespeare's *As You Like It*. John Fletcher's *The Faithful Shepherdess* (1608), an attempt at pastoral drama, follows the traditions of Italian pastorals. The pastoral lyric and especially the pastoral **elegy** were popular in the Renaissance and remained so afterward. Milton's "Lycidas" and Shelley's "Adonais" are the two most famous examples of the latter form.

When the Romantic poets again turned directly to contemporary rural life, the popularity of the pastoral conventions declined. In the modern period, an attempt at a philosophical definition of pastoral was made by William Empson in *Some Versions of Pastoral* (1935). Empson discards the flowers and shepherdesses of tradition as superficial addenda and sees the essence of pastoral as a putting of the complex, such as courtly ladies and gentlemen, into the simple, such as a rustic setting. He then proceeds to analyze several different examples and types of literature, such as the proletarian novel, as examples of pastoral. See **eclogue; idyl(l)**.

See W. W. Greg, *Pastoral Poetry and Pastoral Drama* (1906); William Empson, *Some Versions of Pastoral* (1935); Eleanor T. Lincoln, ed., *Pastoral and Romance: Modern Essays in Criticism* (1969); Harold E. Toliver, *Pastoral Forms and Attitudes* (1971); Laurence Lerner, *The Uses of Nostalgia: Studies in Pastoral Poetry* (1972); Andrew V. Ettin, *Literature and the Pastoral* (1984).

pastoral elegy: See **elegy.**

pastoral idyll: See **idyl(l).**

pastourelle (pastorella): A type of medieval lyric in dialogue form in which a knight or a man of equivalent social rank attempts to court a shepherdess. His suit is usually unsuccessful, though the wooing is sometimes terminated only by the arrival of a father or brother.

patent theaters: See **legitimate theater.**

pathetic fallacy: A phrase originated by Ruskin in *Modern Painters*, Vol. III, Part IV (1856), to describe the attribution of human characteristics to inanimate objects. Such an attribution usually falls short of a full **personification.** Quoting a phrase from Kingsley, "the cruel, crawling foam," Ruskin said, "The foam is not cruel, neither does it crawl. The state of mind which attributes to it these characters of a living creature is one in which the reason is unhinged by grief. All violent feelings . . . produce in us a falseness in all our impressions of external things, which I would characterize as the 'Pathetic Fallacy.' "

Ruskin qualified his condemnation by admitting that examples of the pathetic fallacy, though false to nature, were often very beautiful. This phenomenon, he argued, was usually found in poets whom he placed in the second rank (such as Wordsworth, Coleridge, Tennyson), those who felt strongly but thought weakly. Great poets, who both felt and thought strongly, would not so distort nature unless, under the stress of prophetic inspiration, they were attempting to express something so incomparably above them that no human mind could perceive it truly. Though this distinction in the use of the pathetic fallacy has been criticized as dubiously subjective, Ruskin's term has remained useful. Today, however, it is descriptive and carries no pejorative connotations.

See Josephine Miles, *Pathetic Fallacy in the Nineteenth Century* (1942).

pathos: That quality in a work of literature which evokes from the reader feelings of pity, tenderness, and sympathy. The death of Desdemona is pathetic; that of Othello, however, is tragic. He is a character too heroic in scale and his death is too great a fall to be described as pathetic. A pathetic object usually suffers helplessly, but a tragic hero, such as Othello, always achieves dignity and the resolution of his pain.

Sometimes a writer, trying too hard for pathos or sublimity, stumbles into **bathos.**

pause: A moment of rest in the rhythm of verse. The most commonly recognized pause, that which occurs within the line, is called a **caesura.** There is often a pause at the end of a line and usually at the end of a stanza. These are sometimes called metrical pauses. A pause is often used in verse to offset a missing syllable. (See **compensation.**) Sometimes a pause is used for poetic rather than strictly metrical effects. In the final line of Hopkins's "God's Grandeur," the pause and the exclamation contribute to the power of expression:

> . . . the Holy Ghost over the bent
> World broods with warm breast and with ah! bright wings.

penny dreadful: In England, a novel or novelette of mystery or adventure, cheaply printed and bound in paper, equivalent to the American dime novel.

pentameter: A line of five metrical feet. The pentameter line, the most widely used in English poetry, is the basis of such special metrical forms as **blank verse,** the **heroic couplet,** and the **sonnet.** All the lines in the following quatrain by Thomas Nashe are pentameter:

> Spring, the / sweet spring, / is the / year's pleas / ant king;
> Then blooms / each thing, / then maids / dance in / a ring,
> Cold doth / not sting, / the pret / ty birds / do sing:
> Cuckoo, / jug-jug, / pu-we, / to-wit / ta-woo!
>   "Spring"

penult: The syllable next to the last in a word, as in "cru*ci*fy."

perfect rhyme: See **rhyme.**

periodic sentence: See **loose and periodic sentences.**

peripeteia (peripety): A sudden reversal of situation; a term usually limited to the drama. For Aristotle's use of the term, see **tragedy.** An instance from comedy will be found at the end of Congreve's *The Way of the World* when Fainall, apparently about to succeed in his aims, is suddenly discomfited by a crucial document produced by Mirabell.

periphrasis: Circumlocution—using many words to express something which could be put more briefly. This is one of the devices by which a writer may avoid the commonplace and achieve an elevated style, though its indiscriminate use may lead not to elevation but to pomposity. In this passage from *The Rape of the Lock,* Pope, for comic purposes, elaborates a simple statement, "Hampton Court is on the Thames near Hampton":

> Close by those meads, forever crowned with flowers,
> Where Thames with pride surveys his rising towers,
> There stands a structure of majestic frame,
> Which from the neighb'ring Hampton takes its name.

peroration: See **speech.**

persona: The Latin word for the mask worn by the actors of the ancient Classical theater (thus the term *dramatis personae* for the characters in a play) and by extension, in modern literary usage, the character or "mask" assumed by the speaker or narrator of a poem or work of fiction. No readers are likely to equate the imagined historical personage Andrea del Sarto, the speaker of Browning's poem of that name, with Browning himself; few would look for more than certain tentative similarities in temperament between the young T. S. Eliot, the author of "The Love Song of J. Alfred Prufrock," and Prufrock himself, the timid, frustrated, middle-aged figure who is the speaker of that poem; many readers, however, might well feel that the speaker of such a poem as Wordsworth's "I Wandered Lonely as a Cloud" could be identified with the poet himself. But modern criticism, with its emphasis on the rhetorical strategies of literature, has asserted that the speaker of such a poem, or even the Wordsworth who directly addresses his sister in "Tintern Abbey," is a "persona," a mask which the poet has assumed in order to speak to his audience more effectively. The persona is a literary creation, a part of the poem, not to be confused with the private personality of the poet.

In addition, the term *voice* is sometimes used to designate the creating, ordering artistic intelligence that we recognize behind any narrating persona, even an "objective" third-person one. Though some critics maintain that this voice is also a literary creation, others suggest that it is nearer the author's genuine self. In any case, part of the reader's acceptance of a work depends on his acceptance of this voice and of the values for which, at least by implication, it speaks. See **point of view.**

See M. H. Abrams, ed., *Literature and Belief* (1958); Wayne C. Booth, *The Rhetoric of Fiction* (1961); Robert C. Elliott, *The Literary Persona* (1982).

personification: In Greek: *prosopopoeia.* A figure of speech in which inanimate objects or abstract ideas are endowed with human qualities or action. In morality plays, for example, characters are frequently given such names as Lust, Good Sense, etc., which indicate that ideas, not individualized persons, are being dramatized. Personification is often used in verse when the poet wishes to achieve certain effects, as in Gray's "Ode on a Distant Prospect of Eton College":

> These shall the fury Passions tear,
> The vultures of the mind,
> Disdainful Anger, pallid Fear,
> And Shame that skulks behind,
> Or pining Love shall waste their youth,
> Or Jealousy with rankling tooth,
> That inly gnaws the secret heart,
> And Envy wan, and faded Care
> Grim-visaged, comfortless Despair,
> And Sorrow's piercing dart.

See **pathetic fallacy.**

Petrarchan sonnet: A poem of fourteen lines divided into two parts: the first eight lines called the octave, or octet, rhyme *abbaabba;*

the remaining six lines, or sestet, usually rhyme *cdecde*. The rhyme scheme of the sestet admits some variation but there are never more than a total of five rhymes in the poem. The octave generally contains the "problem" or theme which the sonnet will develop. Sometimes, an expression of indignation, desire, or doubt may occur in the opening lines which will be resolved in the sestet.

Originating in Italy in the thirteenth century, the Italian sonnet, as it is sometimes called, was brought to its fullest development by Petrarch (1304–74). In England, Petrarch's sonnets were translated and imitated for the first time by Sir Thomas Wyatt in the sixteenth century. English imitators, using iambic pentameter, took liberties with the rhyme scheme, though they retained the division of the sonnet form into two parts, as in Keats's "On First Looking into Chapman's Homer":

> Much have I travelled in the realms of gold,
> And many goodly states and kingdoms seen;
> Round many western islands have I been
> Which bards in fealty to Apollo hold.
> Oft of one wide expanse had I been told
> That deep-browed Homer ruled as his demesne;
> Yet did I never breathe its pure serene
> Till I heard Chapman speak out loud and bold:
> Then felt I like some watcher of the skies
> When a new planet swims into his ken;
> Or like stout Cortez when with eagle eyes
> He stared at the Pacific—and all his men
> Looked at each other with a wild surmise—
> Silent, upon a peak in Darien.

See **Miltonic, Shakespearean,** and **Spenserian sonnets.**

Petrarchism: The style introduced by Petrarch (1304–74) in his sonnets to Laura. It was a style marked by grammatical complexity, elaborate **conceits,** and conventional diction. Its influence was widespread, extending to the **Pléiade** in France and the Elizabethan sonneteers in England.

phallocentrism: See **feminist criticism.**

philippic: A speech or piece of writing which denounces someone in harsh and vituperative language. The term derives from the orations in which Demosthenes denounced Philip of Macedon.

Philistine: One devoted to materialism, progress, and wealth with no concern for art, beauty, culture, or spiritual things. In a lecture entitled "Sweetness and Light," his last as Professor of Poetry at Oxford (1867), Matthew Arnold singled out as Philistines those Englishmen who believed that wealth indicated greatness. The lecture, subsequently printed as the first chapter of *Culture and Anarchy* (1869), cites culture as an antidote to the stultifying effects of Philistinism:

> Now, the use of culture is that it helps us, by means of its spiritual standard of perfection, to regard wealth as but machinery, and not only to say as a matter of words that we regard wealth as but machinery, but really to perceive and feel that it is so. If it were not for this purging effect wrought upon our minds by culture, the whole world, the future as well as the present, would inevitably belong to the Philistines. . . . Culture says "Consider these people, then, their way of life, their habits, their manners, the very tones of their voice; look at them attentively; observe the literature they read, the things which give them pleasure, the words which come forth out of their mouths, the thoughts which make the furniture of their minds; would any amount of wealth be worth having with the condition that one was to become just like these people by having it?"

During the nineteenth century, Aesthetes, identifying the term *Philistine* with the middle class, attempted by their dress, behavior, and art to shock the unimaginative middle class—*épater le bourgeois*. For a discussion of the conflict between the Aesthetes and the Philistines, see **Decadence.**

picaresque narrative: An episodic depiction of the adventures of a *pícaro* (Spanish: "rogue") or in English a "picaroon," whose knavery implicates him in imbroglios which take him from one social class to another. Frequently, he is a social parasite or a person of low estate who manages to exploit those in more elevated positions. A vehicle for satire, the picaresque narrative, generally presented in the first person, consists of unconnected episodes held together by the presence of the central character. Realistic detail, usually drawn from the life of the lower classes, tends to be coarse and bawdy.

Emerging as a distinct genre in sixteenth-century Spain, the picaresque narrative became a popular form of entertainment following the success of an anonymous work, *La vida de Lazarillo de Tormes* (ca. 1554). Later writers borrowed extensively from Spanish models, setting their stories in Spain and using similar incidents. A notable French example of the form is Lesage's *Gil Blas*. The first work of this type in English was Thomas Nashe's *The Unfortunate Traveller* (1594), later followed by Defoe's *Moll Flanders* (which deals with a female picaroon), Fielding's *Jonathan Wild*, and Smollett's *Ferdinand, Count Fathom*.

See Harry Sieber, *The Picaresque* (1977); Alexander Blackburn, *The Myth of the Picaro: Continuity and Transformation of the Picaresque Novel, 1554–1954* (1979).

picaroon: See **picaresque narrative.**

pièce à thèse: See **thesis play.**

pièce bien faite: See **well-made play.**

Pindaric ode: See **ode.**

plaint: A lament in verse. See **complaint.**

planh: In Provençal verse, a song of mourning for a deceased patron; it contrasts his virtues with the vices of those who survive. In aim and subject matter, the *planh* is related to the **sirventes.** See **troubadour.**

Platonism and Neo-Platonism: The doctrines of Plato and certain followers, "new Platonists," such as Plotinus (third century A.D.) and other philosophers of the Alexandrian school who elaborated and added to Plato's thought. The ideas of Plato and his followers have at times been profoundly influential in the history of literature even though Plato himself banned most poets—exceptions were made for those who praised the gods and famous men—from his ideal Republic because he feared the distorting influence of poetry. For Plato considered that, since the physical world is merely an imperfect imitation of the divine archetype, the poet in representing the world was imitating an imitation and thus creating something that stood at two removes from truth. This argument, however, has been answered in at least two ways: Aristotle maintained that because the poet imitates general rather than particular ideas, his work is more philosophical than history; Neo-Platonists have suggested that the poet is attempting to imitate not the world but the divine archetype itself.

The Alexandrian Neo-Platonists mingled Platonic ideas with elements from Oriental and Christian thought to form a body of hermetic learning that ultimately influenced such mystical writers as Blake and Yeats. But a broader stream of influence flowed into European literature from the Neo-Platonists of the Renaissance. One of the sources of this stream was the Latin translation of Plato (1482) by the Florentine Marsilio Ficino, leader of a group of friends and scholars called the Platonic Academy, which made Plato's work generally accessible to educated men. Another source, more immediately significant for literature, was the wide dissemination of the concept of Platonic love. (The idea that Platonic love is simply love without sexuality is a gross misunderstanding.) For Plato, as he suggests in the *Symposium*, beauty proceeds in a series of ascending steps from the love of one beautiful body to that of two (thus becoming less exclusive), to the love of physical beauty in general, and ultimately to the love of that beauty "not in the likeness of a face or hands or in any form of speech or knowledge or animal or particular thing in time or place, but beauty absolute, separate, simple, everlasting—the source and cause of the perishing beauty of all other things." When this scheme is Christianized by equating this ultimate beauty with the divine beauty of God, the Renaissance Platonic lover can move in stages through the desire for his mistress, whose beauty he recognizes as an emanation of God's, to the worship of the Divine itself. Much of the love poetry of this period from Petrarch to Spenser is informed by this concept.

Platonism was less sympathetic to the rationalism of the eighteenth century, as these lines of Pope suggest:

> Go, soar with Plato to th' empyreal sphere,
> To the first Good, first Perfect, and first Fair;
> Or tread the mazy round his followers trod,
> And quitting sense call imitating God.
> *An Essay on Man*

During the Romantic period Platonism reasserted its influence. In Wordsworth's "Intimations" ode the ideas of the pre-existence of the soul and of the body as the soul's prison are traditionally Platonic, though the Greeks would not have been sympathetic to Wordsworth's idealization of childhood. Plato's influence on Shelley, in such a poem as the "Hymn to Intellectual Beauty," for example, is central. In America Platonism was important for both Emerson and Poe; through the latter its influence extends to Baudelaire and the modern Symbolists. See *dolce stil nuovo*.

See G. M. A. Grube, *Plato's Thought* (1935); Paul Shorey, *Platonism Ancient and Modern* (1938); Philippus V. Pistorius, *Plotinus and Neoplatonism: An Introductory Study* (1952).

play: A dramatized story designed to be performed onstage by actors. For the major types of plays, see the listing under "Dramatic Types" at the end of this book.

Pléiade: A constellation named for the seven daughters of Atlas, the Pleiades has given its name to several groups of "stellar" poets, of which the most significant was the group that flourished in France in the middle of the sixteenth century. The members were Ronsard, du Bellay, Baïf, Belleau, Thyard, Jodelle, and Daurat. In the famous *Défense et illustration de la langue française*, du Bellay set forth the theories of the group. The *illustration*, or "making illustrious," of the language was to be achieved by expanding the vocabulary to include words from Greek and Latin, newly coined words based on these languages, and both antique and provincial words from French. The poet, accepting his task with high seriousness, was to create a French literature comparable to the literatures of Greece and Rome; and, to this end, he was to ignore the forms of medieval French literature such as the **ballade,** the **villanelle,** etc., and write sonnets in the manner of Petrarch, odes in the manner of Pindar, and in general take the writers of the Italian Renaissance and especially those of Classical antiquity as models. The *Pléiade* not only stimulated French literature but also influenced the poets of the English Renaissance as well.

See Robert J. Clements, *Critical Theory and Practice of the Pléiade* (1942); Grahame Castor, *Pléiade Poetics: A Study in Sixteenth Century Thought and Terminology* (1964).

plot: The organization of incidents in a narrative or play. The governing word in this definition is *organization*, for the happenings of a story are not, in most critical views, the same as the episodes of a plot. In *Aspects of the Novel* (1927), E. M. Forster describes a story as "a narrative of events arranged in their time-sequence," evoking in the reader merely curiosity. "A plot," he goes on to say, "is also a narrative of events, the emphasis falling on causality." Thus, it demands of the reader both "memory" and "intelligence." A writer may find a story anywhere—mythology, previous literature, a newspaper—but only if he shapes it into a plot will it produce an artistic effect and so express his meaning.

The primary discussion of the structure of a plot is that of Aristotle in the *Poetics*. A unified plot, he says, has a beginning (that which is not necessarily caused by something else but which produces other events), a middle (which derives from what has gone before and which something else must follow), and an end (something that depends on what has happened but which need be followed by nothing else). Aristotle says further that the plot should be so constructed that no incident can be displaced or omitted without destroying the unity of the whole. The presence of a single hero is not sufficient, he continues, to give unity. A plot which consists of a series of disconnected incidents, even though it may center on one figure, he calls "episodic" and ranks as inferior. Many writers, however, have deliberately chosen the episodic plot for its freedom and scope.

An organizing device not anticipated by Aristotle is the double plot, one in which the episodes of a subplot—a second complete story—are interspersed with those of the main plot. (Such plots are especially common in Elizabethan and Jacobean drama.) Although a subplot may be largely extraneous and thus destroy the unity of action Aristotle admired, such a plot may also offer a comic variation on the main one (the Sir Politic Would-be plot in *Volpone*) or a serious counterpoint to it (the Laertes plot in *Hamlet*).

Aristotle also raised questions not only about the nature and structure of plot but about its importance. Calling plot "the soul of tragedy," he held it to be more significant than the development of character, a view that has been both defended and disputed. Certainly the recent dominance of the novel, a form inherently discursive and introspective, and the post-Freudian development of psychological knowledge have shifted emphasis toward the exploration of character. But it is doubtful that plot and character can, in fact, be separated. In this regard, the classic statement is that of Henry James in "The Art of Fiction," who —discussing the interrelatedness of description, narration, dialogue, and incident—asks, "What is character but the determination of incident? What is incident but the illustration of character?"

Often, though by no means invariably, two characters in conflict provide the motivating force that drives a plot to its climax and ultimately to its resolution. Plots that follow this pattern have been especially common in drama. For example, in Shakespeare's *Othello*, after the **exposition,** the incidents involving Iago's deception of Othello lead to a **crisis,** the point at which the Moor decides to kill Desdemona. The conflicts of the play now intensified and heightened, the action moves toward the **climax,** the murder of Desdemona. Following this incident, the **denouement** contains the discovery of Iago's treachery, Othello's remorse and suicide, along with Iago's capture and condemnation to torture. In this plot pattern the events preceding the climax are called the "rising action," those following, the "falling action." Because the major climax of *Othello* comes late in the play, the falling action and the denouement are here the same, but in such a play as *Hamlet*, where the climax—the confirmation in the play scene that Claudius is the murderer—comes comparatively early, there is an extended falling action, with the denouement at the end. Though many works do not rigidly follow this pattern, these terms remain useful in discussion of the drama and of other genres as well. For a diagram of this type of plot structure, see **Freytag's Pyramid.** See also **unities.**

See Percy Lubbock, *The Craft of Fiction* (1921); Wayne C. Booth, *The Rhetoric of Fiction* (1961); Robert Scholes and Robert Kellogg, *The Nature of Narrative* (1966); Peter Brooks, *Reading for the Plot: Design and Intention in Narration* (1984).

poem: A composition in which rhythmical, and usually metaphorical, language is used to create an aesthetic experience and to make a statement which cannot be fully paraphrased in prose. Such elements as meter and rhyme are usually but not necessarily present. See **poetry.**

poetaster: An incompetent versifier; a writer of inferior or mediocre verse.

poète maudit: French: the "accursed poet." The phrase embodies the idea that the artist, and especially the poet, is forever rejected by, or at least alien to, the bourgeois society around him. In giving the title *Les Poètes maudits* (1884) to a collection of essays on such then little-known writers as Mallarmé and Rimbaud, Verlaine echoed a phrase from Alfred de Vigny's *Stello* (1832), in which Vigny dealt with such poet-martyrs as Chatterton and Chénier.

poetic diction: In the *Poetics*, Aristotle says that a writer's diction should be clear but that it should also be raised above the commonplace. To achieve this elevation, he maintains, the writer must introduce unusual words, metaphors, and various stylistic ornaments, "for by deviating in exceptional cases from the normal idiom, the language will gain distinction." In this part of the *Poetics*, Aristotle was defending poets who had been condemned for using expressions that would never be found in ordinary speech. A language made up entirely of deviations from the ordinary would, he said, be grotesque where one with no such deviations would be flat.

The debate on poetic diction—the type of language suitable to verse and the liberties allowable in it—has continued since Aristotle's time. In the English Renaissance, Spenser built an elaborate poetic style, using many words which were quaint or archaic even then. The eighteenth century saw the development of an ornate diction full of archaisms, Latinisms, conventionally personified abstractions, and **periphrasis** (*e.g.*, "finny prey" for "fish").

At the beginning of the Romantic period, Wordsworth protested against this style. In the preface to the *Lyrical Ballads*, he said that there was no essential difference between the language of prose and that of verse. The poet, since he was addressing other men, should employ a "selection of the language really used by men." Wordsworth said he had taken as much pains to avoid poetic diction as others had to achieve it. Nevertheless, to the modern ear, Wordsworth's speech reflects the conventions of traditional poetic style:

Thrice welcome, darling of the spring!
Even yet thou art to me
No bird, but an invisible thing,
A voice, a mystery.
    "To the Cuckoo"

Such expressions as *thrice* for *three times*, *thou art* for *you are*, in this stanza, and *oft* for *often*, *whereso'er* for *wherever*, etc., seem to the contemporary reader marks of that "poetic diction" which Wordsworth sought to escape. The poets of the twentieth century have largely avoided the diction of nineteenth-century poetry, just as Wordsworth and his contemporaries attempted to avoid that of their predecessors, the Neoclassicists. The language of poetry, never precisely the same as the language of prose, moves closer to it or further from it as the needs of the age demand.

See Owen Barfield, *Poetic Diction: A Study in Meaning* (3rd ed., 1973); Arthur Sherbo, *English Poetic Diction from Chaucer to Wordsworth* (1975).

poetic justice: A term used by Thomas Rhymer in *Tragedies of the Last Age* (1678) to designate the idea that the good are rewarded and the evil punished. The use of poetic justice has been urged by many who regard the moral function of literature as primary. A writer, these critics say, should carefully distribute rewards and punishments so that the good may be inspired to further goodness and the wicked discouraged from evil. Despite the obvious observation that life does not have such a convenient arrangement, the doctrine is defended on the grounds that the universe is presided over by a beneficent deity who will, at the appropriate time, redress wrongs and punish the wicked who have prospered on earth. Literature, consequently, should present the true state of things.

In the eighteenth century, the critic John Dennis defended this idea of poetic justice by stating that literature which did not function as "a very solemn lecture" was either "an empty amusement, or a scandalous and pernicious libel upon the government of the world." Addison, however, called the idea a "ridiculous Doctrine." In modern times, the use of poetic justice is limited largely to **melodrama** and many motion pictures. In *The Im-*

portance of Being Earnest, Oscar Wilde, ridiculing the notion of poetic justice, has Miss Prism declare that she has written a three-volume novel:

> Cecily: Did you really, Miss Prism? How wonderfully clever you are! I hope it did not end happily? I don't like novels that end happily. They depress me so much.
> Miss P: The good ended happily, and the bad unhappily. That is what Fiction means.

poetic license: The liberty, usually limited to verse, taken by a poet in matters of word order, rhyme, use of archaic words, and figures of speech. Within the conventions of poetic form, license is granted so that the writer may be permitted to achieve certain effects.

poetic prose: Elaborately wrought prose which makes use of the rhythms, figures, and other devices of verse. Many writers have adopted poetic prose for a short work or for passages of particular intensity in a longer one, as here in the description of the mermaid in Oscar Wilde's "The Fisherman and his Soul":

> Her hair was as a wet fleece of gold, and each separate hair as a thread of fine gold in a cup of glass. Her body was of white ivory, and her tail was of silver and pearl. Silver and pearl was her tail, and the green weeds of the sea coiled around it; and like sea shells were her ears, and her lips were like sea coral. The cold waves dashed over her cold breasts, and the salt glistened upon her eyelids.

poet laureate: A title traditionally given to a poet appointed by the British sovereign. The poet laureate was generally expected to compose verse for state functions, but in modern times his title has been chiefly a distinction.

From primitive times, poets have traditionally functioned as singers at the courts of kings who wished to hear their virtues and victories extolled in verse. In the medieval universities, where recipients of academic degrees were customarily crowned with laurel, one who had attained distinction in Latin rhetoric was designated poet laureate. In 1341, the Italian poet Petrarch was honored with a crown of laurel by the Senate of Rome for his achievements.

In England, the first official poet laureate was John Dryden, who held the laureateship from 1670 to 1688, though other poets, such as Ben Jonson and William Davenant, had been "court poets" before him. Though some poets laureate have been writers of little distinction, others, such as Wordsworth and Tennyson, have dignified the office.

In 1986, Robert Penn Warren was appointed for one year as the "first official Poet Laureate" of the United States (the British poet laureateship is a lifetime appointment). The principal duties of the American poet laureate are to give a public lecture and a public reading, advise the Library of Congress on its literary programs, and recommend new poets to be recorded in the Library's archive.

See Kenneth Hopkins, *The Poet Laureate* (rev. ed., 1974).

poetry: Though poetry is sometimes defined as any metrical composition, for the most part a distinction is made between it and verse. Sir Philip Sidney, saying that verse is "but an ornament and no cause to Poetry," expressed the attitude that is commonly, though not universally, accepted. If metrical form is disregarded as a basis for a definition of poetry, a different basis must be found. Wordsworth said that the opposite of poetry was factual or scientific writing, and modern theoreticians tend to agree with him. The meanings of a piece of prose, especially scientific prose, these critics feel, can be stated as intellectual concepts, but those of poetry cannot. By making wide use of the connotations and interrelations of words, poetry presents much that is beyond the expressive ability of prose. Though some critics have maintained that the aim of poetry is to produce pleasure and others that it is to give a unique sort of knowledge, there is considerable agreement that poetry presents an emotional and intellectual experience rather than an abstraction from experience.

See Anthony Easthope, *Poetry as Discourse* (1983).

point of attack: A term, sometimes limited to the drama, designating the point in a story at which the writer begins his action. Because the playwright does not usually make the point of attack coincide with the beginning of the story, he presents preceding material through **exposition.** Easy changes of scene allow him to dramatize most of his action directly: in *Macbeth*, for example, the point of attack is near the beginning of the story. But in such modern plays as Ibsen's *Ghosts*, the conventions of the realistic theater lead the playwright to set the point of attack much nearer to the conclusion of the action.

point of view: The point from which a story is seen or told. Though there are numerous possible arrangements, three principal points of view are most commonly employed: (1) The omniscient, which enables the writer to present the inner thoughts and feelings of his characters. Godlike, he may survey from his Olympian position past and present so that the reader may come to know more of his imaginative world than any single character in it. In *Ulysses*, for example, a work that employs shifting points of view, Joyce reveals the inner thoughts of his three major characters through the **stream of consciousness** and presents actions, unknown to the individual characters, going on in various parts of Dublin. Moreover, the omniscient author may sometimes openly comment on the behavior of his characters, as in Thackeray's *Vanity Fair*. (2) The point of view of a single character who is used by the author as a central observer or participant in the action. Utilizing this device, the writer may, in the third-person narrative, limit the knowledge available to the reader, as in Joyce's *Portrait of the Artist as a Young Man*, in which Stephen Dedalus's consciousness is all the reader knows. (3) The first-person narrative, in which the point of view is solely that of the character telling the story. He may be the central character, as in Defoe's *Robinson Crusoe*, or a minor figure who either observes or participates in the action, as in Conrad's *Heart of Darkness*, in which Marlow does both. This device, the furthest removed from the omniscient point of view, significantly reduces the reader's sense of the author's presence in the work.

In addition, the writer's purposes, conscious or otherwise, may be served by making the narrator unreliable—that is, by casting doubt on whether his presentation and/or analysis of events is to be trusted. In the Sherlock Holmes stories, for example, the limits of Dr. Watson's perspicacity often prevent him from keeping abreast of the hero's designs. More commonly, however, the questions at issue are the narrator's moral comprehension, as in James's *The Aspern Papers*, or mental stability, as in his *The Turn of the Screw* (where the matter has been hotly debated among critics). In Book I of *Gulliver's Travels*, Gulliver's putative obtuseness in being unable to discover the lenity in his being sentenced to blindness and starvation is only an assumed mask for Swift's denunciation of authoritarian cruelty, but in Book IV our ultimate doubts as to Gulliver's sanity make more complexly elusive a final assessment of the author's view of the Houyhnhnms' inhuman virtue.

See Susan S. Lanser, *The Narrative Act: Point of View in Prose Fiction* (1981).

polemic: A work, argumentative in nature, which presents the writer's viewpoint on a controversial subject. Many English authors such as Swift and Milton have written polemical works, of which Milton's *Areopagitica* is perhaps the most famous.

polyphonic prose: Prose which has the qualities and elements of verse. As developed by Amy Lowell (1874–1925) from the nineteenth-century poet Paul Fort, who wrote verse which was printed as prose, polyphonic prose was a fusion of meter, alliteration, assonance, free verse, rhyme, and recurrence of significant images. Amy Lowell's *Can Grande's Castle* (1918) is the most notable example of this kind of writing. John Gould Fletcher, an associate of Amy Lowell, has been credited with giving the name to this prose and, in fact, made use of it himself.

pornography: From Greek: *pornē*, "prostitute"; *graphos*, "writing." Pornography has been regarded by some critics as a subgenre, much like science fiction and the detective story, but others regard it as antithetical to, indeed a negation of, literary art.

Pornography (the terms "hard core" and "soft core" seem to relate merely to the degree of specificity with which the relevant activities are portrayed) has been said to be an attempt to evoke sexual fantasies to the exclusion of other human concerns, to draw the reader into an erotic utopia in which experience is untouched by the conflicts and perplexities of human striving. In such a "pornotopia," to use Steven Marcus's term from *The Other Victorians*, disgust, laughter, ugliness, and sexual failure are excluded so that its inhabitants may be promptly and completely satisfied without emotional or spiritual consequences. Here the reader's sexual fantasies are stimulated by a virtually unbroken succession of images of splendid physical creatures inexhaustibly engaged in sexual activity leading invariably to perfect orgasms. From the ethical point of view, the effect is to dehumanize characters by restricting their responses to a physiological, even mechanistic, determinism.

Literary art, on the other hand, claims to represent a more complex vision of reality, although it remains one in which sexual activity may well have an integral role. Such a vision offers an imaginative grasp of the contradictions, ironies, and failures of life by relating them to humanity's moral and psychological, as well as physical, existence. In literature, then, the imagination reveals essential truths of the human condition, whereas in pornography, fantasy arouses—and perhaps satisfies, if only vicariously—the reader's sexual appetites.

It may be argued, however, that this traditional antithesis, between pornography on the one hand and literature on the other, fails to deal with the complexities of "sexual fiction," to use Maurice Charney's more inclusive and less emotionally loaded term. Work of this sort may offer a vision of life no less imaginatively valid, although undoubtedly far more disturbing, than that of more conventional writing. The novels of the Marquis de Sade, for example, which hardly exclude ugliness or traffic entirely in gratification, have been said to create a special eroticized universe in which the claims of moral conduct have been replaced by the demands of sexual power. Thus they may be seen as offering an artistic vision of an aspect of reality usually repressed. Such fiction would have to be judged, as Charney insists it must be, by the same standards that are applied to more conventional kinds of literature.

The difficulty in determining which literary works are "pornographic" is illustrated by the fact that at one time Joyce's *Ulysses* (1922) and Henry Miller's *Tropic of Cancer* (1939) were called "obscene" or "pornographic" and banned from sale because of certain erotic passages. However, in landmark decisions (involving *Ulysses*) Judge John Woolsey in 1933 and Judge Learned Hand in 1934 ruled that isolated sections of a serious literary work—no matter how sexually provocative—could not be used to determine the intent or value of the entire work. More recent legal tests of pornography have been principally concerned with the socially redeeming value of the work, with the effect of such a work upon the sensibility of the average citizen, and with contemporary community standards—all matters difficult to demonstrate with any precision in a court of law.

See Eberhard and Phyllis Kronhausen, *Pornography and the Law* (rev. ed., 1964); Douglas A. Hughes, ed., *Perspectives on Pornography* (1970); Angela Carter, *The Sadeian Woman and the Ideology of Pornography* (1978); Maurice Charney, *Sexual Fiction* (1981).

portmanteau word: A word formed by combining two or more words. In *Through the Looking Glass*, Lewis Carroll referred to his own inventions in the poem "Jabberwocky" as "portmanteau words": "You see," says Humpty Dumpty, explaining to Alice that *slithy* combines *lithe* and *slimy*, "it's like a portmanteau—there are two meanings packed up into one word." James Joyce made extensive use of portmanteau words in *Finnegans Wake*, as, for example, "bisexcycle."

post-structuralism: Although this term can refer to any developments in literary theory since **Structuralism**, it is frequently used as a synonym for **deconstruction.**

potboiler: A literary work produced for the sole purpose of providing the author with money. Generally potboilers are of inferior literary merit, but occasionally they may have considerable distinction, as in the case of Dr. Johnson's prose tale *Rasselas*, which was written in a week to pay his mother's funeral expenses.

poulter's measure: The alternation of the alexandrine (or iambic hexameter) and the fourteener (or iambic heptameter) used widely in the sixteenth century. The term derives from the poulterer's practice of giving customers twelve eggs in the first dozen bought and fourteen in the second dozen. Poulter's measure is now rarely used; however, a modification may take the form of a stanza containing iambic trimeter in the first, second, and fourth lines and tetrameter in the third. See **short measure.**

précis: A concise summary or abstract of a work.

preface: A brief introduction to a work, stating the author's intention or commenting on the contents. Shaw's prefaces to his plays are notable examples of how such introductions may be extended into significant essays.

Pre-Raphaelites: Established in 1848 by Dante Gabriel Rossetti, William Holman Hunt, and John Everett Millais, the Pre-Raphaelite Brotherhood challenged the dominant style of painting, extolled the purity and simplicity of the Italian "primitives" (those painters preceding Raphael), and insisted on "truth of fact" in art. In their devotion to an uncompromising realism, the P.R.B. provoked attacks in the press (Dickens, for example, condemned Millais's painting "Christ in the House of His Parents"), which prompted John Ruskin to defend its aesthetic principles. The P.R.B.'s notoriety attracted supporters who joined the group, expanding it to seven members: James Collinson, a painter; Thomas Woolner, a sculptor; F. G. Stephens, an artist and critic; and Rossetti's brother, William Michael Rossetti, a poet and scholar, who edited the P.R.B.'s periodicals, *The Germ* (1850) and its successor, *Art and Poetry* (1850), which, in its total of four issues, outlined the relationships between poetry and painting as the P.R.B. saw them.

In 1852 the P.R.B. disbanded, each artist going his separate way; at this point the Brotherhood ceased and Pre-Raphaelitism, as a "movement," began. Within five years a second group of Pre-Raphaelites had formed: Rossetti, who was turning away from the naturalism of Hunt and Millais and filling his canvases with a subjective pseudo-medievalism; Edward Burne-Jones, who became Rossetti's closest disciple; the poet Algernon Charles Swinburne, whose *Poems and Ballads* (1866) created a sensation because of its verbal fleshliness; and William Morris, whose *Defense of Guenevere and Other Poems* (1858) is generally regarded as the first volume of Pre-Raphaelite poetry. As a literary term, *Pre-Raphaelite* usually suggests pictorialism, arcane religious symbolism, medievalism, archaic diction, and sensual imagery. Such imagery in the verse of Rossetti, Swinburne, and Morris provoked an attack by the Scottish critic Robert Buchanan, who published (under the pseudonym "William Maitland," which he later insisted had been added by an editor) an intemperate article entitled "The Fleshly School of Poetry" in the *Contemporary Review* (October 1871). In later years, however, Buchanan admitted that Rossetti was not an advocate or exponent of "immoral" art.

Pre-Raphaelite art and poetry had a considerable influence on the nineteenth century, particularly on the Aesthetes and Decadents, in the latter part of the century, who worshipped beauty and disdained the growing materialism of the age.

See William E. Fredeman, *Pre-Raphaelitism: A Bibliocritical Study* (1965); John Hunt, *The Pre-Raphaelite Imagination, 1848–1900* (1968); Lionel Stevenson, *The Pre-Raphaelite Poets* (1972); Harold Bloom, ed., *The Pre-Raphaelite Poets* (1986).

press numbers: See **bibliography.**

primary and secondary accent: Primary accent is the stress given to the principal syllable of a word, as in *aes / thete* or *bal / ance.* Secondary accent, on the other hand, is the stress given a syllable less heavily emphasized than the principal one, as in *el / e / va / tor,* the primary accent, in the pronunciation of the word, occuring on the first syllable, the secondary on the third.

primary bibliography: See **bibliography.**

primitivism: The notion that primitive peoples and those thought to have lived in the mythical "Golden Age" of ancient Greece were somehow superior to those living in advanced societies. Central to this view is the notion that primitive peoples lead lives closer to the primal reality of nature, hence uncorrupted by civilization. The Bible has, of course, been a significant influence in such thinking, since the Garden of Eden provides the image of an idyllic earthly paradise before the Fall of Man.

The idea of primitive man's nobility in the state of nature was first suggested by Montaigne in his essay "On Cannibals" (1580); Sir Philip Sidney's **pastoral,** *Arcadia* (1590), is one of many such works depicting a happy world of shepherds and shepherdesses; and Aphra Behn's novel *Oroonoko, or the History of the Royal Slave* (1688) develops the idea of the Noble Savage. In the eighteenth century, during the **Enlightenment,** when thinkers deplored the ills of modern society, primitivists brought "savage" peoples to England in order to demonstrate their inherent nobility as compared to the nature of its own brutalized residents. In addition, some "untutored" poets, such as Stephen Duck, the "thresher-poet," and Ann Yearsley, a milkmaid who wrote under the name of "Lactilla," achieved brief fame for their uncontaminated talent.

Primitivism in the eighteenth century was vigorously attacked by such figures as Dr. Samuel Johnson and Edmund Burke, but the idea continued to have its influence in the nineteenth century (for example, in the idealized American Indians of Cooper's novels) as well as in the twentieth century (in such novels by D. H. Lawrence as *The Plumed Serpent,* particularly in its ritualism, and *Lady Chatterley's Lover,* in the character of the earthy gamekeeper).

See Hoxie N. Fairchild, *The Noble Savage* (1928); Michael Bell, *Primitivism* (1972).

printing: See **edition.**

problem play: See **thesis play.**

proem: A preamble or introduction, especially to a speech.

prolegomenon: See **introduction.**

prolepsis: A figure of speech in which an anticipated event is referred to as though it had already happened. A notable example occurs when Hamlet, lying wounded, says to his friend, "Horatio, I am dead."

prologos: See **Greek tragedy, structure of.**

prologue: An opening section of a longer work. The prologue may perform a number of functions. The prologue to Chaucer's *Canterbury Tales,* for example, establishes the situation in which the tales will be told and characterizes the speakers. In many plays of the seventeenth and eighteenth centuries, a prologue, usually in verse, states a moral point or anticipates the theme and action. For a more restricted use of this term, see **Greek tragedy, structure of.**

propaganda play: See **thesis play.**

prose: Literary expression not marked by rhyme or by metrical regularity. Prose is the type of language used in novels, short stories, articles, etc. See **poetic prose; poetry.**

prose poem: A brief composition printed as prose but containing the elements of poetry: carefully designed rhythms, alliteration, assonance, rhyme, figures of speech, and recurrent images. The prose poem as a distinct genre first appeared in Aloysius Bertrand's *Gaspard of the Night* (1836). Baudelaire, influenced by this work, wrote *Little Poems in Prose* (1862). Later writers, such as Oscar Wilde and Amy Lowell, have written such "poems."

prosodic symbols: See the page "Abbreviations" and "Prosodic symbols" at the beginning of this volume.

prosody: The theory of versification, dealing with such matters as meter, rhyme, stanzaic patterns, etc.

prosopopoeia: See **personification.**

protagonist: In Greek drama, the first actor, who played the leading part and doubled in some minor roles. The term now refers to the most important character, usually the hero, in a play or story. See **antagonist; deuteragonist; tritagonist.**

protasis: That part of a Classical play in which the characters were introduced and the situation explained. Today, the term *protatic character* designates one who is brought on by the author only to assist in the **exposition.** In Pinero's *The Second Mrs. Tanqueray,* Misquith and Jayne, both of whom disappear after the first scene, are protatic characters.

prothalamion: A song heralding a marriage. The term was invented by the sixteenth-century poet Edmund Spenser and used as the title of one of his poems. See **epithalamion.**

proverb: A short popular saying, generally an observation or a piece of advice. Though it may be attributed to an individual, as some of the Biblical proverbs are attributed to Solomon and others, most proverbs are anonymous products of the folk.

proverbe dramatique: A term applied by Alfred de Musset (1810–57) to certain of his plays, both one-act and full-length. Each play illustrates an aphorism which forms its title. Among the best known of these are *Il ne faut jurer de rien (One Should Not Swear to Anything)* and *On ne badine pas avec l'amour (One Does Not Jest with Love).*

psalm: A song of praise to God, especially one in the Old Testament book of Psalms.

pseudo-statement: A term originated by I. A. Richards to distinguish scientific from poetic "truth." By the term *statement* Richards designates scientifically verifiable expressions of fact. Pseudo-statements, on the other hand, the kind made in poetry, are not, of necessity, verifiably true or even logically coherent; they serve, rather, to order, or organize, the reader's attitudes and emotional impulses. Such statements, Richards says, cut free of the belief we accord scientifically verifiable ones, are valuable for the psychological function they perform. Subsequently, Richards came nearer the views of those critics who believe that poetry conveys a special kind of knowledge not available elsewhere.

psychical distance: See **aesthetic distance.**

psychoanalytic criticism: The use of psychoanalytic concepts in the analysis of a work of art. Though literary critics in the Romantic era frequently regarded a literary work as an expression of the author's psyche, it was not until the late nineteenth century that a schema for analyzing psychic phenomena emerged in the writings of Sigmund Freud, who, in 1896, coined the term *psychoanalysis* to characterize the "talking cure," a therapeutic method of recovering repressed material from the unconscious.

Freud focused on the ambiguities of language as reflections of mental processes, particularly as they manifest themselves in dreams, symptoms, slips of the tongue, and puns. In addition, Freud's structural concept of the mind involved dynamic relationships that suggest confrontation: the ego mediates between the self and the outside world and between the superego (roughly equivalent to conscience) and the id (the repository of unconscious instinctual drives— often aggressive and sexual—that crave gratification).

Almost from the beginnings of psychoanalysis, the Oedipus complex (derived from the Greek myth involving Oedipus' slaying of his father and marriage with his mother) was central to Freud's developmental theory of human personality. In his application of psychoanalytic concepts to literary works, Freud suggested an unconscious Oedipal struggle in Hamlet; Freud's British disciple, Ernest Jones, expanded this insight into what remains a classic example of psychoanalytic criticism, *Hamlet and Oedipus* (1949), which interprets Hamlet's inability to kill his stepfather, Claudius, as the result of identification with him in his desire to possess Gertrude, a re-enactment of unresolved infantile desires not only in Hamlet but also in Shakespeare.

"Classical" Freudian psychoanalysis has regarded a literary work as an author's sublimation of unacceptable desires—in short, a substitute gratification. Early psychoanalytic criticism, including Freud's, analyzed characters as though they were living persons and the entire work as the expression of the author's infantile or neurotic wishes. In addition, sexual symbolism was too often rigidly employed: long, pointed objects were regularly seen as phallic; open, hollow objects, as womblike. Such "vulgar Freudian symbolism," as it has been called, was characteristic of early reductionistic tendencies in psychoanalysis.

Freud's initial views of the dream, however, have provided particularly useful concepts for the analysis of literature: the manifest content, he states, is the surface narrative, which the dreamer is likely to recall with "secondary revision" (an attempt to make coherent a seemingly incoherent story); the latent content, which requires interpretation to determine its meaning, is that which involves the "dream work"—the method of disguising forbidden wishes through such devices as condensation (two or more figures or desires fused into one) and displacement (a wish transferred from one person to another). These devices have been seen by the French psychoanalyst Jacques Lacan as analogous to **metaphor** and **metonymy** (indeed, Lacan, reinterpreting Freud, contends that the unconscious is linguistically structured, hence suitable for therapeutic dialogue and literary analysis). The telling of stories involving such methods of figurative expression and the transformation of personal experience into personal myth ("lies" revealing truths) is thus of particular interest to both literary critics and psychoanalysts. Literary critics have also been interested in Carl Gustav Jung's concept of **archetypes** in the collective unconscious as universal images embodied in dreams, myths, and literature.

Recent psychoanalytic critics, who have placed more emphasis on the writer's control in structuring an aesthetic object, have been principally inspired by Ernst Kris's *Psychoanalytic Explorations in Art* (1952), which contends that the artist regresses "in the service of the ego," an indication that ego functioning is central to the creative process and that "primary process" (that which regulates the unconscious) is subject to "secondary process" (the cognitive, rational capacity of the ego). Thus, for psychoanalytic critics, "ego-psychology" has substantially replaced the earlier "id-psychology" (with its focus on instinctual drives). The effect has been to regard the artist's creative capacity—as opposed to his personality—as "healthy" rather than neurotic.

Since the 1960's, psychoanalytic criticism has merged with such other critical modes as **feminist criticism, reader-response criticism,** and **Structuralism;** it has, moreover, been increasingly used by biographers, prompting the coinage of the term **psychobiography.**

See Frederick J. Hoffman, *Freudianism and the Literary Mind* (2nd ed., 1957); Meredith A. Skura, *The Literary Use of the Psychoanalytic Process* (1981); Elizabeth Wright, *Psychoanalytic Criticism: Theory in Practice* (1984); Bettina L. Knapp, *A Jungian Approach to Literature* (1984).

psychobiography: A biographical study concerned with the subject's psychological, even psychosexual, development. The writer of such a biography not only analyzes the circumstances of the subject's life but, in the case of literary biography, examines his writings for clues that can be interpreted—usually through the techniques of psychoanalysis—to make evident the course of his psychic existence and offer an explanation of the creative processes underlying his achievements. Few biographers have remained untouched by the work of Freud and his followers, but the type of biography here described is associated particularly with the writings of Erik H. Erikson. For an example of Erikson's work applied to a literary figure, see the pages on Bernard Shaw in "The Problem of Ego Identity," *Identity and the Life Cycle* (1959).

See Leon Edel, *Writing Lives: Principia Biographica* (1984).

psychological novel: A novel which is concerned primarily with the mental and emotional lives of its characters rather than the external events of its plot. Although there have been through the history of literature many works that have analyzed with great subtlety the internal lives of their characters (*Hamlet*, for example), Romantic subjectivity, later reinforced by the psychological researches of Freud and his successors, has led many modern writers to concentrate not so much on the ethical consequences of an action as on the motives that impelled a character to perform it. This term *psychological novel* is descriptive of content rather than form or technique and is applied to work as formally conventional as the novels of C. P. Snow and as unconventional as those of James Joyce.

See Leon Edel, *The Psychological Novel, 1900–1950* (rev. ed., 1964).

puffery: Criticism by clique or coterie. A critic may "puff," *i.e.*, overpraise, the work of a friend or someone to whom he is obligated in the expectation of receiving some suitable favor, such as similar praise of his own work, in return. The false critic of R. B. Sheridan's play *The Critic* is appropriately named Mr. Puff.

pun (paronomasia): Word play involving (1) the use of a word with two different meanings; (2) the similarity of meanings in two words spelled differently but pronounced the same; or (3) two words pronounced and spelled somewhat the same but containing different meanings. Though puns have been called "the lowest form of humor" by many, they have been used for serious purposes, as in John Donne's "Hymn to God the Father." In the following stanza, the word *done* is a pun on Donne's own name; in addition, there is a pun on *Son*, meaning both Christ and the sun:

> I have a sin of fear, that when I have spun
>   My last thread, I shall perish on the shore;
> But swear by Thy self, that at my death Thy Son
>   Shall shine as he shines now, and heretofore;
>   And, having done that, Thou hast done;
>   I fear no more.

See Jonathan Culler, ed., *On Puns: The Foundation of Letters* (1988).

purple patch: A heavily ornate passage which stands out from the writing around it. The term is regularly derogatory, implying a lack of taste in the author. For an example, see the speech in Oscar Wilde's *Salomé* in which Herod describes his treasures.

pyrrhic (dibrach): A metrical foot of two unstressed syllables. The pyrrhic foot is rarely recognized in modern scansion.

Q

Quadrivium: See **Seven Arts, the.**

quantitative verse: Verse, such as Classical Latin, based on **quantity** rather than stress. There have been attempts to write quantitative verse in English, but few have been successful.

quantity: The time needed for the pronunciation of a syllable. In Classical verse, which is based on syllable length, or quantity, rather than stress, as English verse is, a long syllable was one which contained a long vowel or a short plus two or more consonants. A long syllable was considered equal to two short ones; this relationship formed the basis of **substitution** in Classical metrics. Whether or not this regularity was characteristic of these languages as spoken is not known. Long and short syllables exist in English (compare *file* and *bet*) though our system of scanning verse does not take account of them. Just as there are various degrees of stress (we have terms for only two, **primary and secondary accent**), so there are in fact various degrees of length. It is the interactions of these various stresses and syllable lengths that make up the complexity of metrical rhythm.

quarto (abbr. 4to or 4°): 1. A book made from printer's sheets which have been folded twice to form four leaves, or eight pages. See **folio.**

2. The term also refers to the form in which many of Shakespeare's plays were printed. The size of the quarto page at that time was about 9 × 7 inches. The quarto editions of *Hamlet*, for example, published between 1603 and 1637 are referred to as First Quarto, Second Quarto, etc., or simply Q1, Q2, etc.

quatorzain: A fourteen-line poem which does not follow the strict form of the **sonnet.**

quatrain: A stanza consisting of four lines which may follow a variety of rhyme schemes. The quatrain is the commonest stanza form in English verse:

> Oh, Moon! when I look on thy beautiful face
> Careering along through the boundaries of space,
> The question has frequently come to my mind,
> If ever I'll gaze on thy glorious behind.
>   Anonymous

quiproquo: Latin: *quid pro quo,* "this for that." A misunderstanding on the part of two or more characters in a play. The misunderstanding depends upon a word or situation being interpreted differently by characters who believe that their interpretations are the same. Oliver Goldsmith's *She Stoops to Conquer,* for example, begins Act II with a *quiproquo.* The hero, invited to meet his prospective bride, arrives at her home thinking that it is an inn and that her father is the innkeeper. From that point on, a series of misunderstandings motivates the action.

R

raisonneur: A character in a play who acts as the author's spokesman. The *raisonneur,* though he may assist in resolving the plot, is not usually a central figure. He observes the other characters, regularly delivering one or more speeches in which he comments on the action and expresses the writer's views. Most commonly, he is found in such nineteenth-century **well-made plays** as Oscar Wilde's *An Ideal Husband,* in which the aristocratic Lord Goring is the *raisonneur.*

reader-response criticism: A mode of criticism stimulated since the 1970's by the theories of the German critic Hans Robert Jauss, who regards readers' responses, evolving over a period of time, as essential to a determination of meaning and value in a literary work. Critics who subscribe to this approach insist that the text is not a self-contained object (the **New Criticism** had emphasized the text's autonomy) but a reality that is partially defined by our act of perception. The philosophic basis for this view, as enunciated by such twentieth-century German philosophers as Edmund Husserl and Martin Heidegger, is called "phenomenology," involving a merging, through our consciousness, with the object we perceive. Therefore, there can never be only one "correct" meaning of a text but a vast array of possibilities; such critics as Wolfgang Iser and Stanley Fish contend, however, that the controlling text or the "informed" reader prevents gross misreadings.

In *The Act of Reading: A Theory of Aesthetic Response* (1978), Iser regards the effect on the reader, who brings individual experiences to the text, as the principal concern for the critic. Though the text controls, in part, the reader's responses, there are nevertheless "gaps" that the reader must fill in by a creative act. For example, the ironies in Swift's *Gulliver's Travels*—involving a narrator who, although seemingly rational, may at times be actually mad—require the reader's responses to actualize the work—that is, to fulfill Swift's intentions.

The concept of "affective stylistics"—as discussed by Fish in "Literature in the Reader," *Self-Consuming Artifacts* (1972)—focuses on the "psychological effects" of a text on the reader: no text is self-contained; the "meaning" of any utterance is not on the page. Since "*every linguistic experience is affecting and pressuring,*" activating the reader's consciousness, the "informed" reader's responses (including his errors) comprise the total meaning of an utterance. States Fish: "I would rather have an acknowledged and controlled subjectivity than an objectivity which is finally an illusion."

Prominent among those who employ psychoanalytic concepts in reader-response criticism have been Norman Holland and David Bleich. In *5 Readers Reading* (1975), Holland suggests that when we interpret a text, we unconsciously respond with our individual "identity themes" "to symbolize and finally replicate ourselves." In our attempt to defend ourselves against unconscious fears and wishes, we transform the work in order to relieve psychic pressures. In *Subjective Criticism* (1978), Bleich assumes that "each person's most urgent motivations are to understand himself" and that all "objective" interpretations are derived ultimately from subjective responses: therefore, the proper focus of attention lies in the relationship between stated interpretation and its subjective sources.

See Robert C. Holub, *Reception Theory: A Critical Introduction* (1984); Elizabeth Freund, *The Return of the Reader: Reader-Response Criticism* (1987).

realism: Refers to the subject matter of as well as the technique by which a literary work has been created. In theory, the realist, wishing to record life as it is, refrains from imposing a predetermined pattern (based perhaps on a philosophic orientation) upon his materials. He allows the story "to tell itself," for truth, he feels, resides in the events themselves rather than in his imagination. Free of Romantic subjectivity, realistic writing emphasizes truthfulness of detail. This "theory" of realism, however, is not to be taken without reservations, for any artist must shape the materials of his art into a form which derives from his personal vision. Nor does the adoption of an essentially realistic approach limit a writer's access to other techniques. Ibsen, for example, who is rightly considered the founder of the modern realistic drama, is, in such plays as *Ghosts*, *The Wild Duck*, and *The Master Builder*, a profoundly symbolic writer.

As a technique, realism may logically handle any subject matter, but it has chiefly been concerned with the commonplaces of everyday life and the middle and lower social classes. The American novelist and critic William Dean Howells conceived of realism as a device for depicting simple, everyday people with "work-worn, brave, kindly faces," but other realists have strenuously avoided such material in favor of more earthy narratives.

From the beginning of the "realistic movement," which dates from the mid-nineteenth century, there has been no universally accepted set of principles governing the manner or content of so-called realistic works. In French literature, the realism in the fiction of Flaubert, Balzac, and Maupassant is as different as it is in such American authors as Sherwood Anderson and John Steinbeck.

As a term, *realism* is not, of course, limited to the nineteenth and twentieth centuries, for elements may be found in such earlier works as Defoe's *Moll Flanders* and Ben Jonson's *Bartholomew Fair*. Generally, however, "realistic" handling in past works refers to the accuracy of speech and behavior with which a writer has endowed his "low" characters.

In recent years, realists have turned from their concern with accuracy of external detail to the complex workings of the mind. The device of the **stream of consciousness,** with its fidelity to the inner psychological processes of characters, has become part of much modern fiction. Such writers as Virginia Woolf and James Joyce, though not strictly speaking writers of realistic novels, have reported the flow of consciousness of their characters with such faithfulness that some critics have attacked their psychological realism as lacking in artistic selection. See **naturalism.**

See Erich Auerbach, *Mimesis: The Representation of Reality in Western Literature* (1946; English trans., 1953); Georg Lukács, *Studies in European Realism*, (1948; English trans., 1964); George J. Becker, ed., *Documents of Modern Literary Realism* (1963); Harry Levin, *The Gates of Horn: A Study of Five French Realists* (1963); Roland N. Stromberg, ed., *Realism, Naturalism and Symbolism: Modes of Thought and Expression in Europe, 1848–1914* (1968); George J. Becker, *Realism in Modern Literature* (1980).

recessive accent: In poetry, an accent which has been moved to the first syllable of a word for metrical convenience. In *Henry IV, Part I*, Hotspur, speaking of a battle, says, "But I remember when the fight was done, / When I was dry with rage and *éxtreme* toil."

recto and verso: The recto is a right-hand page in a book, the front of a leaf; the verso a left-hand page, the back of a leaf.

redaction: The editing or revising of a work for publication.

redundant verse: See **acatalectic.**

referential language: See **emotive language.**

refrain: A line or lines repeated at intervals during a poem, usually at the end of each stanza. A refrain serves many purposes aside from helping to establish the meter and tone of the poem. It may be simply a nonsense line which lets everyone join the song, as "Inky, dinky, parlez-vous." Or it may be a line which re-establishes the lyric atmosphere at the end of a stanza, as in Spenser's "Prothalamion": "Sweet Thames! run softly till I end my song." Sometimes a refrain becomes an ironic commentary, changing in tone as the stanzas change. Compare the first and last stanzas of the tragic ballad "The Cruel Brother," in which the refrain first reflects the gaiety of the courtship and then contrasts with the mournful lines describing the murdered sister:

> A gentleman came oure the sea,
>   Fine flowers in the valley
> And he has courted ladies three
>   With the light green and the yellow.
>
> . . . .
>
> Now does she neither sigh nor groan:
>   Fine flowers in the valley
> She lies aneath yon marble stone
>   With the light green and the yellow.

See **incremental repetition; repetend.**

regionalism: The representation in a body of literature, created either by a single writer or by a group, of a particular locale. In regional literature, this locale is conceived of as a subject of interest in itself, and much attention is devoted to its description. It may, in fact, become so important as to play a role in the story and influence the lives of the characters. Regional literature is generally realistic and is likely to concern itself with life in rural areas or small towns rather than urban centers. The Five Towns novels of Arnold Bennett are examples of regional literature, as are the novels of Thomas Hardy.

Renaissance: The term *Renaissance,* literally "rebirth," is at once useful and inexact. It is useful not only because it designates the period between the Middle Ages and the **Enlightenment** but also because its name suggests both the revival of interest in the writings of the Classical, pagan world and the sense of a renewal of intellectual and artistic energies, often felt to be the central characteristic of the Renaissance. But the imprecision of the term remains, even as it designates a historical epoch and describes a cultural one. As is the case with most historical periods (created by historians, at least partially as a matter of convenience), the Renaissance offers no universally accepted dates at which it can be said to begin and end; indeed, it does so at different times in different places, beginning in Italy during the later part of the fourteenth century, continuing in Western Europe during the fifteenth and sixteenth centuries, and not ending in England—where it comes late—till well into the seventeenth. Moreover, scholars have come to recognize that much of the Renaissance was deeply rooted in the Middle Ages and that the break between the two periods, if in fact such a division exists, is much less sharp than various writers (even some in the Renaissance itself) have claimed that it is.

Nevertheless, certain characteristics distinguish the burgeoning civilization of the Renaissance from the relatively stable one of the High Middle Ages. Of these none is more significant than the work of the humanists, students of the *litterae humaniores*, the writings of the ancient poets, philosophers, rhetoricians, and historians. They greatly expanded the study of Latin literature and revived that of Greek. (The spread of this new learning was facilitated by the development in the mid-fifteenth century of printing on paper by movable type.) For the humanists the study of Classical literature tended to suggest that man's existence, far from being a brief and painful preparation for the afterlife, could, through the exercise of human reason and talents, offer fulfillment in this life. The extraordinary attraction of this new learning, along with the doubts and guilts it aroused when it conflicted with traditional Christian ideals, is strikingly evoked in Marlowe's *Dr. Faustus*. Although some humanists, like Montaigne, became skeptics and even atheists, most, like Erasmus, retained their allegiance to traditional religious institutions. Whatever their divergences, they were bound together by their reverence for the ancient world.

This admiration for the Classical past had a variety of consequences in literature. It produced the imitation of Classical styles and genres and the rigid codification of "rules" supposed to have been followed by the ancients, who were held up as models of perfection. Literature was polished and enriched by what it learned from the Greek and Latin authors but sometimes hindered in its own development by the attempt to conform to its revered models. In fact, as late as the seventeenth century, Latin continued to be a literary language (even Petrarch, who helped establish literary Italian, wrote a Latin epic). Nevertheless, it is the writings of the vernacular authors—of Petrarch himself, and such writers as Boiardo, Ariosto, and Tasso in Italy; of Rabelais, Montaigne, Ronsard and the other poets of the Pléiade in France; of Cervantes, Lope de Vega, and Calderón in Spain; and the galaxy of poets and playwrights in England, including Spenser, Marlowe, Shakespeare, Jonson, and Donne—that make Renaissance literature one of the major achievements of Western culture.

Moreover, the Renaissance produced a flowering not only in learning and literature but also in the other arts. The burst of creativity in painting, sculpture, and architecture associated with the names of Michelangelo, Raphael, and Leonardo da Vinci, to name only the most eminent, remains unparalleled for achievement and influence. The production of Monteverdi's *Orfeo* at the court of Mantua in 1607 marks the most significant early step in the development of opera.

Beyond the area of the arts the expansion of commerce continued to favor the growth of social mobility, as wealth and power accrued to the mercantile classes. The Medici, for example, were a family of bankers as well as rulers. The search for new trade routes led to the discovery of the new worlds of the Americas and a new expansion of wealth and power, especially for Spain and England. In addition, the Renaissance saw at least the basis for the expansion in the knowledge of and control over the physical universe as the scientific view of the world and the scientific method of investigating it developed in the work of such men as Descartes and Bacon. And beyond the investigation of the earth was that of the heavens. Whereas the older picture of the cosmos (called Ptolemaic from its formulator, the Egyptian astronomer Ptolemy of the second century A.D.) had shown the earth stationary at the center of the universe with the other heavenly bodies rotating around it, the new Copernican view (so called from the astronomer Copernicus, 1473–1543) placed the sun in the central position and made the earth merely one of the planets rotating about it. This new vision of the universe, however, had some disquieting implications: when, for example, after making certain observations with the newly developed telescope the astonomer Galileo Galilei announced his support of the Copernican hypothesis in 1632, he was tried by the Inquisition and forced to recant.

The Church, after all, could ill afford to see the received picture of the universe further threatened at a time when the appeal of Protestantism was already dividing the allegiance of Christendom. When in the early part of the sixteenth century the Reformation made salvation a matter of the individual's direct relationship with God and discounted the mediation of the Church, it gave further impetus to the individualism that was one of the salient characteristics of the Renaissance. Though a historical movement of such complexity, so wide-ranging in time and geographical area, cannot be limited to a single defining feature, the sense of the significance of the individual personality unites such otherwise diverse phenomena as the religious thought of Luther and his followers, the braggadocio of Cellini, the humane self-examination of Montaigne, and the intense, even extravagant, passions portrayed by Marlowe, Shakespeare, and the other Elizabethan and Jacobean dramatists. Indeed, individualism remains a significant concept in the modern world, a part of its vast heritage from the Renaissance.

See W. K. Ferguson, *The Renaissance in Historical Thought* (1948); C. S. Lewis, *English Literature in the 16th Century* (1954); Paul Kristeller, *Renaissance Thought: The Classic, Scholastic, and Humanistic Strains* (rev. ed., 1961); Douglas Bush, *English Literature in the Earlier 17th Century* (2nd ed., 1962); Frederick Artz, *Renaissance Humanism 1300–1500* (1966).

repetend: Any repeated element in a poem. Sometimes this term is used as a synonym for **refrain,** but the two are usually distinguished. Whereas a refrain appears without alteration at regular intervals, a repetend is often varied and does not appear at any predetermined point. Coleridge uses repetends throughout *The Rime of the Ancient Mariner.* For example, he introduces the mariner's "glittering eye" and "skinny hand" at the beginning of the poem, and then works them into a new pattern in Part IV:

"I fear thee, ancient Mariner!
I fear thy skinny hand!

And thou art long, and lank, and brown,
As is the ribbed sea-sand.

I fear thee and thy glittering eye,
And thy skinny hand, so brown."—
Fear not, fear not, thou Wedding-Guest!
This body dropt not down.

repetition: One of the fundamental devices of art. Just as a composer repeats his themes after their development and a painter echoes the line of a figure in another part of his composition, so a writer reuses various elements within his work, for, to be satisfied, the mind demands not only the revelation of the new but also the recognition of the familiar. A sequence of novelties inevitably seems formless; it is the reappearance of something known which the mind requires before it can accept a work as a unified whole, as, in fact, a work of art. The repetitive nature of some devices, such as the **refrain** and the **repetend,** is obvious at once, but many others—**assonance, consonance, alliteration,** for example —are also based on repetition, as are indeed the rhythmical patterns of both verse and prose.

resolution: The events following the climax of a play or story; the term is used synonymously with *falling action.*

Restoration comedy: English comedy as practiced from the restoration of the monarchy (1660) to the rise of the sentimental comedy of the early eighteenth century. Restoration comedies are graceful, elaborately witty, and regularly concerned with sexuality. Set in the aristocratic Restoration world of elegant licentiousness, they usually describe the courtship and marriage of a witty heiress and a town rake. There is much raillery at the expense of age, cuckoldry, rusticity, and persons, such as the fops, who vainly attempt to imitate the manners of the charmed inner circle of true wits. In Wycherley, Restoration comedy produced a satirist of moral force, and in Congreve, a stylist of extraordinary grace. Among its other practitioners are Etherege, Vanbrugh, and Farquhar.

See Bonamy Dobrée, *Restoration Comedy, 1660–1720* (1924); John Harold Wilson, *A Preface to Restoration Drama* (1965); John Loftis, *Restoration Drama: Modern Essays in Criticism* (1966).

revenge tragedy: See **tragedy.**

revue: A theatrical presentation which, devoid of plot, consists of sketches, dances, and songs designed for amusement and frequently containing satirical commentaries on the personalities and events of the day.

rhetoric: In its most general meaning, the principles governing the use of language for effective speaking and writing. Classical theoreticians considered the study of rhetoric essential for effective oratory. To this end, such writers as Aristotle, Quintilian, and Longinus codified the theories of rhetoric, which, along with logic and grammar, became, during the Middle Ages, one of the basic studies of the Trivium. (See **Seven Arts, the.**)

The Greek Sophists at one time made rhetoric a tool for effective argumentation, regardless of the truth or validity of the viewpoint. Plato reported Socrates as saying that he thought rhetoric a superficial art, and in the dialogue *Protagoras* he reveals how the clever Sophist Protagoras argues with the aid of rhetorical devices. Because rhetoric may be used in such a manner, the term sometimes carries pejorative connotations.

rhetorical accent: See **accent.**

rhetorical figure: In general, a specific arrangement of words for rhetorical emphasis. Unlike figures of speech, such as **metaphors** and **personifications,** rhetorical figures do not alter the meanings of the words employed. For individual definitions and illustrations of some rhetorical figures, see **apostrophe; chiasmus; invocation; rhetorical question; zeugma.**

rhetorical irony: See **irony.**

rhetorical question: A question asked, not to elicit information, but to achieve a stylistic effect. Often a writer or speaker adds emphasis to a point by putting it in a question, the answer to which supports his argument. In *The Merchant of Venice*, Shylock uses this device in a speech defending his conduct:

> Hath not a Jew eyes? hath not a Jew hands, organs, dimensions, senses, affections, passions? . . . If you prick us, do we not bleed? If you tickle us, do we not laugh? If you poison us, do we not die? and if you wrong us, shall we not revenge?

Since "Yes, of course" is the answer to all of the questions preceding the climactic one, the same answer is imposed upon it by the pattern, and the speaker's point is confirmed.

rhyme: The repetition of similar or duplicate sounds at regular intervals, usually the repetition of the terminal sounds of words at the ends of lines of verse. (Since the spelling *rhyme* derives by association from *rhythm*, many prefer to use the older spelling, *rime*.) Verse has not always made use of rhyme, and some poets (*e.g.*, Milton) have spoken against it; nevertheless, rhyme is one of the most persistent of poetic devices. It calls attention to the word as sound, which we enjoy for its own sake, as opposed to the word as conveyer of meaning. It also functions as a marker, signaling the end of a rhythmical unit. When a rhythmical and a rhetorical unit coincide, the rhyme reinforces their correspondence; when they do not, the rhyme establishes, in the mind of the reader, an interaction between them. When regularly arranged, rhymes also serve to help mark stanzaic structure.

Of the various types of rhymes, some are distinguished by position, such as end rhyme—one which comes at the end of a line of verse—**internal rhyme, leonine rhyme,** and **beginning rhyme,** but most are marked by different relationships between sounds. **Eye rhymes,** however, such as *weak* and *break* depend on spelling. An eye rhyme which was once a true ear rhyme is called a "historical rhyme." Some of the commonest rhyme types are listed below:

The most usual English rhyme is variously called "true," "full," "perfect," "complete," or *rime suffisante*. In it, the final accented vowels of the rhyming words and all succeeding sounds are identical, while preceding sounds are different, as in *bake–rake*, *heaven–seven*.

A rhyme limited to a single terminal syllable is called "masculine," one that extends over two or more syllables is "feminine." The latter may be called "double rhyme" if it includes two syllables and "triple rhyme" if it includes three (though some critics do not extend the term *feminine rhyme* to include triple rhymes). The ingenuity involved in rhymes of two, and particularly of three, syllables makes them appropriate for humorous verse. In this stanza from Edward Lear's description of himself, the rhymes of the first and third lines are feminine, those of the second and fourth masculine:

> He has many friends, laymen and clerical,
>> Old Foss is the name of his cat;
> His body is perfectly spherical,
>> He weareth a runcible hat.

Rhymes that are not true rhymes may result either from the poet's ineptitude or from his desire to create a particular effect. Among the many names applied to such rhymes are "near," "slant," "oblique," "approximate," "half," and "imperfect."

Analyzed rhyme is a complex arrangement of near rhymes in the four lines of a quatrain ending, for example, thus: *pass, relief, laugh, peace.* Rhymes 1-4 and 2-3 exhibit **consonance,** while rhymes 1-3 and 2-4 exhibit **assonance.** Both of these phenomena, along with **alliteration,** are sometimes considered types of rhyme.

Apocapated rhyme is one in which the end of a word is discounted, as in *rope–hopeless.*

In broken rhyme, one of the rhyme words extends over two lines.

Identical rhyme is the recurrence of two words which have exactly the same sound but are spelled differently and carry different meanings; also called *rime riche.* In the prologue to *The Canterbury Tales*, Chaucer, using identical rhyme, describes the pilgrims:

> And specially from every shires ende
> Of Engelond to Caunterbury they wende,
> The hooly blisful martir for to *seeke,*
> That hem hath holpen when that they were *seke.*

The term *identical rhyme* also designates the use of the same word in the rhyme position two or more times, as in the limericks of Edward Lear.

Linked rhyme, a device from early Welsh verse, is formed by joining a final syllable in one line to the first sound of the following line. In these lines from "The Wreck of the Deutschland," Gerard Manley Hopkins makes use of it by "joining" the word *door* to the initial consonant of the word *drowned* to form a rhyme with *Reward:*

> Dame, at our door
> Drowned, and among our shoals,
> Remember us in the roads, the heaven-haven of the
> Reward . . .

In pararhyme, the consonants both before and after differing vowels are identical, as in *look–luck*. See **consonance, light rhyme.**

rhyme royal: A seven-line stanza in iambic pentameter with the rhyme scheme *ababbcc*. The term has been associated with King James I of Scotland, who himself used this stanza form. Others, however, had used it before him, among them Chaucer in the *Parliament of Fowls*, the "Clerk's Tale" in *The Canterbury Tales*, and in *Troilus and Criseyde*. Sometimes this stanzaic form is called the Chaucerian stanza:

> The double sorwe of Troilus to tellen,
> That was the kyng Priamus sone of Troye
> In lovynge, how his aventures fellen
> Fro wo to wele, and after out of joie,
> My purpos is, er that I parte fro ye.
> Thesiphone, thow help me for t'endite
> Thise woful vers, that wepen as I write.

Other poets who have used this form are Wyatt and Shakespeare, and in modern times William Morris and John Masefield.

rhyme scheme: The arrangement of rhymes in a unit of verse. The four-line stanza, or quatrain, for example, frequently has a rhyme scheme of *abab* (that is, the first and third lines and the second and fourth lines rhyme), though it may have such variations as *aabb* or *abcb* or *abba*. Some rhyme schemes in longer units of verse are complex, as in the **Petrarchan sonnet.**

rhythm: In language, the sense of movement attributable to the pattern of stressed and unstressed syllables in a line of prose or poetry or to the lengths of sounds in **quantitative verse.** In verse, the rhythm is determined by the metrical pattern, whereas in prose or **free verse** it is the effect of an arrangement of words more nearly approximating natural speech. A careful writer arranges his rhythms so that they intensify the expression of what is said. For different kinds of rhythm, see **falling rhythm; rising rhythm; sprung rhythm; meter.**

riddle: A puzzle generally in the form of a question, a statement involving a partial description of an object, or a comparison between two things in which only one is given. Riddles were a popular literary form in the Middle Ages and the Renaissance. Perhaps the most famous of all riddles is the one which the Sphinx presents to Oedipus: "What moves on four feet in the morning, on two at noon, and on three in the evening?" The answer, Oedipus replies, is Man: "As a child, he crawls on hands and knees; as an adult, he walks erect; and as an old man, he walks with a stick."

Riddles have always been a source of delight, and even such notable writers as Swift and Goethe have composed them.

rime couée: See **tail-rhyme stanza.**

rime riche: See **rhyme.**

rising action: The part of a play preceding the climax. See **plot.**

rising rhythm: Occurs when the stress falls on the last syllable of a foot, as in the **iamb** and the **anapest.** Most English verse is written in rising rhythm, as in the following stanza from Lewis Carroll:

> He thought / he saw / an El /ephant,
>   That practiced on a fife:
> He looked again and found it was
>   A letter from his wife.
> "At length I realize," he said,
>   "The bitterness of life!"

rocking rhythm: Occurs when the stressed syllable in a foot of verse falls between two unstressed syllables:

> Believe me, if all those endearing young charms,
> Which I gaze on so fondly today,
> Were to change by tomorrow, and fleet in my arms,
>   Like fairy-gifts fading away . . .
>   Thomas Moore

rodomontade: Vainglorious boasting, empty bragging. The term is derived from the character Rodomonte, a boastful Saracen king in Ariosto's *Orlando Furioso.*

roman à clef: A novel, often satirical, in which actual persons appear under fictitious names. Oscar Wilde and Alfred Douglas were caricatured in Robert Hichens's *roman à clef*, *The Green Carnation* (1894).

romance: Very loosely, a narrative characterized by exotic adventure rather than by the realistic depiction of character and scene usually associated with the novel. Historically, the term *romance* is applied to three distinct bodies of writing.

The Greek romances that survive intact are from the second and third centuries A.D. (*e.g.*, the *Daphnis and Chloe* of Longus) though there are older fragments. These are complicated tales of idealized lovers, separated by pirates, shipwrecks, wars, kidnappings, and other catastrophes, who somehow retain their virtue and are ultimately reunited in happiness.

In the late Middle Ages tales of love and chivalric adventure, in both verse and prose, became popular. The major sources of these romances (originally in French, later in other vernacular languages) were ancient history and literature, the Arthurian legends, and the stories that centered on Charlemagne. In the romances the stress is on the power of love, both legitimate and illegitimate, and on the chivalric virtues—courage, grace, loyalty, and honor—of an idealized court. Among the most famous of the English romances are *Sir Gawain and the Green Knight*, *Le Morte d'Arthur* of Sir Thomas Malory, and Chaucer's *Troilus and Criseyde*. The writings of Chrétien de Troyes are especially admired among the French romances, as are the *Parzival* of Wolfram von Eschenbach and the *Tristan and Isolt* of Gottfried von Strassburg among the German.

Since the nineteenth century, the term *romance* has also been used to delineate works that are predominantly exotic or adventurous, such as some of the novels of Sir Walter Scott. Hawthorne called both *The House of the Seven Gables* and *The Marble Faun* romances, and in the fiction of such American writers as Cooper, Melville, and Mark Twain such romance elements as symbolic quests and characters who are embodiments of good and evil have been distinguished.

See Moses Hadas, *A History of Greek Literature* (1950); Roger Sherman Loomis, *The Development of Arthurian Romance* (1963); Northrop Frye, "The Mythos of Summer: Romance" in *Anatomy of Criticism* (1957); Eleanor T. Lincoln, ed., *Pastoral and Ro-*

mance: Modern Essays in Criticism (1969); John Stevens, *Medieval Romance: Themes and Approaches* (1973).

romantic comedy: A play in which love is the central motive of an action that leads to a happy ending. Though the term is frequently applied to such Elizabethan plays as Shakespeare's *As You Like It*, it may with equal justification be applied to any modern play containing similar features.

romantic irony: See **irony.**

Romanticism: Because the term *Romanticism* designates a phenomenon of immense scope, embracing not only literature but politics, philosophy, and the arts generally, there has been little agreement and much confusion as to what the word means. It has, in fact, been used in so many different ways that some scholars have, in despair, suggested that it be abandoned. However, the phenomenon would not become less complex with the abandonment of the term, and there is no reason to suppose that its successor would be any clearer.

Originally, *Romanticism* referred to the characteristics of romances, or fanciful stories, whose extravagances carried pejorative connotations. But in the eighteenth century the term came to designate a kind of exotic landscape which evoked feelings of pleasing melancholy. (At this time there developed a taste for the Gothic later satirized by W. S. Gilbert, who noted "a fascination frantic / In a ruin that's romantic.") The term *Romantic* as a designation for a school of literature opposed to the Classic was first used by the German critic Friedrich Schlegel at the beginning of the nineteenth century. From Germany, this meaning was carried to England and France.

Since individual Romantics are often in conflict and since no single figure or literary school displays all the characteristics labeled "Romantic," general definitions tend to be imprecise. In addition, these "Romantic" characteristics are often discerned in men and cultural movements not usually so designated. They are not, in fact, the exclusive property of the Romantic period, the end of the eighteenth and beginning of the nineteenth centuries, but it is here that they are dominant and give identity to an era. A discussion of these characteristics will perhaps be more helpful than a strict definition.

One of the fundamentals of Romanticism is the belief in the natural goodness of man, the idea that man in a "state of nature" would behave well but is hindered by civilization. Not only the Romantic admiration for the **Noble Savage** and for the child but also the Romantic faith in the emotions springs from this belief (conversely it inspires the general distrust of the world with its commitment to "getting and spending" and more specifically the dislike of urban life and the fear of its corruptive power). If man is inherently sinful, reason must restrain his passions, but if he is naturally good, then in the appropriate environment his emotions can be trusted. They may even lead him correctly when reason fails.

The idea of natural goodness and the stress on emotion also contribute strongly to the development of Romantic individualism, the belief that what is special in a man is to be valued over what is representative, the representative often being connected with the injunctions and conventions imposed by civilized society. If a man may properly express his unique emotional self because its essence is good, he is likely to assume also that its conflicts and corruptions are a matter of great import and a source of fascination to himself and others. Hence the Romantic delights in self-analysis, the intricate examination and full exposure of the soul. Significantly, both Wordsworth (in *The Prelude*) and Byron (in *Childe Harold's Pilgrimage*), poets of notably divergent temperaments, felt the need to write long poems of self-dramatization. Moreover, the self that Byron dramatized, a projection not identical with his own personality, was especially dear to the Romantic consciousness: the outcast wanderer, heroic but accursed, often pursuing some desperate quest or expiating some recondite transgression, in the tradition of Cain, the Wandering Jew, or the Flying Dutchman. Coleridge's Mariner and Melville's Ahab are such Romantic pilgrims. (See **Byronic hero.**)

For English literature the most significant expression of a Romantic commitment to emotion occurs in Wordsworth's preface to the second edition of the *Lyrical Ballads* (1800), where he maintains that "all good poetry is the spontaneous overflow of powerful feelings." Although Wordsworth qualifies this assertion by suggesting that the poet is a reflective man who recollects his emotion "in tranquillity," the emphasis on spontaneity, on feeling, and the use of the term *overflow* mark sharp diversions from the earlier ideals of judgment and restraint.

Searching for a fresh source of this spontaneous feeling, Wordsworth rejects the Neoclassic idea of the appropriate subject for serious verse and turns to the simplicities of rustic life "because in that condition the passions of men are incorporated with the beautiful and permanent forms of nature." That interaction with nature has for many of the Romantic poets mystical overtones. Nature is apprehended by them not only as an exemplar and source of vivid physical beauty but as a manifestation of spirit in the universe as well. In "Tintern Abbey" Wordsworth suggests that nature has gratified his physical being, excited his emotions, and ultimately allowed him "a sense sublime / Of something far more deeply interfused," of a spiritual force immanent not only in the forms of nature but "in the mind of man." Though not necessarily in the same terms, a similar connection between the world of nature and the world of the spirit is also made by Blake, Coleridge, Byron, and Shelley.

In his desire to identify with a spiritual force, Romantic man often expresses the Faustian aspiration after the sublime and the wonderful, that which transcends mundane limits. Committed to change, flux rather than stasis, he longs to believe that man is perfectible, that moral as well as mechanical progress is possible. Although the burst of hope and enthusiasm that marked the early stages of the French Revolution was soon muted, its echoes lingered through much of the nineteenth century and even survive into our own. If the Romantic often sees his enemy in the successful bourgeois, the Philistine with a vested interest in social stability, political revolution is not always his goal. His admiration for the natural, the organic, which in art leads to the overthrow of the Classical rules and the development of a unique form for each work, in politics may lead him to subordinate the individual to the state and insist that the needs of the whole govern the activities of the parts.

Though these characteristics of Romanticism suggest something of its nature, they are far from exhaustive. The phenomenon is too diverse and too contradictory to be easily encompassed. As Arthur O. Lovejoy whimsically suggests, "Typical manifestations of the spiritual essence of Romanticism have been variously conceived to be a passion for moonlight, for red waistcoats, for Gothic churches . . . for talking exclusively about oneself, for hero-worship, for losing oneself in an ecstatic contemplation of nature."

See Irving Babbit, *Rousseau and Romanticism* (1919) (an anti-Romantic argument); Mario Praz, *The Romantic Agony* (1933); M. H. Abrams, ed., *English Romantic Poets: Modern Essays in Criticism* (1960); Robert F. Gleckner and Gerald E. Enscoe, eds., *Romanticism: Points of View* (1962); Northrop Frye, ed., *Romanticism Reconsidered* (1963); Shiv K. Kumar, ed., *British Romantic Poets: Recent Revaluations* (1966); Harold Bloom, ed., *Romanticism and Consciousness: Essays in Criticism* (1970); M. H. Abrams, *Natural Supernaturalism* (1971).

rondeau: One of the French fixed verse forms which is, along with the **rondel** and **roundel,** characterized by a refrain and the use of only two rhymes. In the rondeau, there are thirteen lines (fifteen if the refrains are counted as lines), usually of eight syllables, arranged in two five-line stanzas separated by a three-line stanza. The refrain, which is the first half of the opening line, is repeated at the ends of the second and third stanzas. The rhyme scheme, with "R" as refrain, is *aabba aabR aabbaR*.

> "To Ethel"
> (Who wishes she had lived—
> "In teacup-times of hood and hoop,
> Or while the patch was worn.")
>
> "In teacup-times!" The style of dress
>   Would suit your beauty, I confess;
> BELINDA-like, the patch you'd wear;
> I picture you with powdered hair,—
> You'd make a charming Shepherdess!
>
> And I—no doubt—could well express
> SIR PLUME'S complete conceitedness,—
>   Could poise a clouded cane with care
>   "In tea-cup times!"
>
> The parts would fit precisely—yes:
> We should achieve a huge success!
>   You should disdain, and I despair,
>   With quite the true Augustan air

> But . . . could I love you more, or less,—
> "In teacup-times"?
>   Austin Dobson

rondeau redoublé: A fixed form of verse more complex than the ordinary **rondeau** (see above). It consists of six quatrains on two rhymes. Each line of the first quatrain is used in order as the final line of the four succeeding quatrains. The last quatrain is followed by a refrain which consists of the first half of the opening line: *abab, baba, abab, baba, abab, babaR.*

rondel: One of the French fixed forms of verse, the rondel consists of thirteen lines (fourteen if the second line of the refrain is repeated at the end) divided into three stanzas. The first two lines are the same as the seventh and eighth and are duplicated again in the thirteenth and fourteenth (if it appears). The scheme is *abba, abab, abbaa(b).*

> Beside the idle summer sea
> And in the vacant summer days,
> Light Love came fluting down the ways,
> Where you were loitering with me.
>
> Who has not welcomed, even as we,
> That jocund minstrel and his lays
> Beside the idle summer sea
> And in the vacant summer days?
>
> We listened, we were fancy-free;
> And lo! in terror and amaze
> We stood alone—alone at gaze
> With an implacable memory
> Beside the idle summer sea.
>   W. E. Henley

rondelet: A brief poem in a fixed form consisting of five lines on two rhymes in a single stanza. After the second and fifth lines, the first part of the opening lines appears as a refrain, thus: *abRabbR.*

round character: See **flat and round characters.**

roundel: Although this term is sometimes used as a synonym for both **rondeau** and **rondel,** it is often limited to a variation on the rondeau developed by Swinburne. The Swinburne roundel consists of three stanzas of three lines each on two rhymes. At the end of the first and third stanzas is a refrain consisting of the first part of the first line, which may rhyme with the second line. The arrangement of rhymes is *abaR bab abaR* ("R" is the refrain). In describing it Swinburne used the form of the roundel itself:

> A roundel is wrought as a ring or a starbright sphere,
> With craft of delight and with cunning of sound unsought,
> That the heart of the hearer may smile if to pleasure his ear
>   A roundel is wrought.
>
> Its jewel of music is carven of all or of aught—
> Love, laughter, or mourning—remembrance of rapture or fear—
> That fancy may fashion to hang in the ear of thought.
>
> As a bird's quick song runs round, and the hearts in us hear
> Pause answer to pause, and again the same strain caught,
> So moves the device whence, round as a pearl or tear,
>   A roundel is wrought.

roundelay: 1. A short, simple song with a refrain; also the musical setting of such a song or a dance based on it.

2. Loosely, any of the fixed forms using a refrain, such as the **rondeau, rondel,** etc.

rubaiyat: From Arabic: *rubai*, "quatrain." A collection of four-line stanzas, or quatrains, as in FitzGerald's translation of the *Rubáiyát of Omar Khayyám*.

rune: 1. From Anglo-Saxon: *rūn*, "secret" or "mystery." A letter of the ancient Germanic alphabet, based perhaps on the Greek or Roman, dating from the third century A.D. Carved on horns, weapons, and amulets, runes acquired magical power and were used in incantations and in healing. Runic writing may be seen in the verse of the Anglo-Saxon poet Cynewulf, who placed in certain of his poems a series of words in runic characters, the first letters of which spelled out his own name. Thus, a rune has meant secret writing.

2. A Finnish or, loosely, an ancient Scandinavian poem. (From *runco*, "poem" or "canto.")

running rhythm: Used by Gerard Manley Hopkins in the preface to *Poems* (1918), the term *running rhythm* refers to a rhythm measured by feet of two or three syllables, aside from imperfect feet at the beginning or end of the line. Each foot contains a principal accent or stress, the remaining part consisting of one or two unaccented syllables called "the slack." The term *running rhythm* is synonymous with *common rhythm*, the usual rhythm of English verse, as opposed to **sprung rhythm.** See **falling rhythm; rising rhythm; rocking rhythm.**

run-on line: A line of verse which continues into the following line without a grammatical break. Enjambement, the running on of such lines, is encountered frequently in English poetry. Byron, utilizing the run-on line, defended himself in the following couplet:

> I say no more than hath been said in Dante's
> Verse, and by Solomon and by Cervantes.

Russian Formalism: The work of two groups of Russian linguists and literary critics, the Moscow Linguistic Circle (founded in 1915) and the Society for the Study of Poetic Language (founded in St. Petersburg in 1916). The initial letters of the latter group's name, transposed from the Cyrillic, form the acronym OPOYAZ, often used as a general term for the movement, which included among its members Viktor Shklovsky, Boris Eichenbaum, Roman Jakobson, Boris Tomashevsky, and Yury Tynyanov. The Formalists (some of whose views anticipated, but did not influence, the **New Criticism**) rejected the idea that literature could be understood through the study of such extraliterary matters as philosophical influences, historical and sociological backgrounds, or biographical circumstances and maintained instead that it was a self-contained enterprise governed by its own laws and susceptible to scientific investigation. This quest for the *literaturnost*, "literariness," of literature and consequent deemphasis of its social substance brought the Formalists into conflict with the Soviet authorities and led to their suppression in 1930.

In examining the work of literary art, the Formalists placed the emphasis not on its content, its presentation or imitation of reality, but on its form, the language and structure of the work itself. Rejecting then current ideas that emphasized imagery as a poetic mode of thought and economy of perception as the core of the aesthetic experience, Shklovsky, the group's leading theorist, argued that imagery was not superior to other techniques and was not a way of thinking but a way of making an impression; moreover, he suggested that poetic language was made more special or difficult precisely to impede understanding. Ordinary habits of perception, Shklovsky said, deadened one's sense of life and thus diminished, even obliterated its value. To reintroduce the lost freshness in the apprehension of reality was the purpose of art, which combated the anesthetizing habituation induced by mundane experience through a "defamiliarizing" of the world.

This *ostranenie*, or the "making strange" of things, was accomplished in literature by using language different from that of ordinary life. The various linguistic devices of literature extended and made more difficult the vitalizing process of perception, which became the artistic goal in itself. Literature was not a way of knowing an object but a way of devising a vision of it. In poetry this aim was accomplished through "roughened" language, in prose through the treatment of **point of view** and the arrangement of **plot** (as opposed to the mere sequence of events in the story) as well as through style. Literary history, for the Formalists, was not a matter of the inheritance of the past but of the struggle to achieve freshness; it was less the expression of new content than the achievement of new form.

The most influential work on prose narrative done in Russia at this time was by a figure generally associated with the Formalists, Vladimir Propp, a professor of philology at Leningrad University. Noting that previous attempts to classify **fairy tales** by such features as theme or character type had been unsuccessful, Propp, in his *Morphology of the Folktale* (1928), proposed a system based on functional elements, thus anticipating a central aspect of **Structuralism**. (Propp's influence was transmitted by Jakobson, a colleague of Lévi-Strauss at the New School in New York during World War II.) Although such tales had an extraordinary variety of surface detail and many different personages, Propp pointed out that these personages performed very few significant acts, or functions. By examining a body of Russian fairy tales, Propp was able to suggest that the functions of the characters (regardless of the personality involved) were the stable elements in these tales, that there were only a small number of such functions, that they always occurred in the same sequence (although not all were present in every tale), and that all fairy tales had one type of structure. Since Propp's detailed analysis of this material emphasized its abstract, structural elements rather than its social content, his work was no more acceptable to the Soviet authorities than that of the Formalist critics, and after 1930 Propp's work was suppressed as well.

See Victor Erlich, *Russian Formalism: History–Doctrine* (1955; rev. ed., 1965); Lee T. Lemon and Marion J. Reis, eds., *Russian Formalist Criticism: Four Essays* (1965); Ladislav Matejka and Krystyna Pomorska, eds., *Readings in Russian Poetics: Formalist and Structuralist Views* (1971); Fredric Jameson, *The Prison House of Language* (1972).

S

saga: A medieval Icelandic or Scandinavian prose narrative involving a famous hero or family or the heroic exploits of kings and warriors. Until the twelfth century, sagas were transmitted orally; in those extant, the authorship is often unknown, the style simple and impersonal. Later writers have attempted at times to imitate the narrative form of the saga. For the *Saga of King Olaf,* for example, Longfellow derived material from the notable saga *Heimskringla.*

Sapphic ode: As practiced by Sappho, an ode written in regular stanzas. The term is sometimes used synonymously with **Horatian ode.**

Sapphics: A quatrain utilizing a meter derived from the Greek poet Sappho. There are eleven syllables in the first three verses and five in the fourth. The verse pattern of the first three lines, in which the fourth and eleventh syllables may be long or short, is —ᵁ|—ᵁ|—ᵁᵁ|—ᵁ|—ᵁ; that of the fourth, which admits variation in the final syllable, is —ᵁᵁ|—ᵁ. An example of a Sapphic stanza is taken from Swinburne's poem "Sapphics":

All the night sleep came not upon my eyelids,
Shed not dew, nor shook nor unclosed a feather,
Yet with lips shut close and with eyes of iron
   Stood and beheld me.

sarcasm: Bitter, derisive expression, involving **irony** as a device, whereby what is stated is the opposite of what is actually meant. In such a statement as "Oh, Hotchkiss, you're unquestionably a genius," the speaker can, by employing the proper intonation, indicate that in reality Hotchkiss is a fool.

satire: In literature, the ridicule of any subject—an idea, or institution, an actual person or type of person, or even mankind in general—to lower it in the reader's esteem and make it laughable. Though a satirist may be attacking a rival or personal enemy (as Dryden did in *MacFlecknoe*, where he castigated the playwright Thomas Shadwell), he will usually claim to be—and indeed often will be—ridiculing some representative vice for the general benefit of mankind. Thus, referring to his own work, Swift claims in his "Verses on the Death of Dr. Swift" that "malice never was his aim" and says, "His satire points at no defect, / But what all mortals may correct."

    Whatever its goal, whether destruction or reform or both, the satiric impulse, which has remained strong from Classical times to the present, is so widespread that it infuses many works not primarily satires. In *The Importance of Being Earnest*, for example, which a critic has gracefully described as "a sort of sublime farce," Oscar Wilde casts, from time to time, a sharp satiric eye on the vanities of Victorian society, as when the languidly witty Algernon notes of a recently widowed lady, "I hear her hair has turned quite gold from grief." But most of the *The Importance* is not satiric; here and elsewhere satire shades off into other kinds of comedy. (The boundaries are often difficult to distinguish.) It is the treatment and attitude rather than the subject matter that mark the presence of satire. For instance, when Ben Jonson in *Volpone* presents the figure of Corbaccio, he fiercely ridicules the greed and vanity of the frail old man who foolishly thinks he will outlive those who are younger. But when Falstaff, fat and old, exclaims while robbing a group of travelers, "They hate us youth," the satiric element is slight or nonexistent; Falstaff's fantasy of himself as a dashing young bandit is so good-humored and self-knowing that, instead of criticizing his vanity, we prefer to share vicariously his momentary triumph over age and girth.

But even within the compass of satire there is a considerable range of tone from restrained mockery to violent denunciation. The Roman poet Horace, scoffing gently at man's foibles, is amused rather than sternly indignant, whereas his countryman Juvenal, severe in his reaction to man's vices, expresses his moral displeasure with trenchant force. The former type of satire has come to be known as Horatian, the latter as Juvenalian. In Swift's *Gulliver's Travels* those sections of the voyage to Lilliput in which Swift gently teases the vanities of the court exemplify Horatian satire, whereas those passages of the voyage to Brobdingnag in which the King fiercely ridicules human cruelty and destructiveness are Juvenalian.

Not only is satire wide-ranging in tone, but it appears in many different kinds of verse, prose, and drama. As a result, it is difficult to define specific satiric forms. Nevertheless, two such forms can be distinguished, though each admits of much variation. One of these is called the "formal verse satire" (or "Lucilian satire," from its originator, the Roman poet Lucilius) and was the sort practiced by Horace, Juvenal, and their imitators. It is a poem of some length involving a "frame" story (see **story within a story**) in which the Speaker, or Satirist, encounters a second figure, the *Adversarius*, who impels him to his satirical attack on vice or foolishness. The second form is the Menippean satire, also called "Varronian satire," from, respectively, the Greek philosopher and satirist Menippus and his Roman follower Varro. The contemporary critic Northrop Frye offers, as an example of the type, Robert Burton's *Anatomy of Melancholy* (1621). Frye characterizes this form as a prose work (though this limitation has been disputed) marked by "a greater variety of subject matter and a strong interest in ideas." In the course of a loosely developed narrative there often occurs a banquet or other gathering at which the characters, representatives of various attitudes, debate with each other and expose their ideas to ridicule. Examples of the form are as diverse as the *Satyricon* of Petronius, Rabelais's *Gargantua and Pantagruel, Gulliver's Travels,* and Aldous Huxley's *Point Counter Point.*

For discussion of related subjects, see **burlesque; invective; lampoon; wit.**

See also Ian Jack, *Augustan Satire* (1952); James Sutherland, *English Satire* (1958); Robert C. Elliott, *The Power of Satire* (1960); John Russell and Ashley Brown, eds., *Satire: A Critical Anthology* (1967); Ronald Paulson, ed., *Satire: Modern Essays in Criticism* (1971).

satyr play: In Greek drama, a comic afterpiece concerned with animals or satyrs, creatures half man and half goat. The satyr play developed from phallic celebrations in honor of Dionysus. In the great age of Greek tragedy, the satyr play, the fourth play of a tetralogy, provided comic relief after the seriousness of the preceding three tragedies. Eventually, retained only by convention, it was transferred to the beginning of the performance. The only extant satyr plays are Sophocles' *Ichneutai* (which survives in fragmentary form) and Euripides' *Cyclops.*

scald: An ancient Scandinavian bard or court singer. See **scop.**

scansion: The analysis of the metrical patterns of verse. Scansion includes the arrangement of accented and unaccented syllables into metrical feet and the grouping of lines according to the number of feet. It also includes the classifying of stanzas according to their rhyme schemes and the number of lines they contain. When a line deviates awkwardly from the basic metrical scheme of a poem, we say that it does not scan. However, a poem in which all lines adhere strictly to a theoretical metrical scheme is rare, for strict metrical regularity is monotonous, and a system of scansion simple enough for practical use cannot adequately reflect the subtleties of verse rhythm. Below is a stanza from Lewis Carroll's "Father William," with the scansion marked.

"You are old, / Father Wil / liam," the young / man said,
  "And your hair / has become / very white;
And yet / you inces / santly stand / on your head—
  Do you think / at your age, / it is right?"

The rhythm of the quatrain is anapestic with iambs at the end of the first line and the beginning of the third. Tetrameters alternate with trimeters thus: $a^4b^3a^4b^3$. Scansion is sometimes a matter of individual judgment, but these lines present no special difficulty. See **meter; prosodic symbols.**

scenario: A plot outline of a theatrical work, giving the order of scenes and the characters involved.

scene: Usually limited to drama, the term *scene* refers to a division of the action within an act, though in some plays only scene divisions are indicated. Various conventions have determined the marking of scenes. The French classical playwrights, for instance, began and concluded scenes by the entrances and exits of characters. The Elizabethans, on the other hand, inconsistent in their practice of marking acts and scenes, sometimes omitted all divisions or, like Ben Jonson, indicated new scenes when there was a new grouping of characters. Many editors of Shakespeare's plays have indicated new scenes with successive changes in a play's locale. (It should be noted that at times the change of locale is assumed, for the text may not indicate a setting for the action.)

In the modern theatrical performance scene divisions may be marked by the use of the curtain, which is lowered at the conclusion of the scene to indicate a change in either time or locale.

scène à faire: French for **obligatory scene.**

school plays: Plays influenced by Roman comedy, performed in schools and colleges during the early sixteenth century in England. As part of the revival of interest in Roman drama, English secondary schools and colleges presented for their own enlightenment and enjoyment the comedies of Terence and Plautus. Occasionally the court or eminent persons might invite the school to perform before them. Soon original plays, based on Classical models, appeared in English and Latin. The earliest extant school play in English, *Ralph Roister Doister*, written by Nicholas Udall while headmaster of Eton (1534–41), follows its Roman predecessors in division of acts and scenes, **unities** of time and place, dramatic motivation, and organization of plot.

Some critics have suggested that the techniques of Senecan tragedy and Roman comedy were important influences on later Elizabethan writers who, as students, had been acquainted with Classical drama in the schools.

science fiction: Novels and stories dealing, usually in a speculative manner, with the achievements of science. At its simplest, science fiction consists of tales of adventure set on other planets instead of more conventional locales, but it can serve as the medium for social comment, as in Arthur C. Clark's *Childhood's End*, or theological speculation, as in C. S. Lewis's *Out of the Silent Planet*. Among the "classic" writers of science fiction are Jules Verne and H. G. Wells.

See Brian W. Aldiss, *Billion Year Spree: The True History of Science Fiction* (1973).

scop: An Anglo-Saxon minstrel. His function was to entertain at the court with songs, either traditional or composed by himself, of heroic deeds.

secentismo: A term used to characterize the bombastic, flamboyant style of the seventeenth-century Italian poet Marino and his followers; used synonymously with **Marinism.** See **Gongorism.**

secondary accent: See **primary and secondary accent.**

secondary bibliography: See **bibliography.**

seer: See *vates*.

semantics: 1. That branch of linguistics which deals with the meanings of words and especially with historical changes in those meanings.

2. The study of the relations between signs (and especially words, or verbal symbols), their meanings, and the actions—both mental and physical—evoked by them. Originally, semantics was concerned with the scientific rather than the imaginative use of language, but some theories of literature as a type of symbolic activity have been based on or influenced by semantics. One of the most notable of these is found in I. A. Richards's *Principles of Literary Criticism* (1925). See **semiology/semiotics.**

semiology/semiotics: The study of signs, not only in such communication modes as language or traffic lights but also in cultural and social behavior. As the critic Roland Barthes has shown, especially in his *Mythologies*, clothes, advertisements, sports activities, and many other objects and forms of behavior are thus systems of "signs" to be interpreted by those who understand their cultural implications. The turn-of-the-century American philosopher Charles Sanders Peirce distinguished various classes of signs on the basis of their differing relationships to what they signified in the study he named "semiotic." But it was the Swiss linguist Ferdinand de Saussure, calling his study of signs "semiology," whose work has been most directly influential in **Structuralism** and **deconstruction**. The terms *semiotics* and *semiology* have come to be used interchangeably.

sense: See **four meanings of a poem.**

sensibility: For most of the eighteenth century, a man of sensibility, a quality supposed to be characteristic of all persons of virtue and breeding, was one who possessed a sympathetic heart, a quick responsiveness to the joys and sorrows of others, and a propensity toward the shedding of compassionate tears. The doctrine of sensibility, a reaction against the seventeenth-century emphasis on reason and the Hobbesian theory of the innate selfishness of man, was founded on the concept of man as inherently benevolent and sympathetic. Many of its manifestations, which would today be described as expressions of **sentimentality**, were criticized in their own time (see Jane Austen's *Sense and Sensibility*). Sensibility carried to excess is sometimes distinguished by the term *sentimentalism*.

Today the term *sensibility* suggests highly developed emotional and intellectual apprehension and particularly a responsiveness to aesthetic phenomena. With varying shades of meaning, this word has been used by a number of the **New Critics** to describe qualities of the temperaments which produce or appreciate poetry. See **dissociation of sensibility; sentimental comedy; sentimentality; sentimental novel.**

sentimental comedy: In the early eighteenth century in England, a type of play that emphasized the distresses of middle-class characters in order to evoke the audience's sympathies. Also called the "drama of sensibility," it not only ends happily but depicts good and bad characters with extraordinary simplicity. The hero may, consequently, be absolutely magnanimous, always acting from a sense of honor, and acutely attuned to the sensibilities of others, including those on lower social levels.

These specific elements of sentimental comedy developed from both theatrical and social changes at the end of the seventeenth century.

As part of a reaction to the "debauchery" of some **Restoration drama,** Jeremy Collier's *Short View of the Immorality and Profaneness of the English Stage* (1698), a work which had considerable influence in bringing about changes in taste, attacked what Collier considered the moral improprieties of English drama in the previous age. Moreover, the rising middle class brought with it a new audience for the theater. To cater to the respectable bourgeoisie, playwrights such as Richard Steele and later Hugh Kelley (*False Delicacy,* 1768) and Richard Cumberland (*The West Indian,* 1771) composed plays which stimulated the tears of their spectators by portraying virtue, first in distress but eventually triumphant. See **sensibility.**

See Arthur Sherbo, *English Sentimental Drama* (1957).

sentimentality: "One must have a heart of stone," said Oscar Wilde, "to read the death of Little Nell without laughing." To the critical intelligence, the tears induced by the demise of the angelic child of *The Old Curiosity Shop* seem excessive, although sorrow, and even tears, at the actual death of a beloved child are hardly inappropriate. The emotion evoked by Little Nell's death, however, appears uncalled for because she is not a child at all; she is so perfect, so angelic, so impossibly good as to be unreal, mechanical rather than human. The critical reader is thus presented with the absurd spectacle of an adult weeping over the death of a doll.

The suspension of the activities of the intelligence, of the powers of ethical and intellectual judgment, is the basis of sentimentality. With these powers in suspension, the reader may accept the sentimentalist's simplified view, usually one in which humanity appears as essentially virtuous (see **sensibility**), and consequently luxuriates in an outpouring of emotion unimpeded by thought.

When, however, a writer presents a sentimental character in a work not designed to elicit floods of emotion, he may wish to evoke in his reader an ethical judgment. In Shakespeare's *Richard II*, Richard, luxuriating in the sensations of the moment, is sentimental, but the play is not, for the spectacle of a weak, ineffectual monarch surrounded by forces he cannot cope with evokes not tears but judgment. Richard is not without sympathy, but it comes about not through an appeal to the spectator's shallow, uncomplicated emotions; it is due, rather, to an appreciation of Richard's eloquence and sensitivity. He engages the spectator's feelings but does not escape his censure.

In eighteenth-century England, when **sentimental comedy** and the **sentimental novel** stimulated the tears of their spectators and readers, emotional expression was considered a manifestation of benevolence. To some extent, sentimentality is today still considered an indication of gentleness, though the term itself has acquired pejorative connotations. In many motion pictures, television "soap operas," and much popular fiction, sentimentality is an important ingredient for those who enjoy the self-indulgent emotionalism.

See Fred Kaplan, *Sacred Tears: Sentimentality in Victorian Literature* (1987).

sentimental novel: In eighteenth-century England, a narrative designed to evoke the sympathies of the reader by demonstrating that unflagging adherence to morality and honor leads to rewards and that a flood of emotion indicates a kind heart. Like **sentimental comedy**, the sentimental novel appealed to the new middle classes, who believed that expression of feeling was a manifestation of virtue. Sensitive to what his readers desired, Samuel Richardson, in *Pamela, or Virtue Rewarded* (1740), portrayed the struggles of a servant girl to remain virtuous in the face of repeated attempts on her honor. Other notable novels of sensibility, as they are also called, are Goldsmith's *The Vicar of Wakefield* (1766) and Henry Mackenzie's *The Man of Feeling* (1771). See **sensibility.**

septenary: A line of seven metrical feet, so called from a verse in Latin prosody. See **fourteener; heptameter.**

septet: A poem or stanza of seven lines. The most common seven-line stanza form is the **rhyme royal.**

serenade: A song written to be sung at night beneath a lady's window and, by extension, a poem in imitation of such a song, as Shelley's "Indian Serenade."

sestet (sextet): A poem or stanza of six lines. The term is often used to designate the second part of the **Petrarchan sonnet.**

sestina: One of the more complicated of the French fixed forms of verse, the sestina originated in medieval Provence. It has six unrhymed stanzas, in which the terminal words of each line are repeated in varying orders, followed by a tercet (a unit of three lines), which may include three of the terminal words or all six, used two to a line. In the diagram below, each letter represents the terminal word of a verse and each line a stanza:

```
a b c d e f
f a e b d c
c f d a b e
e c b f a d
d e a c f b
b d f e c a
  e c a
```

The form has been used by Dante and Petrarch and in English by such poets as Swinburne (who introduced rhyme and varied the word order), Kipling, Pound, and Auden.

setting: The time and place in which the action of a story or play occurs. In the theater, the word *setting* may refer to the physical appurtenances of a production, the scenery and properties, or it may refer to the scenery alone.

Seven Arts, the: In the Middle Ages the seven liberal arts consisted of three studies—Latin grammar, logic, and rhetoric (including oratory)—called the Trivium, which led to the A.B. degree in four years; and the Quadrivium, consisting of four studies—arithmetic, geometry, astronomy, and music—which led to the M.A. degree in three years.

sextet: see **sestet.**

Shakespearean sonnet: A poem of fourteen lines in iambic pentameter divided into three quatrains and a concluding couplet, also called the English sonnet. The rhyme scheme is generally *abab, cdcd, efef, gg,* or *abba, cddc, effe, gg.* Developed by Sir Thomas Wyatt and the Earl of Surrey during the first half of the sixteenth century, the Shakespearean sonnet derives its name from its greatest practitioner. Like many other English sonneteers, Shakespeare used the final couplet to express the central theme of the poem:

> Weary with toil, I haste me to my bed,
> The dear repose for limbs with travel tired;
> But then begins a journey in my head
> To work my mind, when body's work's expir'd:
> For then my thoughts—from far where I abide—
> Intend a zealous pilgrimage to thee,
> And keep my drooping eyelids open wide,
> Looking on darkness which the blind do see:
> Save that my soul's imaginary sight
> Presents thy shadow to my sightless view,
> Which, like a jewel hung in ghastly night,
> Makes black night beauteous and her old face new.
> Lo! thus, by day my limbs, by night my mind,
> For thee, and for myself no quiet find.

See **Miltonic, Petrarchan,** and **Spenserian sonnets.**
See Patrick Cruttwell, *The English Sonnet* (1966).

shaped poem: See *carmen figuratum.*

short couplet: A tetrameter couplet, usually either iambic or trochaic, such as the following:

> The rabbit has a charming face:
> Its private life is a disgrace.
> I really dare not name to you
> The awful things that rabbits do.
>   Anonymous

Couplets such as these, which contain eight syllables to the line, may also be called "octosyllabic couplets."

short measure (s.m.): A quatrain, rhyming either *abab* or *abcb,* in which the first, second, and fourth lines are iambic trimeter and the third iambic tetrameter. The short measure may be formed as a variation on the **hymnal stanza** or by the **poulter's measure** written as a quatrain.

short novel: A prose narrative briefer than the novel but longer than the short story. It combines the concentrated focus of the latter with at least some of the novel's expansiveness in developing character and theme. It is also called the "novelette" and occasionally the **novella;** Henry James referred to it by the French term *nouvelle*. Distinguished examples of the short novel are *Daisy Miller* and *The Beast in the Jungle*, by James, and *Heart of Darkness*, by Joseph Conrad.

short short story: A term which may be applied to any particularly brief **short story** but which is usually used to designate a sketch of a character or incident which is both short in length and simple in form.

short story: A prose narrative briefer than the short novel, more restricted in characters and situations, and usually concerned with a single effect. Unlike longer forms of fiction, the short story does not develop character fully; generally, a single aspect of personality undergoes change or is revealed as the result of conflict. Within this restricted form, there is frequently concentration on a single character involved in a single episode. The climax may occur at the very end and need not involve a **denouement,** though many other arrangements are possible. Because of limited length, the background against which the characters move is generally sketched lightly.

American writers since Poe, who first theorized on the structure and purpose of the short story, have paid considerable attention to the form. O. Henry, for example, popularized the type of climax called the "surprise ending," involving an ironic reversal of expectation. Other writers of short stories, particularly those influenced by late-nineteenth-century **naturalism,** have emphasized the sleazy realities and sordid truths of life. In some later works, interest in the inner psychological processes of character has reduced action to a minimum. Many distinguished writers such as D. H. Lawrence, Katherine Mansfield, and Ernest Hemingway have made considerable reputations as short-story writers.

See Frank O'Connor, *The Lonely Voice: A Study of the Short Story* (1963).

signature: In printing, the original printer's sheet with four or more pages printed on it. When folded and bound, this forms a section of a book. The term *signature* can also refer to a mark placed so that it will appear at the bottom of the first of the pages formed from a single sheet and constitute a guide to the bookbinder as to the order in which these sections, or signatures, are to be bound.

simile: An expressed comparison between two unlike objects, usually using *like* or *as*. "Tom is as ugly as Bill" is a simple comparison, but "Tom is as ugly as sin" is a simile. This stanza from Burns is built around a pair of similes:

> O, my luve is like a red, red rose
>   That's newly sprung in June.
> O, my luve is like the melodie
>   That's sweetly played in tune.

See **epic simile; metaphor.**

sirventes: A type of Provençal lyric verse written to satirize political figures or personal foes or to instruct readers morally. It had no fixed form.

Skeltonic verse: A rough, doggerel-like verse by, or in the manner of, John Skelton (ca. 1460–1529). Skelton's verse, called "tumbling verse" by James VI of Scotland, is composed, for the most part, in short lines with two or three accents and an indefinite number of syllables. These lines rhymed in irregular groups. Below is part of Skelton's "To Mistress Margaret Hussey":

> Merry Margaret, as midsummer flower,
> Gentle as falcon or hawk of the tower,
> With solace and gladness,
> Much mirth and no madness,
> All good and no badness;
> So joyously,
> So maidenly,
> So womanly,
> Her demeaning;
> In every thing
> Far far passing
> That I can indite
> Or suffice to write
> Of merry Margaret, as midsummer flower,
> Gentle as falcon or hawk of the tower.

sketch: A brief story, play, or essay not as fully developed as the

typical examples of these genres. Among the commonest types
are the character sketch, a short description of an interesting
personality, and the sketch composed for a revue, a simple play-
let satirizing some topical trend or event. A group of short pieces
by Dickens are collected under the title *Sketches by Boz*.

slack, the: In a foot of verse, the unaccented syllable or syllables.
In an anapest such as *contrădict*, the slack consists of the first
two syllables.

slant rhyme: See **rhyme.**

slapstick: Low comedy characterized by physical action, such as the
throwing of custard pies. Originally, a slap-stick was a cudgel
made of two flat pieces of wood attached to a handle so that
when a comedian, such as Harlequin of the *commedia dell'arte*,
used it on the buttocks of one of his fellows, a sharp report was
heard.

slice of life: French: *tranche de vie*. This phrase is used to describe
the work of Zola and other practitioners of **naturalism.** It implies
that the writer has simply exhibited a chunk of life, raw and
bleeding, without having made any effort to select his materials
or arrange them. Since no works so composed exist, the term is
better considered an appellation than a description.

s.m.: Abbreviation for **short measure.**

socialist realism: The techniques of traditional nineteenth-century
narrative or dramaturgy combined with themes and attitudes
sympathetic to the socialist cause, in particular as they have been
imposed upon writers by the state literary establishments in the
Soviet Union, especially during the Stalinist era, and in other
communist countries.

sock: See **buskin.**

Socratic irony: See **irony.**

soliloquy: An extended speech in which a character alone onstage
expresses his thoughts. (Since he is by himself, what he says is
presumed to be true, or at least sincere.) A soliloquy may reveal
the private emotions of the speaker, as, for example, Hamlet's

"To be or not to be" and "How all occasions do inform against me"; or it may, often simultaneously, give information directly to the audience and display character, as does Richard III's opening speech, "Now is the winter of our discontent." In the Greek and Roman drama, the soliloquy, though it occurs, is not common. The playwrights of the Elizabethan theater used it regularly and brought the device to its expressive height. Although the modern theater, limited for the most part by the conventions of realism, has made little use of the soliloquy, an example may be found at the opening of W. H. Auden's *The Ascent of F6*.

song: Any poem, even though there is no intention of its being set to music, may be called a song. (See, for example, Kipling's "Song of the Galley-Slaves.") However, this term, which may also designate poetry in general, usually refers to a poem in a regular metrical pattern designed to be sung.

sonnet: A verse form containing fourteen lines, in English usually iambic pentameter, and a complicated rhyme scheme. The sonnet, developed in Italy in the early thirteenth century, was one of the favorite forms of Dante *(Vita Nuova)* and Petrarch, whose sequence of sonnets to the lady whom he called Laura established the conventions of much Renaissance love poetry. In the first part of the sixteenth century, the form appeared in English in the work of Sir Thomas Wyatt. Later developed by the Earl of Surrey, it was used by most of the major Elizabethan poets, such as Spenser, Sidney, Daniel, Drayton, and Shakespeare. After Milton, the form ceased for a time to be popular but was revived by the Romantics and has been much used since. For discussions of various sonnet types, see **Miltonic, Petrarchan, Shakespearean,** and **Spenserian sonnets.**

See John Fuller, *The Sonnet* (1972).

sonnet sequence: A group of sonnets by a single author among which there is a thematic link. The sonnets of such a group are usually love poems which reflect the progress of an attachment or analyze the feelings of the writer. Shakespeare's sonnets are usually considered to constitute such a sequence. Other examples are Sidney's *Astrophel and Stella* and Elizabeth Browning's *Sonnets from the Portuguese*.

sotie: A type of farcical drama popular during the Middle Ages in France.

speech, divisions of a: In setting down the divisions of an oration, the Classical rhetoricians, by no means in complete agreement, named these parts as follows: (1) *Introduction*, also called the Proem or Exordium; (2) *Statement of the Case;* (3) *Argument* or Agon; (4) *Conclusion*, also called the Epilogue or Peroration. Some writers have subdivided the second part into (a) agreed-upon points; (b) the issues involved; and (c) what the speaker intends to establish. Similarly, the third section has been divided into (a) Proof and (b) Refutation of the opponent's argument. In general, modern rhetoricians have retained most of these divisions.

speech act theory: Originated by the English philosopher John Austin and developed in his posthumously published *How to Do Things with Words* (1962), speech act theory posits the idea that language is concerned with a broader significance than its "truth" or "falsity." The purpose of "performatives"—that is, statements that accomplish an act—is not to describe or to inform. As an example, Austin uses the context of the marriage ceremony, with its ultimate question: "Do you take this woman to be your lawful wife?" The response does not involve a description but an act, an event that is not logically "true" or "false" but successful or unsuccessful. The speech act thus involves the first-person present tense ("I do") rather than the descriptive past tense ("I did").

In literary analysis, speech act theorists have examined such elements as dialogue and narration for their forms of linguistic action.

See Shoshana Felman, *The Literary Speech Act* (1983).

Spenserian sonnet: A sonnet whose rhyme is *abab bcbc cdcd ee*. Developed by the Elizabethan poet Edmund Spenser and also called the link sonnet, it has the epigrammatic final couplet of the usual **Shakespearean sonnet,** and often contains no break between the octave and sestet. Below is one of Spenser's *Amoretti:*

> One day I wrote her name upon the strand,
> But came the waves and washed it away:

Agayne I wrote it with a second hand,
But came the tyde, and made my payne his pray.
Vayne man, sayd she, that dost in vaine assay
A mortall thing so to immortalize!
For I my selve shall lyke to this decay,
And eek my name bee wyped out lykewise.
Not so, quod I, let baser things devize
To dy in dust, but you shall live by fame:
My verse your vertues rare shall eternize,
And in the hevens wryte your glorious name;
Where, whenas death shall all the world subdew,
Our love shall live, and later life renew.

Spenserian stanza: A stanza of nine iambic lines rhymed *ababbcbcc*.
The first eight lines are pentameter, but a sixth foot is added to
the final line, making that line an **alexandrine.** Created by Edmund Spenser for *The Faerie Queene* (1590–96), the Spenserian
stanza was little used in the seventeenth century and in the early
part of the eighteenth. Interest in the form revived in the later
eighteenth century, and it was utilized for such significant Romantic poems as Byron's *Childe Harold's Pilgrimage*, Keats's
"The Eve of St. Agnes," and Shelley's "Adonais."

spondee: A metrical foot consisting of two long or accented syllables.
In English, spondees are introduced for variety but never form
the basis of a rhythm. The following contains a number of such
feet:

> One, two,
> Buckle my shoe;
> Three, four,
> Knock at the door;
> Five, six,
> Pick up sticks . . .
>   Anonymous

sprung rhythm: As described by Gerard Manley Hopkins in his
preface to *Poems* (1918), sprung rhythm is measured by feet
consisting of from one to four syllables; however, any number
of unaccented syllables may be used for special effect. In a foot
of sprung rhythm, there is, regardless of the number of syllables,
only one stress, which occurs on the initial syllable. Four kinds
of feet are possible: a monosyllable, a **trochee,** a **dactyl,** and a

first **paeon.** These are mixed, any one foot following any other in no prescribed order. Unlike **running rhythm,** the common form of English meter, sprung rhythm may contain two stresses which may follow one another (each a monosyllabic foot) or which may be divided by one, two, or three unaccented syllables. In addition, Hopkins states, lines in sprung rhythm are "rove over," the scansion of one line being carried over from a previous line; if one ends with one or more unstressed syllables, the following has that many less at the beginning. Consequently, scansion is not limited to the individual lines of a stanza but runs through it to the end.

In the preface to his poems, Hopkins points out that sprung rhythm is that of common speech and written prose as well as most music. Moreover, it is found in nursery rhymes, as in the following:

> Old Mother Twitchett has but one eye
> And a long tail which she can let fly.
> And every time she goes over a gap,
> She leaves a bit of her tail in a trap.

stage direction: Information not part of the dialogue of a play given to the actor, director, or reader. This information may be a description of an action or a setting. Further, the writer may describe a character or analyze his personality. Stage directions range from such laconic instructions as "Exit, pursued by a bear" to the lengthy elucidations which Shaw inserted into the published versions of his plays.

stand: A synonym for *epode.* See **ode.**

stanza: A group of lines which form a division of a poem. A stanza pattern is determined by the number of lines, the number of feet per line, the meter, and the rhyme scheme. Usually, a stanza pattern once established remains unaltered, but slight variations are sometimes introduced, as in Coleridge's *Rime of the Ancient Mariner.* For descriptions of some of the commonly recognized stanza forms, see **ottava rima; quatrain; rhyme royal; Spenserian stanza.** See also **verse paragraph.**

stasimon: See **Greek tragedy, structure of.**

statement: See **pseudo-statement.**

stichomythia: Greek: *stichos*, "a line"; *mythos*, "speech." In drama, dialogue consisting of single lines spoken alternately by two characters. Generally a verbal duel, stichomythia is characterized by repetitive patterns and antithesis, as in these lines from *Hamlet*, Act III, Scene iv:

> Hamlet: Now, mother, what's the matter?
> Queen: Hamlet, thou hast thy father much offended.
> Hamlet: Mother, you have my father much offended.
> Queen: Come, come, you answer with an idle tongue.
> Hamlet: Go, go, you question with a wicked tongue.

Used in Classical dràma, stichomythia was also employed by the Elizabethan dramatists with some frequency.

stilnovism: See *dolce stil nuovo.*

stock and type characters: A stock character is a familiar figure who appears regularly in certain literary forms. Among the most familiar stock characters of contemporary folklore are the hard-boiled private eye, whose achievements with small arms and susceptible ladies are legend, and the strong, silent man of the West, who rides out of the dawn, rights a wrong, and rides into the sunset. Equally familiar are the stock characters of nineteenth-century melodrama: the imperiled heroine, her gallant savior, and the mustache-twirling villain, whose destiny is perpetual frustration. A stock character, however, need not always be a result of the author's ineptitude. Shakespeare's Falstaff, a variation on one of the classic stock characters, the *miles gloriosus*, or braggart soldier, is notable for his individuality; as is Beaumarchais's Figaro, a later version of the clever servant of Classical comedy.

The term *type character*, though often used synonymously with *stock character*, is sometimes distinguished from it. A stock character, though familiar, need not be typical of a group; a type character is a representative of a general class of people. The braggart, consequently, is a type character, whereas the braggart soldier is a stock character.

stock response: A reaction on the part of the reader or spectator which follows a standard pattern, as when the appearance of a mother evokes feelings of reverence no matter what her character may be. The stock response involves a lack of critical judgment which, in melodrama for instance, leads the unsophisticated reader to react with terror to the exaggerated perils facing the virtuous heroine, whereas laughter may be appropriate to the unreality of the situation.

stock situation: A frequently recurring pattern or incident in drama or fiction. The situation involving mistaken identity, for example, has been used from Classical comedy to the present; similarly, the love triangle involving two men in pursuit of one woman or vice versa has appeared frequently in both comedy and tragedy. A stock situation, though often unimaginative, may be developed with such skill as to give it new effectiveness. The triangle of lovers in Shakespeare's *Twelfth Night*, for example, while a stock situation, is so adroitly handled that it acquires its own character.

Storm and Stress: See *Sturm und Drang.*

story within a story: A narrative enclosed within another upon which equal or primary interest is centered. Examples are the short tales which, from time to time, are interspersed among the adventures of Mr. Pickwick and his friends. Certain stories in *The Thousand and One Nights* are interrupted by other stories and only concluded after the new story has been told. *The Thousand and One Nights* also illustrates the techniques of the frame story, a narrative which serves to connect a series of otherwise disparate tales. The frame story is also exemplified by Boccaccio's *Decameron* and Chaucer's *Canterbury Tales.*

stream of consciousness: Coined by William James in *Principles of Psychology* (1890) to describe the flow of inner experience, the term *stream of consciousness* in literature refers to the depiction of the thoughts and feelings which flow, with no apparent logic, through the mind of a character. To create the effect of the chaotic stream that we recognize in reality, the writer presents the seemingly random mingling of thoughts, feelings, and sense impressions of a character at a specific time. The style became influential after it was used by James Joyce in *Ulysses* (1922), from which the following example is taken. Joyce first describes objectively an action of his hero, Leopold Bloom; then abruptly presents his character's inner feelings and thoughts, which are centered on his wife's lover, Blazes Boylan, whom he has just seen:

> Mr. Bloom reviewed the nails of his left hand, then those of his right hand. The nails, yes. Is there anything more in him that they she sees? Fascination. Worst man in Dublin. That keeps him alive.

To give the sense of the flux of experience, Joyce reduces his sentences to fragments freed of linguistic logic but held together by psychological association.

Though it was the power and brilliance of *Ulysses* that attracted attention to the stream-of-consciousness method, Joyce himself acknowledged his indebtedness to a minor French novelist, Edouard Dujardin, whose novel of 1887, *Les Lauriers sont coupés (The Laurels Are Cut Down)*, published in English as *We'll to the Woods No More*, was an earlier and simpler experiment along the same lines. In the discussions that followed the appearance of *Ulysses*, French critics (Valery Larbaud and Dujardin himself) used the term *monologue intérieur*, originated earlier by the novelist Paul Bourget, to designate the verbal techniques of this sort of novel. Dujardin offered a definition of interior monologue as "an unspoken discourse without a hearer present, by which a character expresses his most intimate thought . . . with syntax reduced to a minimum, in such a way as to give the impression of a 'welling forth.' " But certain elements of his definition—such as the phrase "unspoken discourse," emphasizing words and apparently excluding images—have been disputed by later critics. In current usage the term is often interchangeable with *stream of consciousness;* some critics, however, have suggested that the latter term be used to designate generally all techniques for presenting the flow of inner consciousness and that *interior monologue* be reserved for those occasions when there is little or no sense of the author's presence and the fragmentary material of consciousness comes to the reader as directly as possible. (*Direct* and *indirect interior monologue* have also been suggested as terms for making such a distinction.) The passage quoted above would thus be an example of stream of consciousness but not (since a narrator is clearly present in the first sentence) interior monologue. The classic example of the latter is the final section of *Ulysses*, in which Joyce presents in one vast "sentence" the uninterrupted flow of Molly Bloom's thoughts and impressions.

These techniques have been used by such distinguished twentieth-century authors as Virginia Woolf and William Faulkner.

See Robert Humphrey, *Stream of Consciousness in the Modern Novel* (1954); Leon Edel, *The Modern Psychological Novel* (1955); Shiv K. Kumar, *Bergson and the Stream of Consciousness Novel* (1963).

stress: A term sometimes limited to the emphasis placed on a syllable in a word as opposed to the emphasis demanded by a metrical pattern, it is usually a general synonym for **accent.** See **ictus; primary and secondary accent.**

strophe: In Greek prosody, a group of lines of varying lengths constituting the first part of an **ode.** Since this term is sometimes used as a synonym for **stanza,** a poem whose stanzaic structure does not vary is called monostrophic. In **free verse,** the word *strophe* is sometimes used to describe a group of lines which constitute a unit, or **verse paragraph.**

Structuralism: A method of intellectual analysis (or "mode of thought") employed by a number of French linguists, literary critics, anthropologists, philosophers, and psychologists who, since the 1960's, have been called "Structuralists." Though Structuralism has no common vocabulary or specific doctrines, some Structuralists employ interdisciplinary approaches in an attempt to develop an objective method that will unify their diverse fields.

While the concern with "structure" can be traced back to Aristotle's *Poetics*, contemporary Structuralists have been principally influenced by Ferdinand de Saussure, the Swiss "father of modern linguistics," who, in his *Cours de linguistique générale* (1913), a posthumous reconstruction of his lectures from his students' notes, examined language as a system of signs, a study called **semiology.** Saussure views language as an arbitrary, culturally determined system of signs without any intrinsic or "natural" relationship to external reality. (If, for example, there were a natural relationship between the word *tree* and the actual object, the word would—at any rate, should—be used in every other language.) A sign consists of a fusion of two elements: the signifier is a "sound-image" (or its equivalent in writing); the signified is the concept. Since language is instrumental, signs give meanings to things, not things to signs. In analyzing the structures of language, Saussure distinguishes *langue*, the system of signs, from *parole*, individual utterance determined by the system. The science of linguistics is therefore principally concerned with *langue*.

Structuralists, equipped with a theory and method of linguistic analysis, have examined a wide variety of texts, such as fairy tales and myths. Such cultural phenomena as wrestling matches, regarded as "texts" from the Structuralist point of view, have also been examined. In the study of literature, Structuralists have employed linguistic analysis to reveal how structures are formed.

In a now famous essay on Baudelaire's sonnet "Les Chats," the linguist Roman Jakobson and the anthropologist Claude Lévi-Strauss, who has been primarily responsible for the widespread use of the term *Structuralism*, combined their disciplines in a "dissection and articulation," as Roland Barthes characterizes the typical activity of Structuralists. The poem is minutely examined grammatically, prosodically, phonetically, and semantically to determine the functions of each sound, rhyme, rhythm, and meaning as they interact and form patterns. In a prefatory note to the essay, widely regarded as a model of Structuralist activity, Lévi-Strauss justifies the union of linguistics, poetry, and anthropology by stating: "In poetic works, the linguist discerns structures which are strikingly analogous to those which the analysis of myths reveal to the ethnologist." Michael Riffaterre, commenting on this essay, claims that such an analysis fails to reveal those elements that have an effect on the reader —that is, the "poetic structure" (*Yale French Studies*, 36/37 [1966]).

Indeed, Structuralism does not so much focus on the "meaning" of a literary work as on its linguistic structure. Moreover, Structuralists are principally concerned not with the uniqueness of literary works as aesthetic objects but with basic structures of "possible" works; traditional criticism, on the other hand, is more generally involved not only with meaning but also with value in literature.

In its extension of Saussurean linguistics to literary study, Structuralism has attempted to create a new science of literature. As Structuralism evolved into the more radical **post-structuralism** of the early 1970's, critics of its anti-historical and antihumanistic approach to literature have increasingly deplored its putatively subversive nature and have called for a return to an interest in the social, and even political, aspects of literature. See **deconstruction.**

See David Robey, ed., *Structuralism: An Introduction* (1973); Robert Scholes, *Structuralism in Literature: An Introduction* (1974); Jonathan Culler, *Structuralist Poetics* (1975); Edith Kurzweil, *The Age of Structuralism: Lévi-Strauss to Foucault* (1980).

structure: 1. In the work of John Crowe Ransom, the explicit argument or paraphrasable statement made in a poem, opposed to the texture, which is, briefly, everything else—the phonetic pattern, the sequence of images, the meanings suggested by the connotations of words, etc. The texture and structure, which together yield the complete meaning of the poem, combine to give it what Ransom calls its "ontology," the unique status which differentiates it from non-poetic discourse.

2. In speaking of meter, Ransom uses the term *texture* to refer to the variations on the basic metrical pattern, or structure.

3. The inherent relationships among the elements of a work of art. *Structure* usually refers to the organization of elements other than words. For the latter, the term **style** is used. See **form.**

Sturm und Drang: German: "storm and stress." A German literary movement of the latter part of the eighteenth century. In the 1770's, a group of young writers, impatient with the doctrines of the **Enlightenment,** especially as exemplified by French classicism, turned instead to the admiration and portrayal of turbulent emotion and forceful individualism. They preferred inspiration to reason and sought to model themselves on Shakespeare rather than the Graeco-Roman writers. Intensely nationalistic, they investigated and made use of folk literature. The young Goethe's *Götz von Berlichingen*, with its unconquerable hero and its admiration for the medieval past, is a representative *Sturm und Drang* work. Schiller's *Die Räuber (The Robbers)* also shows the influence of the movement. Among the others associated with it were Herder, Lenz, and Friedrich Klinger, whose play *Wirrwarr, oder Sturm und Drang* gave the group its name.

See Roy Pascal, *The German Sturm und Drang* (1953).

style: The word *style* is used in at least two senses that should be discriminated. If we say of a writer, "His thought is intelligent enough, but the poor fellow has no style," we are assuming that style is an immutable quality found in some writers and lacking in others. In this sense, sometimes called the Platonic, style implies the perfect matching of the means with their end. Thus, the term *style* may be used as a general synonym for *excellence*, or it may, more specifically, suggest that a writer has found the unique verbal pattern that precisely expresses the meaning he wishes to convey.

In a second sense, the Aristotelian, style may classify rather than evaluate. Thus, we speak of a satiric style, a Miltonic style, an Italianate style, etc. A critic may not admire a particular style or may consider its use in certain circumstances inappropriate, but distinguishing its presence in a writer serves merely to classify, not to condemn, him. When an analysis of a writer's style is carried far enough, it ends in the man himself. The total of the qualities that characterize an individual writer's style (some of which may be too subtle ever to be discriminated) constitutes his literary personality and reflects his psychological one. The style, said Buffon, is the man.

subjectivity: A quality of writing in which the expression of personal feeling or experiences is primary. In autobiography, for example, the writer, in presenting his private emotions and memories, is generally subjective in his attitudes toward himself and others. Similarly, in semi-autobiographical fiction, such as Thomas Wolfe's novels or Samuel Butler's *The Way of All Flesh*, the writer dramatizes feelings and incidents that are derived from his own experiences. In general, **Romanticism** has encouraged this kind of writing, for the expression of personal feeling, to the Romantic, confirms his individualism. In time, excessive concern with the inner life has given rise to "private" expression of the sort sometimes evident in the poetry of Rimbaud and Dylan Thomas.

Subjectivity, however, may indicate the inner thoughts or feelings of the characters in a literary work rather than the author's. In Browning's dramatic lyrics, for example, the central element is the revelation of the speaker's nature. In literary judgment, the term *subjectivity* refers to personal taste and response, particularly in the type of criticism called **"Impres-sionism."**

See **criticism; objectivity.**

sublime, the: A quality possessed by a work that, as a result of the author's inspiration rather than his reasoned judgment, does not so much convince the reader as it thrills, or transports, him. This idea was formulated by an anonymous Greek rhetorician writing in Rome in the first or second century A.D. Because he was confused with the third-century Greek Platonic philosopher and rhetorician Dionysius Cassius Longinus, he is often called the "pseudo-Longinus." The sublime was much admired by the Romantics, who often sought to achieve it in their own works.

subplot: See **plot.**

substitution: The use of a foot other than the one regularly demanded by the meter. In **quantitative verse,** substitution is made on the basis of equivalence, the doctrine that two short syllables equal one long (a dactyl or anapest may be substituted for an iamb or trochee if the two short syllables are read at double speed). When a trochee is substituted for an iamb or a dactyl for an anapest (and vice versa), the result is an inverted foot, in stress prosody sometimes called "inverted stress" or "inverted accent." The commonest substitution in English verse is the use of a trochee for an iamb at the beginning of a line, as at the opening of Shakespeare's Sonnet 27:

Weary / with toil / I haste / me to / my bed.

subtext: The unspoken content of a dramatic scene. In a Freudian reading of *Hamlet*, for example, the subtext of the Closet Scene, in which the Prince denounces his uncle and rebukes his mother for her sexual misconduct, might be his own erotic desire for Gertrude and his consequent jealousy of Claudius.

Surrealism: A movement, originating in France in the 1920's, that attempted to express in art, primarily in literature and painting, the working of the unconscious. Although the term *Surrealism* was coined by Guillaume Apollinaire, the founder of the movement was the poet André Breton, who, in 1924, issued the first Surrealist manifesto, which explained that a higher reality could be captured by freeing the mind from logic and rational control. Earlier, Breton, influenced by the techniques of Freudian analysis, had been experimenting with automatic writing. The British critic Herbert Read has placed Surrealism in the tradition of **Romanticism,** a central concept of which has been the exploration of the mind.

Among the painters who have worked in the Surrealist manner are Chirico, Picasso, Tanguy, and Salvador Dali; among the poets, Aragon and Eluard. Both Joyce, especially in *Finnegans Wake*, and Dylan Thomas have been called Surrealists, but the element of conscious control in these writers makes the appellation doubtful.

See Wallace Fowlie, *The Age of Surrealism* (1950); Maurice Nadeau, *The History of Surrealism* (English trans., 1965); Anna Balakian, *Surrealism: The Road to the Absolute* (rev. ed., 1970); Mary Ann Caws, *The Poetry of Dada and Surrealism* (1970); Paul C. Ray, *The Surrealist Movement in England* (1971).

suspense: In a literary work, an expectant uncertainty concerning the outcome of the plot. To hold his reader, the writer of a detective story, for example, may resort to sudden disappearances of key characters or the introduction of clues that implicate apparently innocent people, always keeping the final solution just out of sight. In Sophocles' *Oedipus Rex*, suspense is achieved through a withholding of the knowledge that Oedipus himself has killed Laius, his father. During the play, the spectators, aware that Oedipus will eventually make the discovery, share the hero's uncertainties and fears as he pursues the truth of his own past.

syllabic verse: Verse measured not by **stress** or **quantity** but by the number of syllables in each line. In English poetry, Milton and Pope, among others, have written such verse.

syllepsis: A rhetorical figure in which a word brings together two constructions, each of which has a different meaning in connection with the yoking word. Syllepsis may be the result of inept writing or may be used for humorous effect: "Hotchkiss spied on his wife with interest and a telescope." Here, the word *with* involves both accompaniment *(interest)* and means *(telescope)*.

symbol: Before a symbol can be defined it must be distinguished from a sign, an object that signifies something else, such as a red light that instructs the motorist to stop. To be efficient, the sign must have only one meaning. A symbol, on the other hand, is more complex. In its simplest sense, it is also something that stands for something else. The cross, for example, is a symbol of Christianity, the hammer and sickle of communism, John Bull of England, etc. Such symbols are more complicated than signs, however, for they sum up a large number of ideas and attitudes and can mean different things in different circumstances. The cross, standing for the whole complex of Christianity, is an object of reverence to some and of contempt to others. Nevertheless, such symbols are public and generally understood.

These symbols are used in literature as in ordinary discourse, but in literature we often find, in addition, symbols of a different sort. Such symbols do not have a publicly accepted meaning but take their significance from the total context in which they appear. (Symbols may also be taken from a special area of knowledge, such as Freudian psychology, or from a private system of the author's; however, the most powerful symbols are usually formed—or, if borrowed, modified—by the works in which they are found.) Thus, the white whale of Melville's *Moby Dick*, one of the most discussed of literary symbols, is simply the animal that Captain Ahab pursues, but at the same time is much more. As the novel proceeds, Melville associates so much meaning with Moby Dick that the reader accepts him as an object of great significance, as a "grand god": "Moby Dick moved on, still withholding from sight the full terrors of his submerged trunk, entirely hiding the wrenched hideousness of his jaw. But soon the fore part of him slowly rose from the water . . . and warningly waved his bannered flukes in the air, the grand god revealed himself, sounded, and went out of sight." Many critics have discussed the meaning of Moby Dick without final agreement, for such complex symbols do not admit of easy definition and are perhaps expressible only in terms of themselves.

Sometimes, not only an image but an entire work may be taken as a symbol. Thus, the journey of Coleridge's Ancient Mariner may symbolize the universal journey into the depths of despair and back to psychological and spiritual stability.

See W. Y. Tindall, *The Literary Symbol* (1955); Harry Levin, "Symbolism and Fiction," *Contexts of Criticism* (1957); Maurice Beebe, ed., *Literary Symbolism* (1960); Mark Neuman and Michael Payne, eds., *Self, Sign, and Symbol* (1987).

symbolic action: In his critical writings, notably *Attitudes Toward History* (1937) and *The Philosophy of Literary Form: Studies in Symbolic Action* (1941), Kenneth Burke uses the term *symbolic action* to designate the unconscious or conscious "ritual" that the writer undergoes in the creation of a literary work and that he embodies within it. For the creator, Burke states, the work of art is a "strategy" for handling or controlling his own problems. By disguising his identity, the writer, in the act of creation, performs a symbolic action, that "which a man does because he is interested in doing it exactly as he does it." These symbolic acts center on initiation, rebirth, purification, and other ancient collective ceremonies. Thus, T. S. Eliot's *Murder in the Cathedral* is a purification ritual and Thomas Mann's *Death in Venice* involves a scapegoat ritual, in which the immorality of the artist is punished by death.

Despite Burke's apparent emphasis on the relationship of the work to the artist, he does not slight the effect of the symbolic action on the reader, for he states that, though many of the things that the work does for the artist are not the same for the reader, "if we try to discover what the work is doing for the artist, we may discover a set of generalizations as to what works of art do for everybody."

Symbolist Movement: In *The Symbolist Movement in Literature* (1899), Arthur Symons states that symbolism is seen, "under one disguise or another, in every great imaginative writer." By this, Symons meant that these writers had apprehended and expressed "an unseen reality." Whether or not they did so, the work of many distinguished writers undoubtedly contains symbols and so provides support for Symons's remark. The term *Symbolist Movement*, however, is commonly used to designate a literary movement which began in France in the latter part of the nineteenth century. Many literary historians designate the years 1885–95 as the "Symbolist period," when theories and manifestos were most prominent; others, reluctant to exclude major Symbolists who wrote before this period, extend the time limits of the movement to include such earlier writers as Rimbaud and Baudelaire.

A major poem of the Symbolist Movement, Baudelaire's "Correspondances" (in *Les Fleurs du mal*, 1857), profoundly affected later poets. In this sonnet Baudelaire, influenced by the **Platonism** of the eighteenth-century philosopher Swedenborg, envisioned nature as a "forest of symbols," implying correspondences among sensations in the phenomenal world (see **synaesthesia**) and between that world and an ideal one. However, Baudelaire consciously employed symbols not only to suggest a transcendent reality superior to our world but also to express his own spiritual condition. The morbid images of Parisian life with which he filled his poems were, in part, symbolic embodiments of his state of mind and soul. In his poems, as in those of other Symbolists, suggestiveness—along with the music of the verse—was calculated to endow image and **symbol** with evocative power. In 1891, Mallarmé, condemning poetry of description and declamation, defined symbolism as the art of "evoking an object little by little so as to reveal a mood, or conversely, the art of choosing an object and extracting from it a 'state of soul.'" As Symons states Mallarmé's fundamental principle, "to name is to destroy, to suggest is to create."

The Symbolist Movement acquired a self-conscious identity in 1886 when Jean Moréas published a manifesto in *Le Figaro*. He declared that the poetry of the new movement, in keeping with the Platonic basis of much symbolist verse, was to give expression to "primordial Ideas" but not by mere description: "symbolic poetry seeks to invest the Idea with a sensible form" —that is, by employing concrete symbols that have "esoteric affinities" with Ideas in a transcendent world. He praised Mallarmé as one who had given the movement "the sense of mystery and of the ineffable" and praised Verlaine for having broken "the cruel bonds of versification." (Indeed, *vers libre* was of central importance to many of the Symbolists.) Among the poets who joined Moréas in the "Symbolist School," as he called it, were René Ghil, Stuart Merrill, Francis Viélé-Griffin, and Gustave Kahn. Others associated with the movement were Maeterlinck, Villiers de l'Isle Adam, and Jules Laforgue. In England, the

Symbolists were admired and sometimes imitated by such writers as George Moore, Arthur Symons, and Yeats. The effect of the Symbolist Movement has been extensive in the twentieth century: such poets as T. S. Eliot, Paul Valéry, and Dylan Thomas and such novelists as Proust and Joyce have been influenced by it.

See A. G. Lehman, *The Symbolist Aesthetic in France, 1885–1895* (1950; 2nd ed., 1968); Ruth Z. Temple, *The Critic's Alchemy: A Study of the Introduction of French Symbolism into England* (1953); Anna Balakian, *The Symbolist Movement* (1967); Lothar Honnighausen, *The Symbolist Tradition in English Literature: A Study of Pre-Raphaelitism and Fin de Siècle* (1971; English trans., 1988).

synaesthesia: The intermingling of sensations; the sensing, for example, of certain sounds through colors or odors. In the late eighteenth century and in the nineteenth, there was much interest in synaesthesia, and many attempts to mix the effects of the various arts were made. Baudelaire's sonnet "Correspondances," in which he described certain perfumes as "soft as oboes, green as meadows," is probably the most widely known example. Another is the sonnet called "Voyelles," in which Rimbaud associated a specific color with each of the vowel sounds. Among other writers who made use of the theory of synaesthesia were J. K. Huysmans and Oscar Wilde.

synalepha: See **elision**.

syncopation: The simultaneous occurrence in verse of two different accentual patterns, one of the meter, the other of normal speech. In "The Wife of Usher's Well," for example, the basic meter is iambic. The final line of the second stanza would normally be scanned thus:

> That her three sons were gane.

The normal speech rhythm, syncopated against the rigid metrical one, is as follows:

> That her three sons were gane.

The speech rhythm may also bring about syncopation by altering the number of stresses with which a line is read, as in the second line of Shakespeare's sonnet which begins:

> Farewell! thou art too dear for my possessing
> And like enough thou knowest thy estimate . . .

The scansion above reflects the regular metrical pattern. In fact, that pattern contrasts with the actual speech pattern below:

> And like enough thou knowest thy estimate.

syncope: The omission of a letter or a syllable within a word, as in *o'er* for *over*. See **elision**.

synecdoche: A figure of speech in which a part represents the whole object or idea. In Sonnet 55, for example, Shakespeare, expressing the idea that art is eternal, uses the word *rhyme* to refer to the entire poem:

> Not marble, nor the gilded monuments
> Of princes, shall outlive this powerful rhyme . . .

T

tableau: 1. A stationary, silent grouping of performers in a theatrical production (or sometimes on a float) for a special effect. In the final scene of Gogol's *The Inspector-General*, the announcement that the inspector-general has arrived results in a sudden freeze by the corrupt officials, who form a tableau as the curtain falls.

2. An elaborate stage presentation consisting of dance, pantomime, or ballet in impressive settings.

tail-rhyme stanza: A unit of verse in which a short line, following a group of longer ones, rhymes with a preceding short line. Also called by the French term *rime couée*, the tail-rhyme stanza has a number of variants, but a common form is $aa^4b^3cc^4b^3$. Sometimes the tail rhyme is used to connect succeeding stanzas. In Shelley's "To Night," the form of the tail-rhyme stanza is as follows:

Wrap thy form in a mantle gray,
    Star in-wrought!
Blind with thine hair the eyes of Day;
Kiss her until she be wearied out;
Then wander o'er city and sea and land,
Touching all with thine opiate wand—
    Come, long sought.

tale: In its simplest meaning, a narrative. The term has referred to such realistic stories as Chaucer's *Canterbury Tales* and to such bizarre ones as those written by Poe. Generally, the tale is loosely plotted, told by a narrator, and little concerned with development of character. The term, often synonymous with **short story,** can refer to a novel, such as Dickens's *A Tale of Two Cities*. It is now frequently used to designate stories that are exotic or adventurous, as in James Michener's *Tales of the South Pacific*.

telestich: See **acrostic.**

tenor: See **metaphor.**

tension: As used by Allen Tate, the term *tension* designates the totality of meaning in a poem. The term, Tate says, is not used as a general metaphor; it derives from the logical terms *extension* and *intension* (see **meaning**) after the prefixes have been removed. According to Tate, a poem has at once literal meaning (extension) and metaphorical (intension). It is the simultaneous existence of these two sets of meaning that Tate refers to as *tension*. An additional meaning of the term involves what the New Critics call "conflict-structures," some of which Robert Penn Warren has listed as follows: ". . . tension between the rhythm of the poem and the rhythm of speech . . . between the formality of the rhythm and the informality of the language; between the particular and the general, the concrete and the abstract; between the elements of even the simplest metaphor; between the beautiful and the ugly; between ideas; between the elements involved in irony; between prosisms and poeticisms."

In the poem's ability to organize tensions, some of the New Critics find a basis upon which they make value judgments.

tercet: In verse, three lines which constitute a unit. When used interchangeably with the term *triplet*, *tercet* designates a three-line stanza on a single rhyme. However, the word *tercet* may also be applied to half of the sestet of a **Petrarchan sonnet** and to the *terza rima* stanza. The tercets (or triplets) below are from Thomas Carew's "Inscription on the Tomb of the Lady Mary Wentworth":

> And here the precious dust is laid:
> Whose purely-tempered clay was made
> So fine, that it the guest betrayed.
>
> Else the soul grew so fast within,
> It broke the outward shell of sin,
> And so was hatched a cherubin.

terza rima: A series of interlocking tercets in which the second line of each one rhymes with the first and third lines of the one succeeding: *aba, bcb, cdc,* etc. Italian in origin, the form was used by Dante in *The Divine Comedy* as well as by Petrarch and Boccaccio. It was introduced into English by Sir Thomas Wyatt in the sixteenth century but, though used (with variations) by such poets as Shelley, Browning, and Auden, has not become genuinely popular. The most famous example of *terza rima* in English is Shelley's "Ode to the West Wind." The following are the opening verses of the final section, in which Shelley addresses the wind, identifying himself with its power:

> Make me thy lyre, even as the forest is:
> What if my leaves are falling like its own!
> The tumult of thy mighty harmonies
>
> Will take from both a deep, autumnal tone,
> Sweet though in sadness. Be thou, Spirit fierce,
> My spirit! Be thou me, impetuous one!

tetrameter: A line of four metrical feet. Though the following lines contain a variety of feet, they are all tetrameter:

> Fe, / Fi, / Fo, / Fum!
> I smell / the blood / of an Eng / lishman;
> Be he / alive / or be / he dead,
> I'll grind / his bones / to make / my bread.
>   Anonymous

tetrastich: A stanza of four lines; a term used synonymously with **quatrain.**

textual criticism: The study of the available manuscripts or printings of a literary work in order to determine its correct version—that is, the form which the writer originally or, if there are revisions, ultimately wished it to have. Especially in the cases of certain older works, such as the plays of Shakespeare, of which the manuscripts are lost and the earliest printed versions inaccurate, detailed scholarly analysis (and sometimes imaginative reconstruction) is necessary before an accurate text can be established.

See O. M. Brack, Jr., and Warner Barnes, eds., *Bibliography and Textual Criticism: English and American Literature, 1700 to the Present* (1969).

texture: See **structure.**

Theater of Cruelty: A term coined in the 1930's by the French actor, playwright, director, and theoretician Antonin Artaud. By cruelty, Artaud protested, he did not mean exhibitions of sadism, though most of his scenarios deal with images of blood and violence, but a rigorous effort to regain contact, which he believed the literary, psychological theater had lost, with the vital energies of life. Although Artaud's writings are often vaguely hyperbolic and sometimes incoherent (he ultimately spent several years in an institution for the insane), the boldness of his ideas for a predominantly non-verbal theater of symbolic images, in which the conventional barriers between actors and audience would be eliminated, made them influential on many later theatrical innovators.

See Antonin Artaud, *The Theater and Its Double* (English trans., 1958); Bettina Knapp, *Antonin Artaud: Man of Vision* (1969); Naomi Greene, *Antonin Artaud: Poet Without Words* (1970).

Theater of the Absurd: An experimental theatrical style which came into prominence after World War II in the work of such writers as Samuel Beckett, Eugène Ionesco, Jean Genet, and Harold Pinter. Many Absurdist plays contain grotesque and ludicrous elements, but the term *Absurd*, as applied to this movement, carries the sense given it by the Existentialist thinkers, that man is "out of harmony," that without metaphysical beliefs he finds himself an exile in a meaningless universe. Deriving stylistically from the experimental tradition of the modern drama as found in Strindberg, Jarry, and the writers who created literary **Expressionism** and **Surrealism,** the playwrights of the Absurd often dispensed with such traditional elements as a coherent plot (or any plot at all), realistic stage design, and psychologically consistent characters. As with any literary "movement," there is a great deal of thematic and temperamental variety from writer to writer (the violent social hostility of Genet finds no echo in the metaphysical whimsy of Beckett, for example), but the symbolic treatment of Existential themes has produced a recognizably coherent body of work.

The fiction of Joyce and Kafka anticipated some elements of the Theater of the Absurd, and by extension such prose works as the novels of Beckett are sometimes called "Literature of the Absurd."

See Martin Esslin, *The Theatre of the Absurd* (1961); Leonard Pronko, *Avant-Garde: The Experimental Theater in France* (1962); George E. Wellwarth, *The Theater of Protest and Paradox* (1964); Arnold Hinchliffe, *The Absurd* (1969).

theme: Sometimes used to indicate the subject of a work, the term *theme* is more frequently employed to designate its central idea or thesis. A theme may be stated directly or indirectly. When not specifically given, it may be abstracted from the work. Keats's "Ode on a Grecian Urn," for example, embodies the themes of the permanence of art and the impermanence of life.

theory: Since the 1970's a commitment to "theory" has not only suggested a special interest in the more abstract aspects of literary questions but implied a claim to membership in the intellectual avant-garde or at least to a wider cultural discrimination based on a sympathetic understanding of such intellectual heroes as Marx, Nietzsche, Freud, Wittgenstein, Lévi-Strauss, and Lacan, whose contributions transcend standard disciplines. In professional literary circles advocates of "theory" have sometimes found themselves at odds with those "traditional" scholars who are more likely to emphasize biographical elements or social and historical backgrounds.

thesis: 1. A proposition to be maintained, especially one laid down for formal defense or proof.

    2. An essay presented by a candidate as partial fulfillment of the requirements for a university degree.

    3. In Greek verse, *thesis* was "a putting down" and thus the lowering of the hand or foot on an accented syllable while beating time. By extension, *thesis* came to mean a stressed syllable, as opposed to *arsis* (raising), the unaccented part of a foot of verse. In Latin usage, however, *thesis* and *arsis* referred to the lowering and raising of the voice on unstressed and stressed syllables respectively, reversing the Greek usage. In modern prosody, the Latin usage is the one most commonly found; however, since the Greek is sometimes encountered, confusion, as Fowler has said, "is not unknown." Syllables are spoken of as being "in thesis" or "in arsis."

thesis play: French: *pièce à thèse.* A drama in which a social problem is illustrated and, usually, a solution suggested. This form originated in nineteenth-century France with such plays as Dumas *fils's Le Fils naturel.* Other examples are the plays of Eugène Brieux and such early plays of Shaw as *Widowers' Houses* and *Mrs. Warren's Profession.* Two other terms often used to characterize plays of this type are *problem play* and *propaganda play,* though the latter suggests more militant works such as Odets's *Waiting for Lefty.*

threnody: From Greek: *threnos,* "lamentation"; *ode,* "song." A lyric lamenting someone's death. In Classical Greek poetry, the threnody was a choral dirge. See **monody.**

tirade: In a drama, the French term *tirade* designates a long, uninterrupted speech addressed to one or more characters onstage with the speaker.

tone: In general, critics use the term *attitude* to refer to the author's relationship to his material or to his audience, or both. These attitudes, as they appear in the work itself, constitute or determine its tone. A speaker indicates tone, at least in part, by changes in voice and manner, but a writer must rely on the verbal devices at his command. In the quatrains below, for example, both Marvell and Herrick handle the traditional *carpe* *diem* theme, but the former's tone is one of passionate entreaty, the latter's of gentle persuasion:

> Let us roll all our strength and all
> Our sweetness up into one ball,
> And tear our pleasures with rough strife
> Thorough the iron gates of life.
> > Marvell, "To His Coy Mistress"

> Gather ye rosebuds while ye may,
>   Old Time is still a-flying:
> And this same flower that smiles to-day
>   To-morrow will be dying.
> > Herrick, "To the Virgins, to Make Much of Time"

For a more restricted use of the word *tone*, see **four meanings of a poem.**

topos: Greek: "place" (plural: *topoi*). A familiar motif (in effect, a recognized "place" in the *topo*graphy of literature) or standardized pattern of literary usage.

tract: A brief essay, usually in the form of a pamphlet, on a religious or political subject. The famous *Tracts for the Times* (1833–41), for example, were a series of papers presenting the religious views of Newman and others in the **Oxford Movement.**

Tractarian Movement: See **Oxford Movement.**

tragedy: Greek: *tragoidia*, "goat song." The term *tragedy* probably refers to an ancient totemic ritual, the sacrifice of a goat, associated with the god of the fields and vineyards, Dionysus. In time, contests in the writing of tragedies came to be held as part of the ceremonies of the Great Dionysia at Athens, the springtime festival of the death and resurrection of the god. From these contests developed Greek tragedy and later a larger body of dramatic, and even non-dramatic, tragedy in Western literature.

In the still-continuing effort to define the nature of tragedy, undoubtedly the most significant critical document is the first one, the *Poetics* of Aristotle; but in the consideration of it, several things must be kept in mind. First of all, the *Poetics* appears to be a group of somewhat sketchy notes, perhaps lecture notes, rather than a fully developed discussion, and, partly as a result of this circumstance, the precise meaning of Aristotle's key terms has been the subject of much argument. Indeed, his aim may have been as much to defend tragedy against the criticisms of his former teacher, Plato, as to define it. Moreover, though Aristotle, writing after the great age of Greek tragedy had passed, was able to draw upon that literature in formulating his ideas, he could hardly anticipate the developments of the next two thousand years. Attempts to fit all subsequent tragic writing into the Aristotelian mold are of dubious validity, though the influence of the *Poetics* on both writing and criticism has been incalculable. It remains profoundly instructive, the inevitable starting point of all discussions.

Aristotle defined tragedy as an imitation of an action "of high importance, complete and of some amplitude" (trans. L. J. Potts., 1953). It is presented in dramatic, as opposed to narrative, form and utilizes poetic language. The tragic hero, a person of stature who is neither villainous nor exceptionally virtuous, moves from happiness to misery through some frailty or error, called *hamartia*. (Oedipus, for example, kills his father because of his own rashness, marries his mother because of ignorance.) This term has sometimes been loosely translated "tragic flaw," thus emphasizing the question of moral judgment. Though the hero's *hamartia* may be *hubris (hybris)*—the excessive pride and self-confidence that the Greeks so feared—it may also be merely a mistake in judgment. At any rate, it moves the plot to a *peripety (peripeteia)*, a sudden reversal of the hero's fortune from good to bad. At this point, Aristotle suggested, there should also occur the *anagnorisis*, "disclosure" of the true circumstances or "recognition" of the hero's true self or nature. (By extension, these two terms have been applied to comic and other plots.) Finally, the tragic action through pity and fear effects a "purgation of these emotions." The meaning of this purgation, or *catharsis*, has been widely debated. It has been held that the catharsis drains off repressed and dangerous feelings and that it purifies them. In any case, by this term Aristotle seems to be referring not to the experience of depression but to that of exaltation, which great tragedies produce.

In the Middle Ages, when the great tragedies of the Classical period were unknown, a tragedy was a narrative of a fall from good fortune to bad, from high position to low. The depiction of such disasters served, in a Christian epoch, to remind men of the frailty of human life. But the **Renaissance** sought models that would allow for a wider vision. In England, though the medieval tradition of the **mystery** and **morality play** influenced the new drama, the work of the Roman tragedian Seneca was even more significant. Offering to the Elizabethan playwrights in general a model for a serious, passionate drama embellished with rich language, his work was particularly important for the development of the immensely popular genre of the revenge play—or tragedy of blood, as its more sensational examples are sometimes called. In it appear such Senecan elements as ghosts, the theme of revenge, and lurid happenings (murder, mutilation, infanticide, for example). Although Seneca, whose plays were designed for recitation rather than performance (a fact unknown to the Elizabethans), kept such events at a certain distance in having them reported by messenger, the Elizabethans brought them onstage to gratify the popular taste for gaudy action. The form of the revenge tragedy was established by Thomas Kyd's *The Spanish Tragedy*, but its most exalted example—embodying such characteristic elements as madness and the play within the play—is *Hamlet*.

Not only the revenge play but English Renaissance tragedy in general reveals such non-Aristotelian elements as loosely structured action, including multiple plots, a mingling of the comic and the serious, and—as in *Macbeth*—a hero dominated by evil. The Spanish drama of the period shares a number of these characteristics, but a heightened critical consciousness, especially in France, produced a different kind of tragedy. In his *Poetics of Aristotle* (1570) the Italian critic Castelvetro had formulated the doctrine of the **unities** of time, place, and action (only the last of which was truly Aristotelian). The influence of this formulation on the seventeenth-century French tragedians Corneille, Racine, and their imitators, led to a Neoclassic tragedy much more restrained and formalized than that of the Elizabethans. It was not until the 1760's in the work of such critics as Dr. Johnson and Gotthold Lessing that the doctrine of the unities began to be seriously questioned.

Meanwhile, a new kind of serious drama, of which Lessing was not only an advocate but a writer, had begun to appear. Although a few Elizabethan plays deal seriously with the dramatic circumstances of middle-class people, tragedy had almost always been written in verse and centered upon heroes of exalted status. But with the continuing rise of the middle class, the theater began to reflect its interests. In 1731 appeared George Lillo's *The London Merchant: or, The History of George Barnwell*, a serious drama about a merchant's apprentice who ultimately turns to robbery and murder. More such plays and critical justifications of them followed. By 1767 the French playwright Beaumarchais in his *Essay on the Serious Drama* could argue, "The true heart-interest, real relationship, is always between man and man, not between man and king. . . . The nearer the suffering man is to my station in life, the greater is his claim upon my sympathy."

Although serious dramas in an exalted style were still being written (by Schiller, Goethe, and Hugo, for example), the tide had turned toward the **realism** and contemporary subject matter of the modern theater. With such plays as *Ghosts* and *The Master Builder* Ibsen may have created genuine tragedies in this style, but it is often questioned whether in the scope of their action, the dignity of their characterization, and the exaltation of their effect any twentieth-century plays are appropriately called "tragedies." Despite the strenuous efforts such writers as Eugene O'Neill, T. S. Eliot, and Arthur Miller have made to use the techniques and achieve the effects of tragedy in certain works, the question remains unanswered. See **Greek tragedy, structure of; tragicomedy.**

See F. L. Lucas, *Tragedy: Serious Drama in Relation to Aristotle's Poetics* (1928); Elder Olson, *Tragedy and the Theory of Drama* (1961); Barrett H. Clark, ed., *European Theories of the Drama*, rev. ed. by Henry Popkin (1965); Robert W. Corrigan, ed., *Tragedy: Vision and Form* (1965). For examples of opposed views on the question of tragedy in the modern world, see George Steiner, *The Death of Tragedy* (1961) and Raymond Williams, *Modern Tragedy* (1966).

tragedy of blood: See **tragedy.**

tragic flaw: See **tragedy.**

tragic irony: See **irony.**

tragicomedy: A play in which the action, though apparently leading to a catastrophe, is reversed to bring about a happy ending. The term is frequently associated with some of the plays of Beaumont and Fletcher, whose *Philaster, or Love Lies A-Bleeding* (ca. 1610) is an example of the form. The typical tragicomedy concerns noble characters involved in improbable situations. Love, frequently seen as a contrast of the pure and the sensual, is the central motive of the elaborate plot, in which both hero and heroine are rescued from imminent disaster so that the play may conclude happily.

Fletcher, defining the term *tragicomedy* in his preface to *The Faithful Shepherdess*, wrote: "A tragicomedy is not so called in respect to mirth and killing, but in respect it wants deaths, which is enough to make it no tragedy, yet brings some near it, which is enough to make it no comedy. . . ." The term may be used to characterize such plays as Shakespeare's *Cymbeline* and *The Winter's Tale* and, by extension, any play which involves a similar movement of plot.

See Marvin T. Herrick, *Tragicomedy: Its Origin and Development in Italy, France, and England* (1955).

tranche de vie: See **slice of life.**

Transcendentalism, New England: A movement, most prominent from 1835 to 1845, which was essentially religious and which emphasized the primacy of the individual conscience. Influenced by nineteenth-century philosophical idealism and Christian mysticism, the Transcendentalists (a term first used by their opponents but later accepted by the group) never regarded themselves as a school; in fact, they prided themselves on their lack of accord in matters of doctrine. However, on some principles they were in tacit agreement.

Rejecting the authority of religious dogma, they believed that each man's inner consciousness embodied something divine. In nature, man could find God's moral law, and through his personal experiences with God reveal his own moral being. This idea was presented in Emerson's *Nature* (1836), the first extensive statement of New England Transcendentalism:

> We can foresee God in the coarse, and, as it were, distant phenomena of matter; but when we try to define and describe himself, both language and thought desert us, and we are as helpless as fools and savages. That essence refuses to be recorded in propositions, but when man has worshipped him intellectually, the noblest ministry of nature is to stand as the apparition of God. It is the organ through which the universal spirit speaks to the individual, and strives to lead back the individual to it.

The Transcendentalists believed that truth might be discovered by an intuitive process and morality guided by conscience. Similarly, inspiration could be trusted as a source for artistic creation.

For the most part, the Transcendentalists were social reformers, supporting such issues as temperance, public education, and women's rights. Anti-slavery sentiment among them continued up to the Civil War, by which time Transcendentalism had lost much of its force.

In addition to Emerson and Thoreau, some of the other members of the Transcendentalist group were Theodore Parker, Bronson Alcott, Margaret Fuller, George Ripley, Orestes Brownson, and Ellery Channing.

See Brian W. Barbour, ed., *American Transcendentalism: An Anthology of Criticism* (1973); Lawrence Buell, *Literary Transcendentalism: Style and Vision in the American Renaissance* (1973).

transferred epithet: An adjective used to describe a noun to which it does not normally apply. The transferred epithet is a common poetic device; some examples are "sad storm," "embalmed darkness," and "dreamy house."

translation: The Italian proverb *traduttore, traditore* (translator, traitor) embodies a painful truth: that a faithful translation is a contradiction in terms. In the work of a literary artist, effect and, indeed, meaning depend so precisely upon sound, rhythm, connotation, etc., that to alter any of these elements is to cause distortion and even destruction. From lyric poetry, for example, the translator can often extract little more than a metrical paraphrase. From most prose, narrative verse, or works with a strong intellectual content, however, enough can be salvaged so that the translation is at least a likeness of the original. Occasionally a translation, such as the King James Bible, is so striking that, faithful to the original or not, it becomes a notable work in its own right.

travesty: See **burlesque.**

triad: The strophe, antistrophe, and epode of the Pindaric ode. See **ode.**

Tribe of Ben: See **Cavalier poetry.**

tribrach: A foot of three short or unstressed syllables; uncommon in English verse.

trimeter: A line of verse consisting of three metrical feet, as in the first, second, and fifth lines of this limerick:

> There's a not / able clan / named Stein:
> There's Gertrude, there's Ep and there's Ein.
>   Gert's prose has no style,
>   Ep's statues are vile,
> And nobody understands Ein.
>   Anonymous

triolet: One of the French fixed forms of verse, used by English poets, especially the **Parnassians,** in the late nineteenth century. Containing only two rhymes, the triolet has a total of eight lines: the first two are repeated as the last two; the fourth is the same as the first. The rhyme scheme is thus *abaaabab.*

triple meter: One with three syllables to the metrical foot.

triple rhyme: See **rhyme.**

triple rhythm: A synonym for **triple meter.**

triplet: See **tercet.**

tristich: A stanza of three lines. See **tercet.**

tritagonist: In ancient Greek drama, the third actor, added by Sophocles. Generally, the three actors assumed various roles in the play by changing masks and costumes. See **deuteragonist** and **protagonist.**

Trivium: See **Seven Arts, the.**

trobar clus: In the twelfth century, certain of the troubadour poets, such as Marcabru, Peire d'Auvergne, and Giraut de Bornelh, adopted a deliberately difficult, almost private style called the *"trobar clus,"* in which the complexity of phraseology made the poet's meaning difficult to ascertain. This style was opposed to the *trobar clar,* or "open" writing. It has been suggested that an English analogue which gives some idea of the nature and difficulty of the *trobar clus* style is Donne's "Nocturnal upon St. Lucy's Day."

trochee: A foot of verse consisting of two syllables, the first stressed, the following unstressed, as in this example in which the first and third lines are trochaic:

> ′ ‿ ′ ‿ ′ ‿
> Sing a / song of / sixpence
> A pocket full of rye
> Four and twenty blackbirds,
>   Baked in a pie.
>   Anonymous

trope: 1. Used in the eighteenth century to designate elaborate figurative language, the term *trope* (from Greek: "a turn") is less frequently employed in modern literary discussions. The term *figure of speech* is now more currently used to refer to language which departs from its literal meaning. Among the major tropes are **metaphor, simile, hyperbole, personification,** and **metonymy.** Some forms of **irony** are also considered tropes when the ironical expression involves the reverse of the literal meaning.

2. An interpolated amplification of phrases or passages in the services of the medieval Church. See **liturgical drama.**

troubadour: A member of the class of lyric poets whose activities were centered in southern France in the twelfth and thirteenth centuries. Though some of them lived in northern Italy and northeastern Spain, they wrote in *langue d'oc* (the dialects of southern France), loosely called Provençal.

The troubadour, writing of love and chivalry, often addressed his poems to a noble lady, usually married, whom he served and revered in the tradition of **courtly love.** Interest in metrical technique led to the development of many intricate fixed forms.

Among the most famous Provençal poets were William, Count of Poitiers; Arnaut Daniel; and Bertran de Born.

Troubadour poetry, influential in the Renaissance, contributed to the development of the *dolce stil nuovo*, which achieved its greatest expression in the poetry of Dante. See *trouvère*.

trouvère: One of a class of court poets of northern France who wrote at the same time as the **troubadours** of southern France and were much influenced by them. The *trouvères* wrote love lyrics, chivalric romances, and *chansons de geste*. Among the latter are the Arthurian romances of Chrétien de Troyes.

truncated line: See **acatalectic.**

tumbling verse: See **Skeltonic verse.**

type character: See **stock and type characters.**

U

ubi sunt **theme:** So called from the opening words *ubi sunt* (Latin: "where are") of a number of medieval Latin poems. The *ubi sunt* formula often appears within a poem as a **repetend,** or **refrain.** One of the most famous examples of this theme, which expresses the mutability of things, is François Villon's *Ballade (des dames du temps jadis),* of which the most famous line is the refrain, *"Mais où sont les neiges d'antan?"* ("Where are the snows of yesteryear?"). The poem has been translated into English by Dante Gabriel Rossetti as "The Ballad of Dead Ladies."

underground writing: 1. In the United States such newspapers as *The Village Voice* in its earlier years, the *East Village Other*, the Los Angeles *Free Press*, and a large number of radical, especially student, newspapers directed to special cultural and political audiences, and thus of limited circulation, which have reflected such interests as experimental literature and theater, sexual liberation, leftist politics, and the causes of racial minorities.

2. In certain authoritarian states, especially in the Soviet Union, literature and social criticism that, prohibited from open publication, circulates privately.

understatement: See **meiosis.**

unities: The three unities of the drama are action, time, and place. In the *Poetics,* Aristotle said that a play should be the imitation of a single action, the parts of which were to be so arranged that if any of them were removed, or shifted, the whole would suffer. He also indicated that the action of tragedy was limited to a day or slightly more. The Italian and French critics of the Renaissance made the unities strict laws, limiting the action to twenty-four hours and, with the introduction of unity of place, not mentioned by Aristotle, limited the scene to a single place or city. This interpretation of *les unités scaligeriennes* (so called although Scaliger had not insisted on them) often made for a crowded day in the life of the hero, but the rule of the unities, despite protests from such writers as Lope de Vega and Molière, was not really broken till the time of Victor Hugo. In English drama, the unities have not usually been observed, although a writer will sometimes follow them for dramatic intensity. An example of a modern play composed strictly according to the unities is Tennessee Williams's *Cat on a Hot Tin Roof.*

unity: A unified work has a logical relationship of part to part within the whole. Although it has been maintained from the time of the Classical critics that the best works are coherent, self-contained, and free of episodes irrelevant to the work's purpose, the source of this element of unity has not always been agreed upon. The validity of the rules of dramatic construction called the **unities** has been much debated. The *Odyssey,* though episodic, is said to be unified by the presence of Odysseus. Similarly, unity of theme may bind together the disparate parts of such a work as *Henry IV, Part I.* However achieved, unity remains one of the criteria of literary judgment.

universality: A quality which endows a literary work with significance not limited to a particular time and place. A work is regarded as having universality when, through its capacity to reveal human nature and the problems which face man, we recognize the truth contained within it. Sophocles's *Antigone,* for example, is not limited in significance to a specific culture because it is a Greek play based on ancient myth. Rather, by its dramatic skill, its magnitude and power of expression, it presents problems that involve all men as well as the individual characters of the play. Consequently, to call it a "Greek play" is only to describe its origins; its universality lies in its capacity to transcend the limitations of time and space within which the work was created. See **concrete universal.**

University Wits: A name applied to a number of young men who, arriving in London from Oxford and Cambridge in the 1580's, were influential in the development of Elizabethan literature. The wits included John Lyly, George Peele, Robert Greene, Thomas Lodge, Christopher Marlowe, and Thomas Kyd, the last considered one of the group though he had received his education at the excellent Merchant Taylor's School rather than at a university. Although the wits were not a literary school with common principles, among them they established or contributed to a number of the types of Elizabethan drama, such as the revenge tragedy (Kyd), the romantic comedy (Peele, Greene), and the history play (Marlowe, Peele), and did important work in other fields.

unreliable narrator: See **point of view.**

utopian literature: A type of literature in which an ideal society is depicted. The word *utopia* (a pun on two Greek words, *outopia,* "no place," and *eutopia,* "the good place") was first applied to this genre by the Renaissance scholar and politician Sir Thomas More in his Latin work *Utopia* (1516). In more recent times Edward Bellamy's *Looking Backward* (1888), William Morris's *News from Nowhere* (1890), and H. G. Wells's *A Modern Utopia* (1905) have been contributions to the growing body of utopian literature.

The term *dystopia* ("bad place") has lately been used to designate an anti-utopia, a place marked by extreme mechanization or authoritarianism. George Orwell's *1984* (1949) and Aldous Huxley's *Brave New World* (1932) offer such grim visions. In their critical tone dystopias have something in common with such satirical fantasies as Swift's *Gulliver's Travels* (1726) and Samuel Butler's *Erewhon* (1872), whose title is an anagram for "nowhere." These works offer more general criticisms of mankind or more specific criticisms of then contemporary institutions. Works of **science fiction,** extrapolating from current tendencies, may present either attractive or disturbing pictures of future worlds.

See Lewis Mumford, *The Story of Utopias* (1922); Joyce O. Hertzler, *The History of Utopian Thought* (1923); C. A. Doxiadis, *Between Dystopia and Utopia* (1966); Mark R. Hillegas, *The Future as Nightmare* (1967).

V

variable syllable: One which may be stressed or unstressed in the scansion of a line of verse according to the demands of the metrical pattern.

variorum edition: From Latin: *cum notis variorum,* "with notes of various persons." 1. An edition of a writer's work containing variant readings of the text and critical commentary and interpretation by prominent scholars and authors. *The New Variorum Shakespeare,* edited by Furness, is such an edition.

2. An edition presenting variant versions of an author's works, such as *The Variorum Edition of the Poems of W. B. Yeats,* edited by Alspach and Allt, in which a scholar may compare the changes that Yeats made in his poems.

Varronian satire: See **satire.**

vates: Latin: "prophet." From earliest times, the poet has often been considered a seer or *vates,* divinely inspired, and his pronouncements have been accorded the status of prophecy. Vergil, for example, was believed to have predicted the future literally in his *Fourth Eclogue,* which celebrated the birth of a child who was to bring back the Age of Gold. For hundreds of years the poem was read as a pagan prophecy of the birth of Christ and Vergil held to be a *vates.*

vaudeville: In modern American usage, a theatrical presentation consisting of a sequence of songs, dances, and other acts. Originally, the term, as used in France, referred to comic or satirical songs about well-known personalities. It later designated a light play with comic songs, or *vaudevilles,* interspersed. In this sense, the term has been used in English, but is no longer common.

vehicle: See **metaphor.**

verbal irony: See **irony.**

verisimilitude: A quality possessed by a work the action and characters of which seem to the reader sufficiently probable to constitute an acceptable representation of reality. What degree of probability, or likeness to fact, is necessary to achieve verisimilitude has never been finally ascertained. For some, a close depiction of actuality, such as that found in Steinbeck's *Grapes of Wrath*, is required. For others, a degree of imaginative power sufficient to capture the reader's belief gives the work this quality however fantastic the events depicted. In this sense, even such a work as *The Rime of the Ancient Mariner* may be said to have verisimilitude.

verism: The doctrine that literature should represent unadorned reality even when it is sordid and ugly.

vers de société: French: "society verse." A type of light verse which deals gracefully with polite society and its concerns. *Vers de société*, which often makes use of such French fixed forms as the **rondeau** and the **villanelle,** is usually witty, sometimes gently satiric, often elegantly amorous. An example is the mock epitaph suggested by the Earl of Rochester for Charles II:

> Here lies our sovereign lord the King,
> Whose word no man relies on;
> He never says a foolish thing,
> Nor ever does a wise one.

verse: 1. Lines arranged in metrical patterns; the term *verse* is sometimes distinguished from **poetry.**
2. A single line of a poem.

verse paragraph: A group of lines, frequently in **blank verse,** arranged as a rhetorical unit similar to a paragraph in prose. Milton's *Paradise Lost* and Wordsworth's *The Prelude*, for example, are constructed of verse paragraphs.

vers libre: See **free verse.**

verso: See **recto and verso.**

Victorianism: In the most superficial and dubious usage, the term
Victorianism implies that materialism, complacency, and sexual
prudishness were central characteristics of society during Victoria's reign. But the age was far more complex and contradictory
than these conventional associations suggest. Though such characteristics did indeed exist, the most scathing criticism of them
came in fact from the Victorian writers. For the modern reader,
Victorian materialism exists most memorably in the de-
nunciations of Carlyle, Arnold, and Ruskin, and Victorian prig-
gishness in Dickens's depiction of Mr. Podsnap in *Our Mutual
Friend,* waving away anything that might "bring a blush to the
cheek of the young person."

Though Victoria's reign (1837–1901) makes a convenient span,
some scholars prefer to mark the beginning of the period by the
passage of the first Reform Bill in 1832, which enfranchised part
of the propertied middle class, and also to end it sooner, perhaps
as early as 1884 with the third Reform Bill, which gave the vote
to all men (though not to women). That the age should be de-
marcated by such significant political changes suggests another
misconception needing correction. Far from being a period of
order and stability, the Victorian Age was one of stress, doubt,
and change. Especially during the economic depression of the
1840's, the industrial working class lived in such desperate poverty that to many Englishmen (and to the visiting Engels) revolution seemed likely. But despite a theoretical commitment to
an unregulated economy, the Victorians achieved a compromise
—repealing the Corn Laws, which kept the price of grain artifi-
cially high, and passing Factory Acts, which ameliorated working
conditions—that averted violent change.

Even as economic conflicts alienated social classes, religious
differences divided such groups as the traditional Church of
England; the Evangelical sects such as the Methodists, Baptists,
and Quakers; and the Tractarians (adherents of the **Oxford Movement**), who leaned toward an independent, ritualized church
and even toward Roman Catholicism. The great religious crisis
of the age, however, stemmed from the conflict between the
Biblical account of the creation (and particularly the special creation of man) and the view presented by geology, which pos-
tulated a vastly longer development for the earth and its

inhabitants. Though the idea of evolution was very old, the publication of such studies as Lyell's *Geology* (1830), suggesting a
theory of the slow alteration of the earth, produced in many
thoughtful people the spiritual doubt and even anguish reflected,
in literature, in Tennyson's *In Memoriam,* completed in 1850
but begun soon after the death of Tennyson's friend Hallam in
1833. By the time Darwin's *Origin of Species* (1859) appeared,
offering in the theory of natural selection an explanation of the
mechanism of biological development, the way had been prepared for the widespread religious-scientific conflict that the
volume provoked. Even here, however, some Victorians man-
aged a compromise between religion and science in a commitment to the general idea of progress.

As the century continued and brought the commercial com-
petition of the United States and Germany, the cares of impe-
rialism, and the challenges of socialism (even the aesthetically
oriented socialism of Ruskin and the painter and poet William
Morris), something of the confidence of the earlier Victorian age
was lost and the doubts and alienation of **Modernism** began to
appear. Nevertheless, the literary achievements of such poets
as Tennyson and Browning, of such prose writers as Carlyle and
Ruskin, of such novelists as Dickens, Thackeray, and George
Eliot testify to the energy of a great creative age.

See Jerome Buckley, *The Victorian Temper* (1951); Walter
Houghton, *The Victorian Frame of Mind: Ideas and Beliefs of
the Victorians* (1957); Austin Wright, ed., *Victorian Literature:
Modern Essays in Criticism* (1961); J. B. Schneewind, *Backgrounds of English Victorian Literature* (1970); Richard D. Al-
tick, *Victorian People and Ideas* (1973); John R. Reed, *Victorian
Conventions* (1975).

viewpoint: See **point of view.**

vignette: A sketch or other brief literary work characterized by
precision and delicacy of composition. A vignette may also be a
section of a longer work.

villain: An evil character who acts in opposition to the hero. Sometimes, however, a writer centers his interest on a villain (*Macbeth,* Molière's *Don Juan*), and in other cases the villain comes

dangerously close to seizing the major share of the attention in spite of the author (*Othello, Paradise Lost*).

villanelle: One of the French fixed forms. Originally pastoral in subject matter (the name derives from *villa*, a farm or country house), it is often used for light verse. There are five tercets followed by a quatrain, all on two rhymes. The opening line is repeated at the ends of tercets two and four; the final line of the first tercet concludes the third and fifth. The two refrain lines are repeated at the end of the quatrain.

> A dainty thing's the Villanelle
>   Sly, musical, a jewel in rhyme,
> It serves its purpose passing well.
>
> A double-clappered silver bell
>   That must be made to clink in chime,
> A dainty thing's the Villanelle;
>
> And if you wish to flute a spell,
>   Or ask a meeting 'neath the lime,
> It serves its purpose passing well.
>
> You must not ask of it the swell
>   Of organs grandiose and sublime—
> A dainty thing's the Villanelle;
>
> And, filled with sweetness, as a shell
>   Is filled with sound, and launched in time,
> It serves its purpose passing well.
>
> Still fair to see and good to smell
>   As in the quaintness of its prime,
> A dainty thing's the Villanelle,
> It serves its purpose passing well.
>   W. E. Henley, "Villanelle"

virelay (also French: *virelai*): A name applied to either of two verse forms, neither of which is strictly fixed, derived from old French poetry. One, used for a poem of limited length, has only two rhymes; the first and second lines appear alternately as refrains. The other has an indefinite number of stanzas, each having two rhymes, one rhyme in long lines, the other in short. The short lines of one stanza provide the rhyme for the long lines of the next, the short lines of the last stanza rhyming with the long lines of the first. Neither form is common in English.

virgule: A short, slanting line used in prosody to divide lines into feet, as in the following:

> The Owl / and the Pus / sy-cat went / to sea
> In a beau / tiful pea / green boat.

voice: See **persona.**

volta: The turn in thought in a sonnet, usually at the end of the octet. An example is found in Shakespeare's Sonnet 33, part of which appears below, in which he describes the sun first rising gloriously but then clouded over:

> . . . Anon permit the basest clouds to ride,
> With ugly rack on his celestial face,
> And from the forlorn world his visage hide,
> Stealing unseen to west with this disgrace:
> [Volta] Even so my Sun one early morn did shine,
> With all triumphant splendour on my brow:
> But, out alack, he was but one hour mine,
> The region cloud hath mask'd him from me now . . .

Vorticism: A brief movement in literature and the visual arts, centering on the magazine *Blast: Review of the Great English Vortex,* which appeared only twice, once in 1914 and again in 1915. Edited by Wyndham Lewis and designed to shock the Philistines by its eccentric typography and format as well as by its serio-comic belligerence, it contrasted the Vorticist commitment to abstraction, "bareness and hardness," with the emphasis in nineteenth-century literature and art on emotional richness and the representation of nature. (The symbol of this "non-vital" art was the "Vortex," a solid, stable cone spinning on a perpendicular line.) Inspired by the ideas of the critic T. E. Hulme, who praised the static and geometric in contemporary Cubist painting, and precision and impersonality in verse, Vorticism advocated principles similar to those of **Imagism.** Ezra Pound (credited with coining the term *Vorticism*) wrote in *Blast* that the Image was "a VORTEX, from which, and through which, and into which ideas are constantly rushing."

In contrast to the violence of World War I, the contentiousness of Vorticism came to seem merely provincial, and the movement eventually dissolved. Along with Pound and Lewis, those most closely associated with it were the artists and writers Henri

Gaudier-Brzeska, Jacob Epstein, Ford Madox Ford, and Richard Aldington.

See William C. Wees, *Vorticism and the English Avant-Garde* (1972); Reed W. Dasenbrock, *The Literary Vorticism of Ezra Pound and Wyndham Lewis* (1985).

Vulgate: The Vulgate Bible, the Latin translation prepared by St. Jerome late in the fourth century, was the version read during the Middle Ages. In 1546 it was authorized by the Council of Trent as the official Bible of the Roman Catholic Church. It is so called (from the Latin *vulgus*, "crowd"; *vulgare*, "to make common") because it made the Bible available in the common language.

W

Wardour Street English: A style that uses archaic diction in an attempt to achieve elegance. Used pejoratively by nineteenth-century critics to characterize the style of tawdry historical novels, the term *Wardour Street English*, referring to spurious expression, is derived from the London street where many of the shops once sold dubious antiques. Since the 1930's, Wardour Street has been noted for its film companies.

weak ending: A syllable at the end of a line of verse which, though stressed metrically, is unstressed in ordinary speech and which calls for little or no pause before the next line, as in the case of *and* in the following lines from Shakespeare's *The Tempest*:

Thy mother was a piece of virtue, and
She said thou wast my daughter.

well-made play: French: *pièce bien faite*. A type of play constructed according to a formula that originated in France in the early nineteenth century and has remained influential. The inventor and most prolific practitioner of the art of the well-made play was Eugène Scribe (1791–1861), the seventy-six volumes of whose complete works contain some 374 plays, opera librettos, and other theatrical pieces, many of them, however, collaborations. Scribe took the devices that had been part of comedy since the time of Menander and, with great technical skill, wove them into an unvarying formula.

The plot of a well-made play regularly revolves about a secret known only to some of the characters; revealed at the climax, it leads to the downfall of the villain and the triumph of the hero. The action, which centers on a conflict—especially a duel of wits—between the hero and his opponent, builds with increasing intensity through a series of reversals that culminate in the climactic revelation scene. Misunderstandings, compromising letters, precisely timed entrances and exits, and other such devices contribute to the suspense. The **denouement** is always carefully prepared and, within the framework of the manipulated action, believable.

Scribe's disciple was Victorien Sardou (1831–1908), from whose name Bernard Shaw coined the term *Sardoodledom* to describe this type of play-making. Scribe's *The Glass of Water* and Sardou's *A Scrap of Paper* (whose title suggests the sort of props with which well-made plays are replete) are among their best-known plays. The well-made play provided the form for the developing social drama of Augier and Dumas *fils* and influenced Ibsen, Wilde, Shaw, and innumerable others.

See John Russell Taylor, *The Rise and Fall of the Well-Made Play* (1967).

willing suspension of disbelief: A phrase originated by Coleridge in the *Biographia Literaria* (Chapter XIV) while describing his part in the original plan for the *Lyrical Ballads*. It was agreed that Wordsworth was to choose subjects from "ordinary life" but that Coleridge's efforts "should be directed to persons and characters supernatural, or at least romantic; yet so as to transfer from our inward nature a human interest and a semblance of truth sufficient to procure for these shadows of the imagination that willing suspension of disbelief for the moment, which constitutes poetic faith." In this apparently simple phrase, Coleridge has so precisely distinguished the psychological basis of aesthetic apprehension that his formulation continues to be useful in critical discourse. Coleridge himself expands upon his definition later in the *Biographia* (Chapter XXII), where he speaks of the danger of juxtaposing literal fact and imaginative vision: "That *illusion*, contradistinguished from *delusion*, that *negative* faith, which simply permits the images presented to work by their own force, without either denial or affirmation of their real existence by the judgment, is rendered impossible by their immediate neighborhood to words and facts of known and absolute truth." See **Negative Capability**.

wit: The term *wit* has, in critical and general usage, undergone periodic change so that its meanings, overlapping from period to period, have at any one time been numerous. In the Renaissance, the word *wit* meant "intelligence" or "wisdom," as in Spenser's sonnet which celebrates true beauty:

> Men call you fair, and you do credit it,
> For that your self ye daily such do see:
> But the true fair, that is the gentle wit,
> And virtuous mind, is much more praised of me.

During the seventeenth century, the term *wit* meant **fancy**, implying such nimbleness of thought and such originality in figures of speech as was found in the **Metaphysical poetry** of John Donne and others. In the latter half of the century, the meaning of *wit* changed. For Hobbes (in the *Leviathan*, 1651) judgment rather than fancy was the principal element of wit, and, in fact, he felt that wit could be achieved by judgment alone. The excess of fancy, he remarked later, resulted in a loss of delight in wit. As a poetic faculty, true wit was the poet's ability to see similarities in apparently dissimilar things. False wit, as later described by Addison, involved the association of words rather than of ideas; such linguistic devices as puns, anagrams, acrostics, etc., he listed as types of such wit.

In a famous passage from *An Essay on Criticism*, Pope contrasts true wit, guided by judgment, with merely fanciful writing:

> Poets, like painters, thus, unskilled to trace
> The naked nature and the living grace,
> With gold and jewels cover every part,
> And hide with ornaments their want of art.
> True wit is Nature to advantage dressed,
> What oft was thought, but ne'er so well expressed.

In modern times, *wit* is limited to intellectually amusing utterances calculated to delight and surprise. See **humor**.

word accent: See **accent.**

wrenched accent: See **accent.**

Z

zeugma: A rhetorical figure in which a single word, standing in relationship to two others, is correctly related to only one. Unlike a **syllepsis,** which is grammatically correct, a zeugma involves a failure of the single word to give meaning to one of the pair with which it is connected. In the commonly recognized zeugma from Shakespeare's *Henry V* "Kill the boys and the luggage!" the verb *kill* does not apply to *luggage;* instead, a word such as *destroy* must be supplied to complete the meaning of the statement.

A selected list of entries arranged by subject

CHARACTER

alazon
antagonist
anti-hero
Byronic hero
caricature
confidant
deuteragonist
flat and round characters
hero
miles gloriosus
protagonist
raisonneur
stock and type characters
tritagonist
villain

CRITICAL TERMS

aesthetic distance
affective fallacy
ambiguity
anxiety of influence
archetype
autotelic
bathos
concrete universal
contextualism
criticism
deconstruction
decorum
didactic
dissociation of sensibility

donnée
epiphany
fancy and imagination
feminist criticism
four levels of meaning
four meanings of a poem
Freytag's Pyramid
genre criticism
Heresy of Paraphrase
hermeneutics
imitation
inscape and instress
intentional fallacy
intertextuality
Kitsch
l'art pour l'art
mimesis
New Criticism
New Historicism
objective correlative
pathetic fallacy
pornography
pseudo-statement
psychoanalytic criticism
reader-response criticism
semiology/semiotics
speech act theory
Structuralism
symbolic action
textual criticism
tone
verisimilitude
willing suspension of
  disbelief

DRAMA

DRAMATIC ELEMENTS

act
action
agon
aside
catharsis
chorus
comic relief
conflict
coup de théâtre
denouement
deus ex machina
dumb show
exposition
hamartia
hubris
obligatory scene
parabasis
peripeteia
plot
point of attack
quiproquo
scene
soliloquy
stichomythia
unities

DRAMATIC TYPES

boulevard drama
bourgeois drama
burletta
capa y espada
Cavalier drama
chronicle play
closet drama
comédie larmoyante

comedy of humours
comedy of intrigue
comedy of manners
commedia dell'arte
comoedia erudate
curtain raiser
domestic tragedy
drama
Epic Theater
farce
folk drama
heroic drama
high comedy
history play
interlude
Kabuki
kitchen sink drama
liturgical drama
living newspaper
low comedy
masque
melodrama
mime
miracle play
morality play
mystery play
New Comedy
Nō drama
passion play
Restoration comedy
revenge tragedy
satyr play
school plays
sentimental comedy
Theater of Cruelty
Theater of the Absurd
thesis play
tragedy
tragicomedy
well-made play

FIGURES OF SPEECH

conceit
epic (or Homeric) simile
hyperbole
metaphor
metonymy
oxymoron
paradox
personification
pun
simile
synecdoche

HISTORICAL AND PHILO-SOPHICAL CONCEPTS

ancients and moderns,
   quarrel between
Apollonian and Dionysian
baroque
Chain of Being
courtly love
dolce stil nuovo
Enlightenment
Existentialism
Hebraism—Hellenism
mannerism
Modernism
Platonism and Neo-
   Platonism
primitivism
Renaissance
sensibility
Transcendentalism
Victorianism

LITERARY MOVEMENTS AND GROUPS

Aestheticism
Angry Young Men
Beat Generation
Bloomsbury Group
Cavalier poetry
Chicago critics
classicism
Dadaism
Decadence
Expressionism
Fugitives and Agrarians
Futurism
Georgian poetry
Graveyard School
Harlem Renaissance
Imagism
Impressionism
Irish Literary Renaissance
Lake Poets
Modernism
Movement, the
naturalism
Neoclassicism
Oxford Movement
Parnassianism
Pléiade
Pre-Raphaelites
realism
Romanticism
Russian Formalism
Sturm und Drang
Surrealism
Symbolist Movement
Vorticism

NARRATIVE AND DRAMATIC ELEMENTS

anticlimax
climax
conflict
crisis

denouement
description
dialogue
Double, the
exposition
fantasy
flashback
illusion
imagery
irony
motif
peripeteia
persona
plot
satire
stream of consciousness
symbol
voice

legend
New Novel
novel
pastoral
picaresque narrative
psychological novel
roman à clef
romance
saga
science fiction
sentimental novel
short novel
short story
tale
utopian literature

PROSODY

NARRATIVE TYPES

allegory
autobiography
beast epic
bestiary
Bildungsroman
biography
confessional literature
detective story
dream allegory
epistolary novel
exemplum
fable
fabliau
fairy tale
fiction
Gothic novel
historical novel
Künstlerroman

PROSODIC ELEMENTS

acatalectic
accent
alexandrine
alliteration
amphibrach
amphimac
anacrusis
antistrophe
assonance
caesura
consonance
feminine rhyme
foot
free verse
incremental repetition
leonine rhyme
masculine rhyme
meter
quantitative verse

quantity
refrain
repetend
rhyme
rhythm
running rhythm
run-on line
slack, the
sprung rhythm
verse

PROSODIC FORMS

aube, or *aubade*
ballad
ballade
ballad stanza
blank verse
Burns stanza
canso
canto
canzone
carmen figuratum
chanson de geste
clerihew
complaint
couplet
crown of sonnets
curtal-sonnet
dramatic monologue
eclogue
elegy
epic
epithalamion
georgic
haiku
heroic couplet

hymn
idyl(l)
lay
limerick
Miltonic sonnet
mock epic
ode
ottava rima
pastoral
Petrarchan sonnet
rhyme royal
rondeau
rondel
roundel
rubaiyat
sestina
Shakespearean sonnet
Skeltonic verse
sonnet
Spenserian sonnet
Spenserian stanza
tail-rhyme stanza
terza rima
triolet
villanelle
virelay

RHETORICAL FIGURES

apostrophe
chiasmus
hendiadys
invocation
litotes
rhetorical question
zeugma